WITHDRAWN FROM TSC LIBRARY

Policing in England and Wales, 1918–39

Also by Keith Laybourn

BRITAIN ON THE BREADLINE

BRITAIN'S FIRST LABOUR GOVERNMENT (*Co-authored with John Shepherd*)

Also by David Taylor

HOOLIGANS, HARLOTS AND HANGMEN

POLICING THE VICTORIAN TOWN
The development of the police in Middlesbrough c. 1840–1914

Policing in England and Wales, 1918–39

The Fed, Flying Squads and Forensics

Keith Laybourn
Professor of History, University of Huddersfield, UK

David Taylor
Emeritus Professor of History, University of Huddersfield, UK

© Keith Laybourn and David Taylor 2011

All rights reserved. No reproduction, copy or transmission of this publication may be made without written permission.

No portion of this publication may be reproduced, copied or transmitted save with written permission or in accordance with the provisions of the Copyright, Designs and Patents Act 1988, or under the terms of any licence permitting limited copying issued by the Copyright Licensing Agency, Saffron House, 6-10 Kirby Street, London EC1N 8TS.

Any person who does any unauthorized act in relation to this publication may be liable to criminal prosecution and civil claims for damages.

The authors have asserted their rights to be identified as the authors of this work in accordance with the Copyright, Designs and Patents Act 1988.

First published 2011 by
PALGRAVE MACMILLAN

Palgrave Macmillan in the UK is an imprint of Macmillan Publishers Limited, registered in England, company number 785998, of Houndmills, Basingstoke, Hampshire RG21 6XS.

Palgrave Macmillan in the US is a division of St Martin's Press LLC, 175 Fifth Avenue, New York, NY 10010.

Palgrave Macmillan is the global academic imprint of the above companies and has companies and representatives throughout the world.

Palgrave® and Macmillan® are registered trademarks in the United States, the United Kingdom, Europe and other countries.

ISBN 978–0–230–23245–7 hardback

This book is printed on paper suitable for recycling and made from fully managed and sustained forest sources. Logging, pulping and manufacturing processes are expected to conform to the environmental regulations of the country of origin.

A catalogue record for this book is available from the British Library.

A catalog record for this book is available from the Library of Congress.

10 9 8 7 6 5 4 3 2 1
20 19 18 17 16 15 14 13 12 11

Printed and bound in the United States of America

Dedicated to Julia and Thelma

Contents

List of Illustrations and Tables   viii

Acknowledgements   x

Abbreviations   xii

1 Introduction   1

Part 1 The Problem of Public Order and the Professionalisation of the Police

2 Police Trade Unionism and the Federation   13

3 Policing Public Order in the Inter-war Years   49

4 Detective and Scientific Work: A New Vista   81

Part 2 The Prophecy of Nahum: Motor Vehicles, the Police and the Public in Inter-war Britain

5 'A Mere Traffic Signalling Device'? The Debate on Policing and Traffic Control   107

6 The Police and the Practicalities of Traffic Management   135

7 Motoring Offences and the Enforcement of the Law   151

8 Cars, Crime and Coppers: Combating the 'Smash and Grab' Raider   186

9 Conclusion   208

Notes   211

Bibliography   243

Index   249

List of Illustrations and Tables

Illustrations

Front cover photograph is of the Lancashire Flying Squad in 1933. There are 14 MG Mag(n)ettes on display (Lancashire County Police, permission given by the Lancashire County Records Office, Preston).

Tables

1.1	Selected police statistics: county and borough forces in England and Wales (excluding London) 1919–39	5
1.2	Distribution by size (authorised strength) of police forces in England and Wales, 1919, 1929 and 1939 (excluding London)	8
2.1	The war record of the dismissed policemen: men with a military or naval record	31
3.1	Removed and cautioned magistrates as a result of the General Strike	66
3.2	Total number of magistrates named as examined in the Home Office files	68
3.3	Prosecutions arising from the General Strike	73
3.4	Prosecutions connected with the General Strike and coal lock-out 1 May 1926 to 19 December 1926	74
4.1	Returns on cases involving forensic science and detective work for 1939	102
P2.1	Motor vehicles in use in Britain, 1919–38 (000s)	105
5.1	Prime causes of fatal street accidents	132
6.1	Home Office Experimental Motor Patrol Scheme	148
7.1	Selected offences (per million of population)	152
7.2	Selected traffic offences, 1934–38 (by category of road user)	152
7.3	Convictions and punishments for traffic offences for selected groups, 1934–38	153
7.4	Numbers imprisoned for traffic offences, 1934–38	154
7.5	Speeding offences, 1931–38	158

7.6	Serious motoring offences, 1931–38	161
7.7	Manslaughter (motoring) outcomes, 1930–38	163
7.8	Traffic offences, Leeds, 1937 and 1938	172
7.9	Prosecution rates (per 000,000 population) for serious motoring offences in selected towns and cities in Lancashire in the 1930s	176
7.10	Prosecution rates (per 000,000 population) for serious motoring offences in selected towns and cities in the West Riding of Yorkshire in the 1930s	177
7.11	Failure to stop and insurance offences, 1931–38	180
7.12	Prosecutions for neglect of traffic directions, 1935–38	180
7.13	Mechanical offences, 1931–38	181
8.1	Motor vehicle thefts reported to the police, 1921–27	198
8.2	Motor vehicle thefts and recoveries in London, 1924–38	199
8.3	Taking motor vehicles without owner's consent, 1931–34	200

Acknowledgements

Any academic journey inevitably entails great debts to others and it is impossible to pay too fulsome a tribute to the many individuals, library staff and institutions who have contributed to this book. Our colleagues, and former colleagues, at the University of Huddersfield provided much academic advice and friendship, and we should particularly like to thank Paul Ward, Philip Woodfine, Bill Stafford, Tim Thornton, Barry Doyle and Sarah Bastow for the immense help that they have given us during the research and writing of this book. The University of Huddersfield also enabled us to more easily gather the records of police together in digital form through the work of Neil Pye, a PhD research student at Huddersfield. Clive Emsley, Chris A. Williams and various anonymous reviewers have also been invaluable guides as this book has evolved from 'Citizens in Uniform' into its present form and title. More generally we were supported by Mike Russ, Dean of the School of Music and Humanities, and Professor John Shepherd who has recently become an Honorary Professor at Huddersfield.

We owe a particular gratitude to the various archivists and librarians who have provided us with help in our research. Above all, we must thank Duncan Broady, Museum Curator of the Greater Manchester Police Museum and Archive, whose immense knowledge of the nuances of police history guided us to some significant developments in the process of measuring the professionalisation of policing in the interwar years. In addition, we would like to thank the staff of the Birmingham Archives and Heritage section of Birmingham Central Library, Lancashire Record Office at Preston (particularly Bruce Jackson and David Tilsley), the Liverpool Record Office and the West Yorkshire Archives Service. The majority of the primary material was drawn from the National Archives at Kew who gave us permission to quote from their manuscript collection. We would also like to thank the Intellectual Property section of the Metropolitan Police for permission to use some of the Metropolitan Police (MEPO) files. We also thank the Controller of Her Majesty's Stationery Office (Norwich) for permission to quote from Crown Copyright material. Also we would like to acknowledge the Chief Constable of Lancashire Constabulary for permission to use the photograph of the Lancashire Flying squad of 1933, which adorns the front cover of this book.

The vast majority of this book is drawn from the primary evidence gathered in the above-mentioned archives. However, in providing the historiography of debate, we have referred to the vital secondary books and articles that have shaped our thinking. These have generally been referred to within the context of the debate. Occasionally, there have been very short quotes, but these in no way have reached or exceeded the guidelines normally accepted by publishers. In every case we have given them full attribution amongst the 800 or so notes we have supplied.

Every effort has been made to trace copyright holders and to avoid infringement of copyright. However, we apologise unreservedly to any copyright holder whose permission we have inadvertently overlooked.

Our many thanks go to Ruth Ireland and Priya Venkat for their editorial help.

Finally, though in fact both first and last, our love and thanks must go to our families and in particular to Julia (Laybourn) and Thelma (Taylor).

Abbreviations

AA	Automobile Association
CCA	Chief Constables' Association
CID	Criminal Investigation Department
DORA	The Defence of the Realm Act
HMIC	His Majesty's Inspectors of Constabulary
MPD	Metropolitan Police District
MPU	Metropolitan Police Union
NUPPO	National Union of Police and Prison Officers
PLP	Parliamentary Labour Party
RAC	Royal Automobile Club
SJC	Standing Joint Committee
TUC	Trades Union Congress

1
Introduction

Despite the continuing interest in the inter-war years and the recent rapid development of police history there has been surprisingly little research on the general development of policing in the 1920s and 1930s. Further, much of what has been written paints a negative picture of policing in the period. However, it is our contention that the inter-war years witnessed the start of certain fundamental changes in policing that laid the foundations of later, and more publicised, developments that took place, particularly in the 1960s and 1970s. The focus of the book will be on two complex but important drivers of change. The first encompasses concerns about police organisation and politicisation in the immediate aftermath of the Great War with wider concerns about the growth of extremist ideologies, their infiltration into British society and their impact on public order. This resulted in a drive to professionalise the police through better pay and conditions, better training and greater use of science and technology but also involved a change in the relationships between individual police forces, their local authorities and the Home Office. The second set of influences relate to the impact of the advent of a motorised society, which set in motion changes that altered basic policing practices, encouraging specialisation and moving (some) policemen off their feet and onto their seats and that also recast the wider relationship between police and public.[1] This is not to suggest that there were not other important developments. Clearly there were; and some, for example, the emergence of women police, have been analysed elsewhere.[2] Nor is it to deny that there were important elements of continuity in policing that ran through the first half of the twentieth century. Equally clearly there were; but such continuity is but one part of a more complex story and one that has been allowed to overshadow important changes that first emerged between the wars.

Clive Emsley, the doyen of British police historians, in his most recent book, *The Great British Bobby*, stresses the continuity with Victorian practices. 'The Bobby still plodded his beat on foot...largely unchanged from the system that had developed during the Victorian period.'[3] It is almost as an afterthought that he notes 'the succession of new and major challenges' before 1939 and it is only in the 1960s that he sees significant change taking place.[4] A variation on the theme of significant post-war change is to be found in Philip Rawlings overview, *Policing: A Short History*, in which he writes of 'fundamental changes...in the air [and]...a dizzying array of...experiments' that preceded the much-praised changes in Kirkby, immortalised in the TV series *Z Cars*.[5] To a large extent both Emsley and Rawlings were repeating the argument advanced by earlier writers. The first modern police historian, T. A. Critchley, who had been secretary to the Royal Commission on Policing in 1960–62, was impressed with the modernisation that took place in and after that decade after the delays of the 1950s when reform was 'on an ebb tide'.[6] Similarly, Martin and Wilson saw the inter-war years as a period in which '[t]he police service changed less ... than did many other aspects of life.'[7] There was the occasional dissenting voice. Philip Stead, writing in 1985, noted that 'the inter-war period saw much police innovation'.[8] But this was the exception. The new orthodoxy in the general police histories is reflected in a number of local studies, most notably Brogden's study of policing in inter-war Liverpool which puts great emphasis on the routine of the beat and, somewhat surprisingly, in view of the chief constable's concerns with and actions on traffic problems, makes no reference to traffic policing in the city.[9] However, Weinberger's oral history of English policing from the 1930s to the 1960s, while recognising the importance of 'traditional' beat work, is well aware that even before the Second World War 'the car...changed life drastically for the police'.[10] The idea that there were 'real-world' changes has been argued provocatively (though not entirely convincingly) by Howard Taylor who sees the criminal statistics in general and traffic offences in particular as being the product of supply-side politics that had more to do with an existential threat to the police in the harsh economic conditions of the years after the Great War.[11]

Developments in policing have also been widely discussed by labour and social historians concerned with other questions. The policing of strikes in general, and the General Strike in particular, has generated a significant specialist literature; so too has the policing of public protest. Fearing that many of these events were perpetrated by the communists inter-war governments prepared for the threat by introducing the 1919

Police Act to form a Police Federation, in place of a trade union, to stabilise the police and to organise bodies for their representation. Most historians who have written about public order policies suggest that inter-war governments worked closely with chief constables, the army and other interested bodies, in order to co-ordinate an effective response to threats of public order. They generally maintain that public order was better organised in dealing with disturbances and, consequently, that the police response to public disorder was more effective and less violent than might have been expected, although the police were still prone to organising baton charges and effecting local abuse of their power.[12] This is a view with which we would concur.

In 1929 the *Report of the Royal Commission on Police Powers and Procedures* was being disingenuous when it rejected out of hand the claim of some of its witnesses that the police frequently abused their powers. In particular it dismissed the claim that there was amongst the police a 'post-war mentality' that was 'more arbitrary and oppressive to the public than...before the war' but it could not help boasting that there had been a 'post-war magnification of the executive' and that pay, conditions and training had created 'in spirit if not in form' a 'unified National Force'.[13] The mindset of the Royal Commission was clear: it was one of an unequivocal rejection of the evidence it received of the high-handedness of the police and the abuse of their powers. However, the Home Office papers on this matter cannot be denied, for they show that the Home Office was aware of abuse of police powers and was informing and advising chief constables, for instance, in the art of obfuscation in matters of law during the coal dispute and the General Strike of 1926.[14] Even before then, as is evident from Chapter 3, the local control of the police had certainly been circumvented by secret arrangements between the Home Office and chief constables.

Similarly, the growth of motor traffic has attracted attention from historians who, to a greater or lesser extent, commented on the attitudes and actions of the police. Thorold's *Motoring Age* is not primarily concerned with the policing of traffic but on a number of occasions presents the police in a negative light, persecuting innocent drivers.[15] Other historians have been less sympathetic to the plight of the driver and have focused more on the (pedestrian) victims of the emerging motorised age. O'Connell and Moran have emphasised the social and political influence of the motor trade and the motoring organisations in deflecting criticism from perpetrators to victims (the careless pedestrians in particular) and helping to shape government traffic policy in their favour.[16]

O'Connell sees the police as part of the wider problem facing road safety reformers, singling out (as if typical) the Chief Constable of Salford, Major Godfrey, for particular criticism for demanding coroners to return suicide verdicts in certain cases of road fatalities.[17] A more nuanced and more convincing account of the demonising of the 'road hog' is given by Emsley, but even he fails to do justice to the variety and complexity of police responses to this most pressing problem.[18]

Before moving to our main themes it is important to sketch in the background – both specific and general – that will provide the backcloth for the detailed discussions that follow. The general economic background is well known and only the most salient points need to be mentioned here. Despite more positive interpretations of the inter-war years, no historian has seriously questioned the undoubted financial difficulties that faced successive governments during the 1920s and 1930s. The cost of fighting a world war combined with the severe economic downturn of 1921 put immense pressure on governmental resources – pressure that was intensified by the conventional, neo-classical economic thinking that prevailed. Barely had the economy recovered in the late 1920s than it was hit by another economic downturn which, though not as severe as that experienced in America or Germany, was a depression of sufficient dimensions to make exceptional demands on governmental resources. The search for government economies was a recurring theme. The (perceived) need to cut back on public expenditure impacted dramatically on the police. As a consequence there was an ongoing tension for the police (and those responsible nationally and locally for policing) between, on the one hand, the demand to be more professional and to take on more responsibilities, which required more resources, and, on the other hand, the need to be economical by operating on reduced or static resources. These tensions were particularly evident after the economy cuts of the Geddes' Axe in 1921 and the cuts imposed by the National Government in 1932. A second general factor was the concern for social and political stability in an era when threatening ideologies appeared to be undermining national institutions and fomenting popular discontent.

Any discussion of inter-war policing must start with recognition of the weak position of the force as a whole at the end of the Great War. The 'collection of Victorian bric a brac', as Critchley rather harshly described the police at the outbreak of hostilities, was subjected to immense pressure as the demands of war increased. The total authorised strength of the 58 counties and 128 boroughs in 1918 was 35,536 regular police – in theory a small increase over the figure for 1914; but, in practice, the actual strength was 21,113, or just under 60 per cent of the authorised strength. The situation was worse in the boroughs where the figure was just under 56 per cent. The deficiency was made good, in part at least, by the employment of thousands of special constables, almost one thousand of whom were actually deployed on duty on any one day, and by the use of a small number of specialised women's patrols.[19] Leonard Dunning was of the view that 'the war has taught them [citizens] to rely upon their own powers for the protection of themselves and their property instead of leaning on the police.'[20] It was a prospect that filled him with anxiety – and not just for the wellbeing of the country at large. At a time when increased demands on the police suggest that there had been a quick return to the habit of 'leaning on the police' restoring numbers to something like pre-war levels was seen as essential. A further problem, clearly identified by the Desborough Committee, which dealt with police pay and conditions in 1918 and 1919, was the proliferation of small police forces across England and Wales. Table 1.1

Table 1.1 Selected police statistics: county and borough forces in England and Wales (excluding London) 1919–39

	Authorised strength	Vacancies	Vacancies as % authorised strength	Population per constable	Police women attested
1919	35,780	3308	9.25	805	37
1920	36,033	1795	4.98	800	33
1921	36,439	850	2.33	835	31
1922	36,415	2065	5.67	835	36
1923	36,488	2436	6.68	834	42
1924	36,562	2203	6.03	832	48
1925	36,604	1643	4.49	831	56
1926	36,640	1165	3.18	831	65
1927	36,751	1029	2.8	827	62
1928	36,895	974	2.7	824	65
1929	37,088	951	2.56	820	66
1930	37,187	833	2.24	818	71
1931	37,352	733	1.96	850	70
1932	37,294	842	2.26	851	81
1933	37,368	954	2.55	850	84
1934	37,573	843	2.24	845	89
1935	38,113	759	1.99	833	92
1936	38,799	819	2.37	818	89
1937	40,530	1216	3.00	783	93
1938	41,107	902	2.19	772	98
1939	42,708	1279	2.99	743	99

Source: HMIC Annual Reports.

summarises the overall situation regarding English and Welsh county and borough forces. The authorised strength grew unspectacularly over the two decades and did not match the growth in population.[21] Particularly in the early 1920s, vacancies ran at a much higher level than had prevailed before 1914, though part of this was in response to governmental demands for economies.[22]

For His Majesty's Inspectors of Constabulary (HMIC) recruitment, in both quantitative and qualitative terms, was a matter of deep concern. Dunning was concerned with 'the dearth of the best stamp of recruit' in 1919 but counselled against 'undue haste and the appointment of less suitable men' even though there was a need to rebuild overall police numbers.[23] His hopes that the situation would improve with time were not fully realised. Experience varied across the country and some chief constables, as for that in Oldham, reported no significant problems in recruiting suitable men; others did. The number of recruits failing their probationary period was worrying. In 1922, one of the worst years it should be said, 27 per cent of recruits were discharged before they had completed the first year. A year later Dunning was baffled by the continuing high failure rate. 'One might have thought,' he wrote in his annual report, 'that when recruiting was restricted, selection would be stricter and failures would be fewer, but this does not seem to be the case.'[24] A greater problem was the pool from which the police drew. At times Dunning's reports read like the lament of a eugenicist bemoaning the physical and moral decline of the nation.

> The general deterioration of the nation's physique and the after effects of war-time privations... account for the large number who are rejected on medical examination; but perhaps 90 per cent of the applicants for appointment never get so far as the doctor because they are manifestly unsuitable, while the simple educational test knocks out so many more that a Chief Constable is lucky if he finds five suitable men among a hundred applicants.[25]

Despite the fact that overall educational standards were improving 'the average quality of candidates [for the police] is not a bit better than it was years ago.'[26] Despite some positive comments on police training in the following years, the same complaints were being made over a decade later. '[F]or the Service as a whole the supply of recruits cannot be considered as satisfactory', wrote one of Dunning's successors, Brook, in 1937.[27] Expectations of the police had changed over the two decades and, despite the recruitment of better-educated men and improvements

Introduction 7

in initial training, there was a still a shortfall, more particularly in terms of the quality of police recruits.

The problems of recruitment and training were also related to a broader structural weakness in the police of England and Wales. There was a proliferation of forces in general and the persistence of small forces in particular. To compound matters the strength of localism in the thinking of police chiefs (and their political masters in both counties and boroughs) meant that practices varied considerably from force to force. Despite pressures from the centre to rationalise the distribution of police forces and to standardise training, localism proved remarkably resistant. Nowhere can this be more clearly seen than in the resistance to proposed amalgamations of police forces.

The variation in the size of both county and borough forces was quite staggering. At one extreme was the massive Metropolitan Police force, just under 20,000 strong in 1919. Small in comparison were the 1000 plus forces in Birmingham, Liverpool and Manchester, but these were giants compared with the borough forces in Louth and Tiverton, numbering 11 each, if at full strength, or Carmarthen and Congleton, each with an authorised strength of 12. There were also marked discrepancies in the size of county forces, itself a product of the variation in acreage and population between the counties of England and even more so of Wales. In 1919 the authorised size of English county forces varied from 16 in Rutland, 51 in Westmorland and 60 in Huntingdonshire to almost 2000 in Lancashire, nearly 1500 in the West Riding of Yorkshire and exactly 1000 in Staffordshire. In Wales the largest county force, by far, was that of Glamorgan which numbered over 700 men. Only 2 others (Carmarthenshire and Denbighshire) were more than 100 strong and 6 (i.e., half of the Welsh county forces) were less than 50 strong.[28]

There was an obvious logic to the merger of such small forces into a larger entity. The Desborough Committee considered this question of amalgamations at some length. His Majesty's Inspectors, notably Dunning and Atcherley, were strongly in favour, believing that police efficiency could be made as well as savings. Despite strong opposition, particularly from the non-County Boroughs Association, the committee 'strongly recommend that the small borough forces should be merged in the county forces... [and that] the necessary measures should be taken at the earliest possible date'.[29] It didn't happen as Table 1.2 illustrates. There was a brief flurry in the early 1920s. The borough forces of Barnstaple, Berwick, Durham, Louth, Ryde, Truro and Weymouth were abolished between 1920 and 1922. Thereafter mergers were confined to two: Banbury, which was absorbed into the Oxfordshire force

Table 1.2 Distribution by size (authorised strength) of police forces in England and Wales, 1919, 1929 and 1939 (excluding London)

	1919	1929	1939
Under 20	13	6	4
20–49	30	26	21
50–99	37	36	41
% Under 100	62	56	55
100–199	31	31	32
% 100–199	24	26	26
200–299	7	10	9
300–399	3	3	4
400–499	3	3	4
500–999	3	3	3
1000+	3	3	3
% 200+	15	18	19
Total	129	121	121

Source: HMIC Annual Reports.

in 1926, and Beverley, which was merged with the East Riding force in 1928. Tiverton, with its establishment of 11 and described as 'a little island police district' survived.[30] The frustration of the inspectorate was undisguised. Writing in 1928, Dunning bemoaned the failure to agree terms on the merger of Tiverton into the Devon force. 'This was unfortunate ... police districts like Tiverton are anachronisms in these days of modern facilities of travel, fenced in as they are by boundaries of which nobody but the police takes notice.'[31] In 1929 and 1930 chief constables in five small boroughs resigned but the opportunity to negotiate a merger came to nothing in every case.

Such was the concern with lack of progress that a select committee was established in 1932 to consider the matter. Once again the arguments for and against merger were rehearsed. The Home Office, in the formidable person of A. L. Dixon, argued for the merger of all police forces in boroughs of less than 75,000 but was unable to win over committee members. Nor were they persuaded that there were circumstances in which county boroughs should be deprived of their right to have a separate police force. However, they did recommend that the limit for non-county boroughs to have a separate police force should be raised from 10,000 to 30,000.[32] The cautiousness of the committee was also reflected in their decision not to comment on the merger of smaller county forces and the expansion of certain (smaller) borough police districts even though it had heard evidence as to the greater efficiency and economy that would ensue.[33] Hopes of change, albeit limited, quickly disappeared and the frustration of police chiefs grew in the late 1930s as demands upon the police increased. Brook summed up feelings in 1937.

> The increased burdens imposed on the police and the developments in the police service and in the police forces have made more apparent the administrative disadvantages of small forces and intensified their difficulties.... [T]he time is appropriate for a renewed plea for the merging of small forces.... Some of the forces are too small to justify the police administration, and cannot procure even simple police equipment. For example, in some forces criminals who should have been photographed have not been so photographed, because there are no means available to take a photograph. In other instances financial difficulties arose when it was considered necessary to send recruits and others to appropriate courses of training.[34]

Brook concluded that the problem was one of 'local sentiment... [but] while one must have great respect for local tradition and local patriotism' but felt 'the service as a whole... [cannot] be handicapped by such sentiment'.[35] The point was well made and any discussion of the positive developments of the 1930s in particular must always be qualified by the fact that there remained a significant 'tail' of conservative thinking and practice in the police forces of England and Wales. Nevertheless, it was against this unpromising and unpropitious social and economic climate of financial restraint and social conservatism that changes in policing began to change to meet the needs of governments convulsed with the fear of communism and consumed with concern about motorised transport and the 'road holocaust'. In the end policing in England and Wales was driven to change and modernise.

Part 1
The Problem of Public Order and the Professionalisation of the Police

The Great War of 1914–18 fundamentally changed many aspects of life and politics in Britain. Apart from destroying lives in war it undermined traditional industries, enhanced the role of the state and challenged old social and political values. But above all, as Ross McKibbin has recently reminded us, it was 'disruptive' of English politics, helped to destroy the Liberal Party, enhanced the political position of the Labour Party and reshaped the electorate 'such that about 80 per cent of it had never voted before'.[1] The result was that many politicians of the 1920s, and particularly, Stanley Baldwin, talked of the new experiment in democracy, and saw the rise of communism and the emergence of the Soviet Union as a challenge to the embryonic democracy that had emerged in Britain. What is clear is that throughout the inter-war years British politicians were concerned about the growth of extremist ideologies, particularly those of the communists, and the prospect that they might infiltrate British society and undermine public order. This became evident in the case of the police strikes of 1918 and 1919, in the industrial unrest of 1919–21, in the General Strike of 1926 and throughout the 1930s when communists clashed on the streets and with fascists. All inter-war British governments therefore wished to professionalise the police to ensure that, among other things, they were not susceptible to extremist ideas and this led to attempts to improve the pay and conditions, to improve the training and efficiency of the forces, to use the new scientific and forensic techniques that were emerging and to change the relationship between the Home Office, the chief constables and their local authorities. Governments were largely effective in these moves.

In Part 1 of this book Chapter 2 deals with the threat posed by the police strikes of 1918 and 1919 which clearly unnerved the British government and forced it to develop strategies to organise police opinion within a structure which inhibited future militant action by the police. In addition, successive governments ensured that the 2430 police who went out on strike in 1919 would never be re-employed by the police. It also examines the way in which the Police Federation was formed by the state to act as a representative body for constables, sergeants and inspectors in the forces throughout England and Wales and as an alternative to trade union militancy. The Federation and the state worked together closely despite the pay cuts of 1922 and 1931 temporarily undermining that relationship. However, the Federation was more a social club than a bargainer for improved working conditions, and Chapter 3 deals essentially with the way in which inter-war governments used chief constables to maintain public order and to avoid having to deal with the local police authorities and magistrates, some of whom may well have been reluctant to operate with the Home Office in times of strikes and public disorder. Chapter 4 examines another aspect of police professionalisation, the growth of detective and scientific work in policing, and reveals the progress that occurred from the early and mid-1930s which laid the foundation for the creation of modernised scientific detective work; it does give the lie to the impression that the inter-war years were simply dominated by the old style and values of Victorian and Edwardian policing. The fact is that major changes were afoot in the training that occurred to meet the challenges of the English and Welsh police forces.

2
Police Trade Unionism and the Federation

In 2009 the police and prison officers of England and Wales became increasingly frustrated at the way in which successive Home Secretaries had neglected them as their pay, conditions and benefits were being eroded. Many also become frustrated at the way in which the Police Federation of England and Wales seemed powerless to push forward with their wage demands.[2] Yet the right to strike has not been won, no police union has emerged and members of the Police Federation have simply protested in various provincial cities and towns, in London and near Downing Street, on their off-duty days. None of this is surprising when one remembers that the Police Federation was formed in 1919 by the Police Act, following the Desborough Committee recommendations, which passed its second reading in the House of Commons on 31 July 1919 before gaining Royal Assent on 15 August 1919. Its purpose was to counter the emergence of the militant National Union of Police and Prison Officers (NUPPO).[3] NUPPO was formed in 1917 but had emerged out of an earlier police union and went on to foment the Metropolitan Police Strike of August 1918 and the national Police Strike of July/August 1919.

Historians have often written briefly on these two police strikes in both the context of their own particular research and the revolutionary changes that were taking place in the Soviet Union and Eastern Europe at the end of the Great War. The central issue that they address is state control and the revolutionary threat to public order in Britain. James Cronin argues, for instance, that the threat that the police strikes and Bolshevism presented to public order has been greatly exaggerated since the British 'governing elite never lost the capacity or will to rule'.[4] Others, indeed probably the majority, beg to differ. Raymond C. Challinor, an International Socialist, asserts, in his *The Origins of British*

Bolshevism, that a revolutionary opportunity was missed because Lenin condemned the British left-wing demands for an immediate revolution as an 'infantile disorder' and ensured that the British communists would seek to work through the reformist Labour Party. He argues that that was the wrong message and that British communism should have pressed for revolutionary change at a time when the army and police were mutinying.[5] Historians of the British police either make passing remarks about the great dangers that the police had to face, usually emphasising the loyalty and duty of the police if they are local and individual studies,[6] or they agree with the revolutionary implications suggested by Challinor and others. T. A. Critchley, writing a wide-ranging history of the British police, sees the conflict as a struggle between the state and the trade union movement to preserve the 'neutrality' of the police.[7] Owen Jones's more focused study also sees the revolutionary potential of these strikes in linking them to the 'Spirit of Petrograd?' and suggests that the Police Union radicals were concerned to 'sever the connection between the police and the State in favour of the labour movement which in of itself had revolutionary connotations'. Apparently, the radical members of NUPPO believed that the police 'had always been the tool of the employing classes to defeat the legitimate claims of the workers' and as a result 'the ordinary worker was forced to the conclusion that the policeman was his natural and avowed enemy'.[8] To Jones the police strikes were part of a revolutionary moment and that the government outmanoeuvred the strikers, who were divided and lacked the support of the wider trade union movement. Other studies, such as R. Bean's article on the Police Strike of 1919 as it affected Liverpool, tend to tell a story rather than attempt to analyse the dispute within the wider framework of the industrial relations and general public order of the times.[9] In addition, the formation of the Federation may have been seen as a way for the state to head off trade unionism but one historian has suggested that the state was suspicious of the Federation in the inter-war years, thus calling into question the extent to which the police became a professional part of the state.[10]

The prevailing view appears to be that the police strikes of 1918 and 1919 were a revolutionary threat that failed because the wartime and coalition governments took them seriously. In addition, whilst the state created the Police Federation as an alternative non-industrial forum for police opinion, it is clear that there are doubts about its effectiveness during the inter-war years. However, like Cronin, we are not convinced that there was a serious revolutionary threat to the state and public order in Britain, although there is no doubt that the wartime and coalition governments convinced themselves of the revolutionary dangers. We argue that the 1918 and 1919 police strikes strengthened the conviction of inter-war governments that the police should have a formal, but largely toothless, influence over their pay and conditions, through the Federation, and that, as vital servants of law and order, the police would never be allowed to endanger the state by any action that, in the army, would be regarded as mutiny. Inter-war governments favoured the professionalisation of the police at the end of any trade unionism that might place them into conflict with the state. That required harsh treatment of those who struck in the name of trade unionism.

Indeed, the 2430, or so, police strikers and prison warders who struck in 1919 were made an example of by successive inter-war governments and watch committees, lost their jobs and were never allowed to return to their former posts, although, contrary to the general impression, some did recover their pension rights. The Special Branch of Scotland Yard kept a check on the ex-strikers and reported regularly to the Home Office on their vicarious activities. Chief constables and the representatives of watch committees in turn advised the Mackenzie Committee of 1924, a body formed as a result of pressure on the first Labour government from Jack H. Hayes (Labour MP for Edge Hill and a leading figure in the Police Union), the impossibility of re-employing a group of men who had endangered public order by their strike activities.[11] In the end, there was a wide and unbridgeable gulf between the chief constables, watch committees and local government organisations, who opposed the reinstatement of the strikers, and the representatives of the strikers, who demanded reinstatement. The Mackenzie Committee merely endorsed the existing situation and its meetings ceased as it became clear that no compromise was possible. The police authorities prevailed and the NUPPO was isolated from mainstream policing forever. As a result, many of the dismissed police officers became involved in organising public demonstrations against the British governments of the inter-war years and a small but active number became closely identified with the Communist Party of Great Britain and the All-Russian Co-operative Society which organised trade with Britain through Moorgate House, London.[12]

Instead of attempting to appease the strikers, successive inter-war governments channelled the frustrations of police officers into the arms of the newly formed Police Federation of England and Wales, diminishing even its limited influence further during the 1930s by reducing the higher-ranked inspectors from membership. The strikes of 1918 and

1919 were therefore defining moments in the organisational history of policing in England and Wales in the twentieth century.

Indeed, the Police Federation of England and Wales emerged to represent the 55,000–62,000 police officers employed in all forces in England and Wales during the inter-war years. Each police force set up a Branch Board that brought together the representatives of another three boards that represented constables, sergeants and inspectors in the force separately. They passed on their resolutions and concerns to their equivalent national organisations, the Constables' Central Committee, the Sergeants' Central Committee and the Inspector's Central Committee whose representatives joined together as the Joint Central Committee. They met every three months in various locations throughout the country and also held an annual meeting. This structure of local boards and central committees channelled the concerns of the police to the Joint Central Committee whose main function was to report the views of the members of the Police Federation to the Home Office and to circulate its replies. Much of this administrative traffic was concerned with the routine discussion of allowances and payments but occasionally, as in 1922 and again in 1932, there were serious concerns about the pay cuts occasioned by the 'Geddes axe' or 'Geddes blip' and the 10 per cent pay cut imposed by the national government in 1932.[13] The Federation also occasionally became involved in other issues, such as opposing women police officers having their own representation on the Federation and the appointment of chief constables. However, it is clear that the Police Federation carried little negotiating strength and it is evident that its very existence, and the limited formal influence it did carry, was due, almost entirely, to the industrial unrest amongst the police at the time of the Great War. Indeed, as is clear elsewhere, it was the Desborough Committee's reports of 1919 and 1920 that defined basic police pay and conditions during the inter-war years and neither NUPPO nor the Police Federation carried sufficient industrial muscle to force their demands upon governments.

The National Union of Police and Prison Officers and the 1918 and 1919 police strikes

Throughout the nineteenth century there had been many instances in which the police were 'in dispute' with their local watch committee over conditions and pay. In 1870 the Newcastle-upon-Tyne police were 'in dispute' but did not withdraw their labour. In 1872, 179 members of the Metropolitan Police refused to report for duty but 110 of them were back on duty within a matter of hours, having apologised for their actions, and the other 69 were dismissed. These strike actions led to government moves to address the issue of police pay and conditions in the 1880s. Nevertheless, there was a subsequent stoppage in the Metropolitan Force in June 1890 over police pensions. On this occasion the government declared that it would not be held hostage to demands of police officers but nonetheless rushed through Parliament the Police Pensions Bill of 1890. The Superannuation Act of 1906 offered improved police pensions. In effect, then, a small number of disputes led the central and local authorities to improve police pay and conditions in a haphazard way to neutralise attempts to form a police union.

The formation of such a union would, in any case, have been difficult. The Crime Act of 1885 made it illegal for anyone to interfere with police in the course of their duty. Local chief constables were not therefore inclined to encourage union activity. Indeed, Joanne Klein's recent book *Invisible Men: The Secret Lives of Police Constables in Liverpool, Manchester, and Birmingham, 1900–1939* examines the attempts of police officers to form unions alongside their lifestyle, marriage and working conditions. She concludes that 'Beginning around 1900, at the same time as that unionism was spreading through many working-class occupations, policemen struggled to find a voice within the police force.'[14] She notes that there were spasmodic efforts to organise police trade unions in the Victorian age but that they came to nothing although in 1893 John Kempster founded the *Police Review and Parade Gossip* to allow the lower ranks to air their grievances and to compare local conditions.[15] Nevertheless, in the late Edwardian years and in the years immediately before the Great War the frustration at the aggressive high-handedness of senior police officers in the Metropolitan Force changed during a decade which saw significant industrial unrest that had to be dealt with partly by the police.

The Metropolitan Police Union (MPU) was formed in October 1913 following years of protest against alleged corruption within the Metropolitan Force. On 21 September 1913 a protest meeting was held in Trafalgar Square, attended by 2000 supporters, against the dismissal of ex-Inspector John Syme from the Metropolitan Force and as followed up by several more, including a substantial one again at Trafalgar Square on 1 November, with an attendance of about 500.[16] Syme had been dismissed on 31 January 1910[17] for protesting at the 'corruption that exists among the superior officers in the Police Force today. It is because Sir Edward Henry [Metropolitan Commissioner] himself is a corrupt official and will not defend himself against our charges.'[18] The John Syme

League was formed in August 1913 to support the campaign, and was led by J. R. Penfold, T. G. Gamble, G. T. Brown, John Syme and H. E. Linnell, who acted as Honorary Secretary; most of whom do not appear to have been policemen.[19] It supported John Syme who was openly accusing the Metropolitan Police Commissioner of collusion and corruption and invited prosecution for libel, which did not occur at that time – although between 1913 and 1924 he was imprisoned on eight occasions and in early 1921 the Home Secretary informed the Cabinet that he had been transferred from prison to the Broadmoor Asylum.[20]

A pamphlet entitled *Fighting Officialdom*, which sold about 6000 copies, outlined the Syme case and the charges he was making and 'is sold at two pence' and 'A good many thousand of these have already been sold and passed on....'[21] It accused Sir Edward Henry, the Metropolitan Police Commissioner, of condoning 'tyranny of superior over subordinate, manufacturing of charges', and of approving of 'the tyrannical methods of Chief Inspector Shervington and Sub-Divisional Inspector Read of "B" Division', and that in the judgment that led to Syme's dismissal. It is Syme added that 'Sir E. R. Henry further deliberately misrepresented the facts of the official judgement in order to justify my punishment.'[22] Syme was later supported by Philip Snowden, the Labour MP for Blackburn, who took his case to the House of Commons.

The dramatic and tumultuous moment in the campaign occurred at a meeting in Trafalgar Square on 21 September 1913 when Syme stated that

> We are going to form a Union in London within the next month at the very latest, and we hope to be able to inform the Police of London that this Union has been formed but the disgraceful part of the business is that not one of our Police Officers dare join it openly. They will all require to join it secretly, trusting myself as the Honorary Secretary, whatever it may be to keep their names secret and confidential....[23]

In the event it seems that the MPU was formed on a Friday towards the end of October 1913, probably on the 27 October, with Syme as Secretary, a position he held until May 1917, and with the motto 'Tyranny is NOT Discipline'.[24] The management committee consisted of J. Gilbert Dale (the Chairman), Mackenzie Bell (Hon. Treasurer), J. R. Penfold as well as Syme (Secretary); Syme later lost his position in the union claiming that 'I was treacherously robbed of by Charles Duncan and a few treacherous policemen.'[25]

Open to all police officers in the Metropolitan Force the union had six main objectives: 'To safeguard the Members against official tyranny and injustice; To improve the conditions of the Police Service; To secure to each man equal chances for position or special appointment; To maintain just and effective discipline; To purge the Service of corrupt and unjust Members; To secure the Police and efficient Police Administration.'[26] Although the improvement of pay and conditions was one union objective it is clear that there was initially greater emphasis placed upon a just, efficient and effective police force and the removal of petty tyranny. But pay was a very important issue and there was concern that a 'Constables' highest rate is only a little higher than a road sweeper, and is lower than a postman, yet he is expected to live on a higher scale.'[27] The entry cost was set low at a shilling in order to make it accessible to a wide range of members.

From the start the MPU was realistic about the opposition it would face and, in what was essentially a panegyric, stated that 'That the Police Union will be strongly opposed by the Police Authorities cannot be denied....'[28] The police officers in the MPU were in fact informed by 'Circular on 23 December 1913 that the union was not recognised by the Commons'.[29] As a result its members inundated the Home Secretary, Sir Reginald McKenna, with letters evidencing the bullying and petty tyranny within the Metropolitan Police Force.[30] Syme kept up his campaign and union activities throughout the rest of 1913 and into 1914. Indeed, on 2 January 1914 *The Police Review and Parade Gossip*, which sought to be the organ of the British police, attempted to remain neutral by attacking Syme for 'attempting to invoke a spirit of rebellion throughout the Police' whilst stating that 'we are bound to say that the authorities themselves are largely responsible for the [police] protests.'[31]

Throughout the Great War the MPU sought to spread its influence and reorganised to form the NUPPO in 1917, for all police and prison officers, even though Sir Edward Henry insisted that any member of the Metropolitan Force who joined would be dismissed with a loss of all pension rights. In February 1917 seven policemen were dismissed for attending a NUPPO meeting. Nevertheless, NUPPO attracted the widespread support of both police officers, frustrated at their relatively low pay levels, and some prison officers who had became increasingly annoyed at the failure of the government to pay wartime bonuses commensurate with the cost of living paid to police officers.

Before the Great War there were seven different levels of pay for constables (paid from 23s 4d to 29s 2d) and six different rates for sergeants

(26s to 36s 4d), plus allowances, and sergeants within the Metropolitan Force were paid the higher standard of 30s–42s. These levels had not been revised since they had first been laid down in 1886.[32] At the beginning of the Great War changes were suggested and although the Home Office refused to sanction increases in pensionable pay they authorised the County Police Authorities, at their own discretion, to meet the increased cost of living by an allowance and encouraged flexibility in this direction by the borough forces, although they had always set their own levels of pay since they were subject to watch committees rather than the Home Secretary. Improved pay and conditions occurred. The Metropolitan Police officers, for instance, gained a three shilling (15p) allowance in 1915 and this had been increased to eight shillings (40p) by 1917 and 12 shillings (60p) by December 1917. There was also a children's allowance.[33] The government feeling was that these arrangements, which allowed for cost of living allowances alongside pay, would solve the problem of police pay and conditions and staunch any potential unrest amongst police forces. The assumption was incorrect as the Metropolitan Police Strike of 1918 so emphatically proved.

The fact is that Metropolitan Police pay had increased substantially from a total of about 47 shilling per week in 1917 to 69s 9d at the end of 1917, although the actual amounts varied according to the years of service, but that was still considered to be behind the rises needed because of wartime inflation.[34] Indeed, the *Westminster Gazette* of 30 August 1918 recorded a City policeman stating that 'we policemen see young van-boys and slips of girls earning very much more money than we get, and – well, it makes us feel sore.' Thomas Scott, the London organiser of NUPPO, was also reported as stating that 'We are sick of being messed about and being told that they are being considered, considered, considered.'[35] This frustration occurred against an increased working load for policemen who, as noted in the introduction, were greatly under Establishment strength during the Great War, a situation only partly offset by the re-employment and employment, on a temporary basis, of 1200 police pensioners and 30,000 voluntary special constables, the vast majority of whom were not on duty at any particular time. Indeed, as the introduction reveals, the Establishment strength of the police of England and Wales was well above the number actually employed on the Great War. The generally assumed estimate that 4000 policemen had volunteered to go to the front was undoubtedly a gross underestimate of the true level of loss of police to the armed forces.

By the summer of 1918 NUPPO was claiming a membership of 10,000, soon afterwards 12,000, of the 20,000 or so officers in the Metropolitan

Force alone. It also claimed about 300 members in the Manchester Police Force.[36] However, membership of NUPPO was not for the faint hearted and Jack Hayes later complained for NUPPO, in a letter to Lord Breadalbane, of the victimisation of men 'whose only crime was to object to the violation of the agreements entered into on 31 August 1918, between the Government and the men's representatives', that

> To be a member of the Union was a guarantee against any position, besides carrying with it dismissals, fines and penalties. This went on until August 29th 1918 when the new force was organised and meetings were held with David Lloyd George, the Prime Minister and the union was recognised following a pay demand of 12.5 per cent on 28 August for immediate effect.[37]

Hayes's comment was, of course, a skewed, and possibly misleading, version of the events but it was the victimisations of officers, just as much as pay, that appears to have been the driving force to action.

Constable 'Tommy' Thiel, of the Metropolitan Police, was dismissed on 25 August 1918 for being both an organiser of the union and a socialist. This case was one which encouraged NUPPO to campaign almost incessantly for a raft of measures including the reinstatement of Thiel, pay increases, improved war bonuses, an extension of the pension to include the policeman's widow, a shortening of the pension entitlement period and an allowance for the school children of police families. NUPPO informed the police authorities that there would be a strike unless their demands were met by midnight on 29 August 1918.

The government and the authorities were taken aback by the swiftness of union action and the Home Office collected evidence of the widespread refusal to work on the morning of the 30 August and throughout 31 August. There are detailed police records, mainly in the form of hundreds of Metropolitan Police telegrams, and later reports, indicating the extent of the strike, and the threatening behaviour that occurred when between about 5000 and 6000 officers in the Metropolitan Force, about 30 per cent of the force, went out on strike, although other reports suggest that this figure might have been as high as 12,000.[38] There were numerous examples of clashes between the strikers and the non-strikers and threatening behaviour on that date related in the various telegrams. At 5.45 am on 30 August 1918, 500–600 striking policemen threatened the on-duty officers at Paddington police station. At 7.50 am 20 men in M District 'refused to go out on duty, on the grounds that they were not receiving a living wage'. At 9.10 am that

'6 PCs at Clapham Station have refused to go on point duty. The cause is the dismissal of PC Thiel and they desire his reinstatement before they will return to duty. They have been suspended.' Another telegram indicated that 'About 200 apparently suspended police offices in plainclothes intimidated 4 police constables who remained on duty with the result that the officers were obliged to come to the police station. A number of them still remain in the vicinity of Hammersmith whilst others have apparently gone to other districts to carry out the same tactics.' At noon PC Benstead requested that the military authorities should be asked to conduct a 'number of military patrols in the Strand and District from 7.00 pm tonight'. At 1.34 pm it was reported 'About 300 strikers now passing along Piccadilly towards Piccadilly Circus.' Yet another telegram claimed that 'About 2,000 police strikers gathered at 9.30 pm at Marleybone Police station and attempted to close it.' In the following two weeks there were further reports and investigations of many of these incidents. In them, one police officer reflected that the police were 'mutinying in the face of the natural enemy'.[39]

The strikers were encouraged by other trade union organisations. In particular, the Ilford Branch of the National Union of Railwaymen sent a letter to Sir Edward Henry congratulating the 'Metropolitan Police on their magnificent stand for recognition of their Trade Unions…'.[40] In early September 1918, Sylvia Pankhurst wrote in her Marxist paper *Workers' Dreadnought* about the 'Spirit of Petrograd! The London police on strike!', adding that 'After that, anything may happen. Not the army, but the police force is the power which quells political and industrial uprisings and maintains the established fabric of British society.'[41]

In order to control the dispute and maintain public order, the army was called out, but on 31 August David Lloyd George, the Prime Minister, acted quickly and met the union leaders. He appeared to accept NUPPO's right to exist, as already referred to, something which the Home Secretary was later to admit to the House of Commons in December 1918, as long as the union did not interfere with police pay and conditions.[42] He also offered an increase in pay for all ranks of 13 shillings (65p) per week in pensionable pay, raising the minimum pay to 43 shilling (£2.15) per week. The right to a pension was to be established at 26, rather than 30, years of service and widows were awarded a pension of 10 shillings (50p) per week. Constable Thiel was also to be reinstated.

The Prime Minister, however, argued later that he had not given the union recognition, as he felt that he could not do so in the wartime situation, but there was a sense that the union would be tolerated, and its members not subjected to dismissal, as long as it made no further attempt to determine police pay and conditions. The situation was clearly nebulous and open to wide interpretation. James Marston, the union president, and Jack Hayes, by then NUPPO secretary, constantly reminded the public that the union had been recognised in 1918. Indeed the government may well have been more responsive than it had intended to be for in the wake of the 1918 Metropolitan Police Strike policemen in Manchester threatened to strike, although this was averted when they were offered the same conditions as the Metropolitan Force. By October 1918, several other police forces throughout the country had been given pay increases. As a result it was claimed that union membership had risen from about 200 in 1916 to 10,000 in August 1918, and to about 50,000 in November 1918, and the union claimed 200 branches by January 1919. If this last membership figure is correct then about five out of six police officers in Britain were union members, attached to a body that could potentially be in conflict with the state. However, as indicated in the introduction, police forces were greatly under their authorised strength and the figure of 50,000 has to be an exaggeration despite the deep discontent of police officers.

Given the Menshevik and Bolshevik revolutions in Russia in 1917, and the changing political system, it is hardly surprising that there was sensitivity about the forces of law and order in Britain asserting their right to strike. Lord Wittenham, speaking in the House of Lords, stated 'Stamp out Bolshevism and you will have no more of these untimely strikes.... Get the enemy in our midst by the throat, and get Bolshevism by the throat, and you will have no more of these strikes whose end and aim has been to paralyse the war.'[43] He concluded that the sinister enemy was Bolshevism which was attempting to paralyse the war effort. David Lloyd George, the Prime Minister, informed Andrew Bonar Law, the Conservative leader, that 'Unless this mutiny of the Guardians of Order is quelled the whole fabric of law and order may disappear. The Prime Minister is prepared to support any steps you make, however, grave, to establish the authority of social order.'[44] Revolution in Britain had seemed a very real prospect to some, particularly the political elite, after the Russian revolutions of 1917 and the industrial disturbances in Britain of 1918 and 1919, although the next chapter reveals that there was initially little concern about the prospect of revolution.

Nevertheless, the government acted quickly to deal with the threat of police unionism. It removed Sir Edward Henry, the Commissioner of the Metropolitan Police and replaced him with much more dominant and commanding General Sir C. F. Nevil Macready whose real function, in his brief appointment, was to destroy the union. He created a Police Council, the Metropolitan Representative Board, under the Police Orders, on 16 September 1918, and it held its first meeting on 17 October 1918.[45] This representative police body consisted of a committee of 1 inspector, 5 sergeants and 26 constables, which meant that there was 1 delegate being appointed by secret ballot for each division irrespective of ranks. In addition there were *ex officio* members of NUPPO.[46] This body clearly anticipated the formation of the Police Federation of England and Wales. Macready also refused to deal with union officials. The government also set up the Desborough Committee to examine both the pay and conditions of policemen in England, Wales and Scotland, and the structure of policing.

On 20 December 1918, the government was also being advised by General Macready, General Horwood, Sir Leonard Dunning and Major General (sometimes referred to as Lt. Col.) Atcherley about the danger that a police union might cause a national or general strike and that that 'would be pure Bolshevism and would if successful mean an end to all discipline. It should be dealt with immediately and by strong measures: failure would lead to complete anarchy.'[47] They also suggested that a circular should be sent around to all chief constables advising the retention and careful use of special constables, and that the public should be allowed to express their dissatisfaction before the military were called in. In January 1919 Macready informed Lloyd George that 'As regards official recognition, I can say that, in my opinion, not only is it impossible but I believe to be quite impossible for the Union to exist... if the country is to have an efficient body of Police on whom the Authorities can absolutely rely.'[48]

NUPPO was not intimidated by the government actions. James Marston declared in the first issue of NUPPO journal *The Police and Prison Officers Magazine*, on 19 December 1918, that 'The Representative Board would be taken notice of once the Union was behind it...'.[49] On 23 January 1919 the *Magazine* reported PC Patterson's view that 'every member of the Board must be a Union member'. On another occasion, it was argued that

> Recognition would come, and the Representative Board will collapse, for the recognition at present is the Alpha and Omega of the Union.... are we to have a representative Board or a Union? We certainly do not require both. The larger the Board's acknowledged by the Executive Committee of our Union, the greater the fight for recognition.[50]

However, recognition did not come. The Union won the right to representation on the Metropolitan Board and the Board was dismissed and Macready instigated a policy of repression. On 17 March 1919 Macready informed the police that the government was against union recognition and demanded that all policemen should cease to be union members. It dismissed those who refused and this led to further union action when a mass meeting was held at Trafalgar Square on 4 May to protest against the 'barbarous punishment meted out to Constable Spackman, Metropolitan Police'.[51] Spackman had been brought before the Disciplinary Committee of the Metropolitan on 1 April 1919 for 'gross insubordination' and effectively sacked for putting up a notice, proclaiming 'All Out', in a police station and attempting to provoke strike action.[52]

At the end of 1918 the Home Secretary admitted to the House of Commons, what Lloyd George had intimated to the men on 31 August 1918, that 'the men shall be entitled to join any lawful body which they may wish to join, including a Police Union'.[53] This position had clearly changed by 1919. On 28 May the Home Secretary informed the House of Commons that there was no policemen's union because any policeman who joined a union was no longer to be employed.[54] On 30 May 1919 a 'Memoranda of the War Cabinet' was circulated within government by the Home Secretary stating that the 'Union would not be recognized'. Interestingly, the memoranda declared that the representative board idea in the Metropolitan Force had been a failure given a circular produced just ahead of the decision to introduce a Police Bill in August 1919 that intended to end union power by extending the principle of representative boards to the nation's police as a whole. On the advice of Macready, it appears that the Home Secretary had come to the conclusion 'that the maintenance of discipline in the Police Force cannot be maintained if the men are allowed to belong to any Union'.[55] The concern was that NUPPO had sought to 'control the Representative Committee and its Executive Committee' and had sought to interfere 'with Police Regulations', in contravention of the 1885 Crime Act.

Before these tensions intensified further, the (Lord) Desborough Committee was set up in 1918, to report, in the first instance, on police pay and conditions for England, Wales and Scotland. There was at that time no uniform system of pay structure for police forces and it was the local watch committees who determined police pay and conditions. The Desborough Committee discovered that the average constable serving in a provincial county or borough force received about £2 15s 0d (£2.75), including their allowances for rent and children, and a 10 shilling (50 p) war bonus.[56] There was, of course, immense diversity. A constable in the West Riding Force earned between 28s 7d and 32s 8d, those at Sheffield between 28s and 39s, and those at Manchester between 28s and 40s.[57] This suggests that, with the war bonus and allowances, police officers in the West Riding earned below the average figure given by Desborough whilst those in the larger urban forces earned around or slightly above the average. Sergeants in these three forces earned, respectively, 39s 5d to 44s 4d, 41s 6d to 46s 6d, and 41s to 48s before the addition of a war bonus and allowances.[58] The average constable in the Metropolitan Police received about £3 7s 0d, including a war bonus of 12 shillings. The pay for the higher ranks of all other ranks throughout the country, short of assistant chief constable and chief constable, varied from £325 for first year inspectors up to £625 for a chief superintendent with county and borough forces and from £325 to £700 for inspectors up to the rank of superintendent.[59] However, it was the pay of constables and sergeants that most interested the Desborough Committee which found that in comparison a street cleaner in Newcastle-upon-Tyne was on about £2 15s 0d per week, a dock gate worker in Liverpool about £3 8s 0d and in Glasgow some unskilled street worker earned up to £4 per week.[60] As a result of the low pay for constables, and to a lesser extent sergeants, the Committee offered more generous increases (incorporating war bonuses and raising pay by almost 100 per cent) in Part 1 of its report which appeared on 1 July 1919 but not widely published until 1920.[61] (Part 2, which appeared in 1920, dealt mainly with the structure of policing in Britain.) These pay increases, which saw constables' pay raised to between £3 10s and £4 10s, were announced on 30 May and backdated to 1 April 1919 and were also linked with the formation of the Police Federation in the Police Act of 1919. The idea was to undermine the demand for trade unionism amongst the police but NUPPO was not to be denied and trade union activities were soon afoot to widen its appeal and its demands.

Although limited in their action, size and influence it is clear that some prison officers did agitate for and join NUPPO. Prison officers from Wormwood Scrubs and Brixton prisons had been present at a meeting of NUPPO held on 18 January 1917, at its headquarters at 26 Marston Street, Pimlico, where it was made clear that NUPPO was not recognised by the government.[62] After the apparent success of the Metropolitan Police Strike prison warders began to join NUPPO in small numbers in the hope that they would get pay, pensions and allowances in relation to those paid to police officers.[63] Indeed Edgar Percy Brown sent a letter to the Prison Commission on behalf of prison warders on 3 May 1917 about poor pay and conditions, and five other prison warders sent a separate letter on the same day.[64]

NUPPO organised a strike ballot for 29 May 1919 for which it claimed 53,000 ballot papers were issued to the police officers and police warders. Of the 48,863 returned, 44,581 were in favour of strike action.[65] Again, as already previously suggested, these figures are likely to have been greatly exaggerated. Nevertheless, the result was announced in time for a demonstration of the union at Hyde Park on 1 June 1919 out of which emerged a number of demands on pay and conditions which were presented to the Home Secretary on 26 June 1919. However, before the government was able to respond a strike broke out, between 31 July and 3 August 1919, amongst the Metropolitan Force and some of the English and Welsh provincial forces, most obviously in Liverpool, Birkenhead and Birmingham.

The union issued a short leaflet on 1 August 1919 which suggested that courage was required in the face of a strong enemy and 'JOIN OUR RANKS AND LET THE FIGHT BE YOURS'.[66] It argued that its 'Sole Grievance' was the Police Bill, 1919, which was passing through Parliament because, and particularly clauses 1, 2 and 3, 'These clauses take from Parliament their Civil Rights as Citizens, and aim at the destruction of Trade Unionism throughout the country.' Clause 1 was the formation of the Police Federation; clause 2 forbade policemen from being members of a trade union for the control or influence of pay, pensions and condition; and clause 3 allowed for any person causing 'disaffection amongst members of the Police Force, to be imprisoned, with or without hard labour, for two years, or given a summary conviction of three months and a fine not exceeding £50.' In the final analysis, NUPPO insisted that its main work was not so much to fight for improved conditions, which it assumed would arise from its recognition, but to establish the essential right of a police union to exist.

At first it was estimated that around 3000 police officers and prison warders refused to work but in fact the Home Office figures generally indicate that 2364 police officers and 73/74 prison warders came out on strike. Even then the Home Office official figures do vary a little, but it is generally claimed that 1054 or 1084 (1056 or 1156 in some sources from a force of 18,200 men) of the Metropolitan Force came out on strike, that 954 (sometimes indicated as 932, 936 or 1014) men from the Liverpool Force did the same and that remaining 400 or so policemen struck in the City of London (8), Birkenhead (106 or 114), Bootle (63), Wallasey (1) and Birmingham (118).[67]

There were threats of violence in London with numerous Special Branch reports of the subsequent speeches and actions of the strikers and their leaders. Hayes, on the 3 August, spoke at Croydon stating that 'The Police Union... was fighting for the principle of Trade Unionism.'[68] At a Hyde Park meeting on 18 August 1919, ex-PC Martin stressed 'the part they are playing in destroying the Prussianism which has been manifest in the Police for some time'.[69]

The Liverpool Police responded to the strike call far more favourably than did the Metropolitan Police with more than half of them coming out on strike – 954 from 1874 members of the force. On the day of the strike the striking police formed into ranks and marched around the stations attempting to persuade all of their colleagues to join the dispute. By the third day of the strike 'the Police Force of the Borough was practically non-existent' and the watch committee 'decided to approach the Lancashire constabulary with a view to obtaining a loan of constables from outside the Borough'.[70] Left without an effective police presence there was, according to the *Liverpool Daily Post* of 4 August 1918, an orgy of looting and rioting in the Scotland Road area of Liverpool between 1 and 3 August. This lasted for three or four days before the remnants of the police force and the army brought matters under control. Indeed, 'Soldiers with fixed bayonets were drawn up across the end of London Road and behind these were a large force of Special Constables and several loyal Policemen (All plain clothes).' In the event, several lives were lost in the disturbances and about 420 people were arrested, many of whom were later imprisoned. Between 35 and 40 shops were destroyed in Birkenhead, with £45,000 of damage.[71] Many of those arrested were given sentences of two, six or nine months, with hard labour.

In Bootle there was widespread support for the strike and it was reported that the police force was 'practically non-existent on the third day of the strike'.[72] Similar stories emerged elsewhere. Ex-PC Potter stated at a meeting at the Bull Ring in Birmingham, on 8 August 1919, that 'The police are out for their freedom.'[73] At a meeting at the Bull Ring, on 9 August, Harry Shepperson, a member of the Amalgamated Society of Engineers and the Independent Labour Party, stated that 'This Police Bill is a deliberate attempt on the part of the Government to smash trade unionism.'[74] At the Bull Ring, on 10 August 1919, ex-Superintendent Doughty attacked clauses 1, 2 and 3 of the Police Bill, stating that 'if you let it go through it will not only smash the Civil Service Forces, but it will be the thin edge of the wedge for the Government to smash the unions.'[75]

Macready of the Metropolitan Force, the Home Office, and the various police authorities and watch committees throughout England and Wales took a stern approach towards the strikers and dismissed them instantly, never reinstating them despite immense pressure to do so during the inter-war years. Indeed, Macready was quick to distinguish between the reprehensible values of the strikers from the loyalty of the majority of continuing police officers who were obedient to 'Authority and discipline necessary to maintain their objectives to the State'.[76] Prominent and leading figures in NUPPO – Spackman, Hayes, Thiel, Marston and others – were constantly under the surveillance of Special Branch, whose general view was that they were communists and potential revolutionaries and had their speeches recorded.[77] On 2 August 1919 Thiel was reported to have told a meeting 'Don't take any notice of having the sack, that is all kid.' Hayes, speaking at Croydon on the same day, stressed that 'The Police Union... were fighting for the principles of Trade Unionism...' and warned other trade unions of the dangers if the government smashed the Police Union.

The 1919 'national' Police Strike had collapsed quickly. The reasons were obvious from what has been written but there were internal divisions, the details of which need no detailed examination here. In the end, only about 4 per cent of the policemen of England and Wales had struck and the majority had continued to work tempted by the improved pay and fearful of losing their jobs, salary and pension. There had been tensions within the union, many of the more right-wing figures remaining aloof from the main leaders because of the threat of revolution,[78] and the British Labour movement offered moral support but did not offer industrial action in support – a general strike.

In the ensuing years successive governments were determined to ensure that the strikers were never reinstated in what became a vicious vendetta by the state. There were numerous police reports on the dismissed strikers suggesting their Marxist credentials. Ex- Police Superintendent Sell was reported as stressing the socialist principles of NUPPO on 4 August at Barking Broadway in London. At Battersea on 11 February 1922 and ex-PC Howard complained that 'the Prime Minister and Sir Alfred Mond were the two most leading enemies of the working class organisations' and attacked Sir Eric Geddes for causing difficulties for the police by recommending 'a reduction in pay.'[79] At NUPPO meetings at Tottenham on 4 and 7 August 1922 it was asserted that 'Mr. Lloyd George, once a Socialist but now a Capitalist, was the worst enemy of the ex-police.'[80]

The assumption of those reporting was that NUPPO's strikers were all communists. Allegedly, and damagingly, Jack Hayes addressed a meeting on 6 February 1922 along 'with other communist speakers'.[81] The ex-Police Constables W. Wheeler, Hutchings and Howard spoke at Battersea with other dismissed men on 11 February 1922, Howard referring to 'the Prime Minister and Sir Alfred Mond as the two most deadly enemies of the working class organisation'. Mond, he dubbed as a 'German Jew born in Cologne who did not like English people'. On 8 March 1922 there was a meeting of 150 people at Memorial Hall, Farringdon Street, London at which about a dozen dismissed policemen were present including ex-Police Sergeant William Sell, a member of the executive committee of the NUPPO, who was also felt to be communist.[82]

These claims were greatly exaggerated in the climate of the 1920s when the Soviet Union and international communism was seen as posing a threat to Britain but they were not without some justification. The irrefutable evidence for the Special Branch was a report to the Home Office on 14 February 1923 which suggested that all NUPPO officials were communists, although this cannot be verified since the Communist Party of Great Britain kept few membership lists, for obvious reasons of surveillance, and they may have simply been fellow travellers. According to Special Branch, all, except for Hayes who was by then a Labour MP, seem to have been employed by Soviet House, 43–49 Moorgate, London, where the Soviet Union organised its purchases from and sales to Britain in the early 1920s through the All-Russian Co-operative Society.[83] Thomas John Currie Scott, previously of the Metropolitan Police, was housekeeper there at £25 per month with his wife paid £3 10s per week; James Marsden who had been on the Metropolitan Police was employed as a clerk; Frederick W. Howard was night-watchman at £5 per week; William Sell, ex-Police Sergeant in K Division of the Metropolitan Police, was employed and his two sons were employed as clerks; ex-Prison Warder Brodrip, late of Wormwood Scrubs, was a clerk; Daniel Diness, ex-Police Sergeant in S Division of the Metropolitan Police, was employed there but had left; ex-PC Sidney Rupert Taylor was employed as a housekeeper; Arthur Lakey, ex-Police Sergeant of F Division of the Metropolitan Police, was the private and confidential exporting agent of Nicholas Klishko, Secretary of the Russian Trade Delegation.[84]

Throughout the 1920s, Hayes and the Police Union constantly pressured the Home Office, the police authorities, watch committees, parliament and even the newly formed Police Federation, formed by the 1919 Police Act, to reinstate the dismissed police officers. In a letter to the Home Office, dated 21 November 1919, Hayes objected to the dismissal of men 'whose only crime was to object to the violation of the agreements entered into on 31 August 1918, between the Government and the men's representatives' in their direct negotiations with David Lloyd George.[85] He added that those 'dismissed from the Force are now regarded as black sheep' but that on the contrary that the character of the men dismissed was of 'such an excellent nature' that 'without fear of contradiction, these men are the cream of the Service' and that many of them had served their country with distinction, a fact supported by the evidence he produced and indicated in Table 2.1.[86] Hayes also noted under the Police Act of 1919 that police officers were not allowed to be members of trade unions, though they could be a member of the Police Federation, that questions about conditions would be settled by the Ministry of Labour and that those striking could lose pension rights.

NUPPO did not relent upon the need for the reinstatement of their dismissed members and the removal of the 1919 Police Act.[87] However, the Police Federation now came into existence, holding its first annual national meeting at the end of May and beginning of June 1920 when PC Farling, of the Metropolitan Police, was elected as Chairman of the Joint Central Committee.[88] Its very existence was designed to be a challenge to NUPPO, although the union did approach the Police Federation for support. Hayes sent a letter requesting support in the campaign for the reinstatement from both the Metropolitan Police Board (sergeants) and Metropolitan Police Branch Board (constables). Neither responded positively to the request and at a meeting on 22 June 1920 Police Sergeant Vennell stated that 'there was great sympathy for a good many of those who came out, but at the same time we know that they were misled... by their trusted leaders.'[89]

Table 2.1 The war record of the dismissed policemen: men with a military or naval record[90]

Town	In HM Armed Forces	Medals	Wounded
London	443	795	145
Liverpool	398	584	92
Birkenhead	65	128	40
Bootle	44	76	?
Birmingham	54	76	4
Sub-total	1004	1426 [sic]	281 plus wounded
Others		236	
Total		1662	

Note: These are the figures given although the medals total comes to 1659, plus 236 others.

Hayes had by that time already approached both the Labour Party Conference and the Trades Union Congress (TUC) for support. The Labour Party Conference held at Scarborough on 27 June 1919 received the union representatives favourably. The TUC Conference at Glasgow on 8 September 1919 saw the Police Act as a fearsome attack upon trade unionism. Indeed, Labour MPs J. H. Thomas, Vernon Hartshorne, T. Tootill and R. Griffiths, and TUC representatives Henry Gosling and Fred Bramley, visited the Home Office as a deputation on 12 November 1919 where the Home Secretary stated that he had 'no authority' over the actions of the watch committees and the Standing Joint Committee. In other words, he would take no action to ensure the reinstatement of the strikers.[91]

NUPPO achieved little from its efforts throughout the 1920s. None of the strikers got their jobs back although a few did receive some of their pension rights. The Liverpool City Police Watch Committee did, reinstate the pensions of Charles Henry Johnson and John Auchterlonie, after protracted discussions in 1921 and 1922.[92] Also, the Liverpool Watch Committee and the Courts did allow some strikers with over 25 years service to draw their pensions under both the 1906 Superannuation Act and the 1926 Superannuation Act. Ex-PC Rigby won £800 damages in the High Court in December 1920 against the Bootle Watch Committee for 'wrongful dismissal' when failing to report for duty and hoped for reinstatement, and other cases for compensation were fought.[93] There was clearly some support for compensation from local authorities and watch committees, although reinstatement was clearly out of the question. Indeed, Major Clem Attlee, the then Mayor of Stepney and future Labour leader and prime minister, stated that means should be found 'if you cannot reinstate these men to seeing what you can do to assist them. We feel of course that they were misguided.'[94] Many other mayors expressed similar sentiments.

Also, Jack Hayes's pressure on the Labour Party carried some weight and support when he reminded the Labour Party and the Parliamentary Labour Party of its promise to examine the case for the reinstatement of the strikers at the moment that the first Labour government was formed in January 1924. It set up the 'Sir William Mackenzie' Committee to examine the issue. The initial indications were that the Labour government would reinstate the strikers and a meeting organised by NUPPO at Clapham Common on 3 February 1924 was disappointed at the 'stand that the Labour government had made' not to reinstate the dismissed policemen.[95] Notwithstanding this, Hayes sent letters, demanding reinstatement, to the Home Secretary, Arthur Henderson, on 25 March, 7 and 12 April 1924. However, Henderson was advised by the relevant police chief constables and commissioner, and his own officials, that it was impossible to reinstate the strikers because they had been warned that striking would lead to their dismissal, there were dangers that their reinstatement would lead to disruption and potential conflict with those ex-colleagues who did not strike, there were no jobs available, that many strikers were now potential revolutionaries and that most would now be unsuitable for employment. The outcome was an inglorious moment in the career of Henderson and the life of first Labour government. Henderson informed the Cabinet in a report of 31 March 1924 that 'I am regretfully forced to conclude that the objections to reinstatement and the difficulties that are in the way are of the most formidable character.'[96] Henderson presented similar comments to Hayes who then asked Henderson, in a letter of 7 April, 'what are these formidable practical difficulties'.[97] The reinstatement issue was then raised at a meeting of the Parliamentary Labour Party (PLP) on 29 May 1924, along with Henderson's subsequent suggestion that he would form a committee to examine the position of the dismissed police and prison officers. The PLP declared that Henderson's statement was 'directly contrary to Party policy' and that 'the dice would be loaded against the men with an inquiry composed of two lawyers and only one trade union representative.'[98]

Nevertheless, it was in the hands of the Mackenzie Committee that lay the fate of 2364 policemen and 73/4 prison officers.[99] Many of these were clearly vastly experienced policemen who had found their careers terminated. Indeed the evidence Mr Frances Caldwell, Chief Constable of Liverpool, was that 49 were sergeants and 965 constables (figures that do not tally with the other official figures given for the Liverpool Police strikers) and that between them 90 had 20 or more years of service, 105 between 15 and 20 years, 188 between 10 and 15 years, 332 between 5 and 10 years, 78 from 1 to 5 and only 153 under 1 year experience (indicating 936 in total which again differs from the figures given in the same evidence).[100] In other words, it was an experienced force of police who struck and were being judged.

The evidence presented to the six sittings of the Mackenzie Committee was extensive but reflected the imbroglio that reinstatement presented.[101] Hayes and NUPPO demanded clemency for the strikers, stressing that many of the strikers had fought with valour for their country in the Great War. In contrast, the Non-Urban Associations, the Metropolitan Association and other similar police authorities, and the police chief constables, responded by suggesting that there could not be any forgiveness for those who had been responsible for the dereliction of their duties. The issue was one of law and order and Sir Neville Macready, in a letter to the Home Secretary at that time, referred to the fact that reinstatement would be seen as rewarding 'Mutiny', an accusation repeated by him in the evidence he presented to the Mackenzie Committee.[102]

Macready had already advised the Home Secretary that 'The machinations and tyranny of the Union seriously undermined the discipline and efficiency of the service, and the evil effects have not even yet been entirely eradicated. Any reversal of the decision arrived at in 1919 will, inevitably', he argued, 'lead to lesser efficiency and weakened discipline'.[103] He further emphasised that the Police Orders introduced on 30 and 31 May 1918 stressed the loyalty of the police to the service and should not be changed. In a letter to Harwood, at the Home Office, dated 21 March 1925, Macready emphasised that Hayes had been beaten 'all along the line' and reflected that PC Spackman, who had sent a letter to the Home Secretary seeking a return to his post, 'was never anything but a very mediocre officer and after 6 years of loafing would be beneath contempt as a constable. His letter is nothing but "sob stuff" of the worst type.' As for the rest of the situation the 'Gospel of Hayes and the Union' had to be ignored.[104] These views were presented to the Mackenzie Committee on 5 June 1925 where it was stated that there was Mutiny because 'the men withdrew themselves from the duty which they had sworn to perform and were liable to penalties under the Police Act of 1839.'[105]

The attitude of the police authorities and the police was overwhelmingly against reinstatement of the strikers. T. B. Browne, Chief Constable of Bootle, stated to the Committee that 'I am strongly opposed at the re-appointment and re-instatement of police strikers for the following reasons – refusal to duty knowing full consequent, no hope of reinstatement, unfair to loyal men.'[106] Mr Alfred Henry James, the late Chairman of the Watch Committee in Birmingham, said some police officers had been 'misled and coerced'.[107] Mr Charles Houghton Rafter, Chief Constable of Birmingham, said much the same and read out the Statutory Declaration of police officers at Birmingham that

> I do solemnly, sincerely and truly declare and affirm that I will well and truly serve our Sovereign Lord the King in the office of constable of the City of Birmingham, etc, etc,. and that while I continue to hold the said office I will discharge the duties thereof to the best of my skill and knowledge, faithfully according to the law without fear, favour, affection, malice or ill will.[108]

This was very similar to the evidence and the oath given by the Police authorities in Liverpool, the oath being that

> I will declare that I will well and truly serve our sovereign Lord the King in the office of constable for the City of Liverpool without favour or affection, malice or ill will and that I will to the best of my powers cause the peace to be kept and prevent all offences against the persons and property of His Majesty's subjects; and that while I continue to hold the said office I will to the best of my skill and knowledge discharge all the duties thereof faithfully according to the law.[109]

The Mackenzie Committee was never going to more than act as a conduit for government and local police authority opposition to reinstatement. The local police authorities, the police and the Home Office were anxious not to upset the delicate balance of agreement and trust that was developing in the early 1920s. The government had allowed expenditure on policing to almost double between 1919 and 1922 and, despite the 'Geddes axe', the 'Geddes blip' or the Geddes cuts, the local police authorities were not anxious to argue with flexible and compliant governments, and, indeed, the situation was reciprocated. Indeed, in 1922 the Home Office fine-tuned the Geddes cuts, only pruning £1.8 million in the police pay and allowances in the hope of not upsetting more than necessary the chief constables, the police authorities and even the Police Federation of England and Wales. There was little possibility that the evidence given to the Mackenzie Committee by any of the formal establishment was going to suggest reinstatement. In the end it practically faded into oblivion leaving the strikers to their fate.

Further evidence submitted to the Home Office suggests that by the late 1920s about two-thirds of the dismissed strikers had found new jobs. If true that left about 800 or so men who had become disaffected, some of them threatening to be at the forefront of a British Bolshevik Revolution – the constant fear of successive British governments. Some individuals, such as ex-policeman Walter Edwin Dale, on whom the Home Office kept personal files, were seen as particularly dangerous. Indeed, in Dale's case there is evidence that in 1925 he spent some time following a female member of MI5, Miss Dorothy Saunders, and that he was 'Known to be a member of an organisation engaged in espionage on behalf of Russia'.[110]

The calls for reinstatement continued well into the 1930s and were often related to the decision of the national government to cut the wages and salaries of civil servants and by 10 per cent in the case of police, achieved in two stages. Though the police could not strike, about 3000–4000 policemen, delegates of the Police Federation of England and Wales, met at the Manchester Free Trade Hall on 19 January 1932 incensed by the first 5 per cent cut in pay.[111] They were addressed by Jack Hayes MP who saw the cuts as 'an insidious attack on the Desborough standards'.[112] Rhys Davis, another Labour MP, was also present to make the same point. There was speculation that the protests seemed to have worked for the second 5 per cent cut was rumoured to have been dropped in October 1932, though in the end it was applied.

What then are we to say of the experience of trade unionism amongst the British police? The fact is that although a police union was formed in a number of guises before and after the Great War it carried very little influence and was quickly neutralised by the wartime and inter-war governments. The authorities were committed to spending considerably more on the police in the hope of undermining police trade unionism, even though the pay cuts of 1922–25 and 1932–35 presented problems. Also, the state created the Police Federation through the Police Act of August 1919 as a foil to trade unionism. In the end, the police did well out of the final recommendations of the Desborough reports, Part I and Part II, which improved the pay and conditions of the police and preserved the commitment to local autonomy amongst the police, confirming them as 'citizens in uniform', at the same time as encouraging amalgamation where it was possible and desirable. Conditions in policing certainly improved. However, it was government oppression, as much as improved conditions, that did much to undermine police unionism. Conditions worsened again during the Second World War and there were renewed calls for police unionism; and the Oaksey Committee reported in 1948 to resolve the problem, but that is another issue. One central plank in the government's strategy of creating a loyal police was, of course, the Police Federation, an attempt to professionalise the police force, and providing it with a forum, without giving it industrial bargaining powers with the state. The Police Council, which was formed at the same time as the Federation with the purpose of bringing together police representatives and local authority representatives, exerted rather more influence on the wages and conditions of police officers.

The Police Federation of England and Wales, 1919–39

Formed by the Police Act of 1919 the Police Federation of England and Wales was the representative body of police opinion from constables to inspectors. Yet even though it represented around 56,000–60,000 or more police officers during the inter-war years its powers were confined and constrained to police welfare rather than pay.[113] Indeed, one speaker at a Federation meeting reflected, glowingly, that 'The Police Act, 1919, gave us the right to confer on all matters affecting our welfare and efficiency. But it went further, it gave us an organisation.' 'The Federation is not an agitating organisation. The very word itself means "United Bodies".'[114] Most of its business was a matter of regular and routine business connected with pensions, welfare measures, rent allowances, police orphanages and the return of representatives to the Police Council which had been set up at the same time to allow the Home Secretary to seek the views of the county and borough police authorities, some leading chief constables and representatives from various ranks within the police. Most of the business it conducted was about the pedestrian, day-to-day activities of policing. These were often local concerns but nothing of major national importance. However, routinely the Police Federation was consulted on issues of national issues and government policy such as the powers of women police officers and their representation in the Federation, the two periods of pay cuts that occurred between 1921 and 1925 and between 1931 and 1935 – and particularly the latter, when the relationship between the Federation and the government was strained. It was involved in the discussions about the possible amalgamation of smaller forces, the creation of what became the police college at Hendon, and the development of forensic and detective work in policing.

The grass-roots and national structure of the Federation, already outlined, was responsible for an inevitable repetitiveness of its business. Issues would be discussed at the three local force branches, to be discussed further at the force central committee, and then sent up to the three national committees representing the three ranks covered (constable, sergeant and inspector), and then by the joint central committee that represented these three committees of the ranks. The whole structure reflected an organisational upward repetitiveness. The matters discussed might be about unpaid expenses within the force or the issue of pensions, the financing of sports and support for the various police orphanages. The Northern Police Orphanage, which offered accommodation and education for the orphaned children of policemen families, contained 42 boys and 31 girls in 1928 and received regular funding from the Federation.[115]

At the Open Meeting of the Federation in September 1928 Staff Sergeant George Strangeways, of the Newcastle Force, sometime chairman of the Sergeants' Central Committee, called for a Defence Fund and better provision for widows and orphans and noted that the Police Act of 1919 gave them the 'right to confer'. Indeed, 'We had no card of membership; not even an annual subscription, but we had a fellowship of ideas.... The Federation stood for a clean service.'[116]

Organising in the various police forces in England and Wales throughout the end of 1919, and introducing changes to the existing structure in the Metropolitan Force, the Federation held its first national meetings in May and June 1920. But it was not alone in representing the various interests of the police force. It existed alongside the Superintendent Committee for Chief Constables and Assistant Chief Constables, the Chief Constables' Association (for English and Welsh borough forces), which earned an important position in determining police methods and policy in the inter-war years, and the Police Council which represented the views of local authorities, watch committees, chief constables and the Federation. Its main purpose was to gain a status equal to these other organisations, something which it might be fairly said to have more or less achieved by the 1930s.

The Federation was almost inevitably involved in all types of social, sporting and welfare activities that emphasised its social function at the expense of political clout. In June 1929 the National Police Fund it had set up provided £200 for the Aberdere City Police Athletic and Recreation Unit, £120 to the Salford City Police and Fire Brigade Athletic Society, £100 to the Grimsby Borough Police Athletic Club, £75 to the Stalybridge Borough Police Recreation Club, £173 to the Liverpool and District Police Orphanage, and similar sums to many other bodies.[117] There were testimonials for retiring members who had been prominent in their work for the Federation, such as that mentioned at Federation meetings between 23–26 July 1930 for Sergeant Philcox.[118]

In effect the Federation dealt with anything connected with the conditions of police except, in a direct sense, that of pay. In July 1930 the Federation's Joint Central Committee dealt with 'refreshment allowances' for members of the Caernarvonshire Police Force who had not been paid their expenses whilst working away from the force on 17 September 1928, and also the ongoing issue of the rent allowance for the River Tyne Police Force.[119] The vast amount of routine business in effect reflects the immense variation of local police practice throughout the country, and when advice was sought from the Home Office the advice was often that the local watch committee would have to make a decision and that the Home Office had no jurisdiction over the complaint that had been raised. Sometimes these complaints were turned into more general appeals.

Between 15 and 17 July 1930 there were appeals to the Home Office for the more general rent allowances for the police of England and Wales to be increased.[120] In a flowering relationship with the Home Office, the Federation was asked for its advice and support with regard to government initiatives. Inter-war governments favoured the centralisation of police forces and policing as far as possible but were met with much local resistance and found it difficult to reduce the 180 or so police authorities in England and Wales. Although the Home Office was thwarted in this objective, it was successful in its campaign to establish a central police college, which was eventually opened at Hendon, to create an elite body of highly trained police officers, those who would lead the police throughout England and Wales in the future. The Joint Central Committee of the Police Federation of England and Wales met with the Home Office officials on 4 March 1930. At this meeting Sir John Anderson stressed that the service was not developing and that 'far too little is known of technical and other developments' in police work, a view endorsed by Sir Leonard Dunning. The Central Committee of the Federation gave its support for the scheme in the summer of 1930.[121] On 13 November 1930 the Home Secretary, J. R. Clynes, attended the annual conference of the Federation and stressed that the intended college would be 'a centre for research and inquiry into certain technical and administrative branches of Police work'.[122] A. L. Dixon, one of his senior officials, then explained the 'Police College Scheme', although the Federation was already well aware of the development since it had three of its members, including Strangeways, on the committee that had been set up to examine the possibility of a central police college. Dixon stressed that 'many men who have plenty of brain and ability have not all the choices they should have because they have not the advanced training they require, and there are too many members of the Service who are quite content to argue that because a certain thing has been done for a century or so it can go on being done so for ever.'[123] He added, quite openly, the following comment about the elitist nature of the plan.

> This scheme is intended to give a higher instruction to those who are going to be our Chief Officer, Chief Clerk, Detective Inspector, and others in the higher ranks, not to train recruits: It may be that every recent recruit carries a Chief Constable's baton in his pocket, but I think that you will agree that every one is not quite fitted to be

a Chief Constable. The idea was that both the large and small forces would both benefit from the intended college, that any man could apply, that there would be independent selection, and the emphasis would be placed upon whether or not the candidate could benefit from attending the college.[124]

The Federation's involvement and general support for this development seems to have been part of this process of professional development for which it had come into existence. As a consequence of such professionalisation it became restrictive and sectional in its interests, just as any other exclusive body tends to become, and saw itself as a male preserve. Indeed, on 4 March 1930 a meeting of the Federation representatives and the Home Office, which included Sir John Anderson, noted the Royal Commission on Police Powers and Procedures (1929) advice that except in the capacity of matrons, police duty was essentially a man's work though 'the experiment with police women was not at an end' and that 'steps should be taken to regularize their conditions of services and further define the scope of their employment'.[125] The members of the Federation's Council 'were adamant that women were not required in the Police Service'.[126]

Women had first been employed in police work during the First World War, often under the auspices of the National Union of Women Workers of Great Britain and Ireland. Edith Sharples (née Haigh) acted as a lady police officer in Huddersfield from 1915 to 1918 and Phyllis Lowell was a sergeant at Birkenhead between 1915 and 1919.[127] Small groups of women were also employed in patrol work, usually with a male police officer, to discourage improper behaviour between soldiers, women and girls in wartime Britain. In Liverpool, these patrols operated from 8.0 pm to 10.30 pm in Lime Street and other streets in Liverpool.[128] In London there were numerous women patrols in the vicinity of Victoria Station, Piccadilly and Leicester Square to suppress 'gross indecency'. After the war, various police forces employed small numbers of women and by 1940 there were 282 women police officers, about half of them in the Metropolitan Force.[129]

The hostility of the Federation made it hard for the women police to establish themselves, but they were gradually accepted to be the 'soft arm of the law', sometimes the 'Left Arm of the Law', who dealt with women and children as they were employed by the larger forces such as Sheffield, Manchester, Liverpool and the Metropolitan Police Forces. It was, largely due to Dorothy Olivia Georgina Peto that both the women police, in general, and the Metropolitan Police, in particular, developed.

Appointed in 1930 as Staff Officer, and, in 1931, as Superintendent for Women Police in the Metropolitan Force she raised police women numbers up from 47 to 136 officers in the 1930s.[130] She fought hard for the representation of women police officers on police bodies. In a letter to the Deputy Metropolitan Commissioner, sent shortly after her appointment in 1930, she complained that women officers were not allowed to vote on the Metropolitan Police Board, whose boards for inspectors, sergeants and constables all voted to send representatives to the Police Federation from which representatives were further sent to the Police Council, which brought together representatives from all the main bodies with policing. She also noted that, under the 1930 Police Orders for the Metropolitan Force, women were allowed to vote 'with the men of their respective ranks' to return representatives.[131] His reply was that there were many practical problems and that the 'men didn't like it'.[132] Peto, constantly pressured the Federation, through the associate Metropolitan Board, to gain voting rights and representation for women but she did not win her battle until 1941 when Charles Drummond, Metropolitan Commissioner, admitted, in what seems to be a draft letter to the Home Office, that Peto was right and that Police Orders did allow women police to vote at elections or stand as representatives to the Metropolitan Board and thus the Federation. Whilst admitting that 'Personally I do not see any great harm in Women Police being members of the Branch Board' though he felt that there would be resentment from the men.[133]

The Federation was eventually forced to accept the rights of police women to vote for Federation representatives or to stand for election but it was reluctant to do so and many of its minutes for the inter-war years, often short, terse and to the point, saw the women police as less than full members of the constabulary whose job, with male help, was to look after women and children, in sensitive cases, and to escort prisoners from police goals, courts or prison.

The new era of motorised road traffic was another inter-war development that occupied the local and national organisation of the Federation. Despite some early equivocation on the role of traffic wardens, the Federation became increasingly protective in its assumption of the responsibility for traffic policing, a role which was strongly enhanced by the Select Committee of the House of Lords in 1938. This is discussed in far more detail in Part 2, Chapter 5. It is sufficient, here, to say that the Federation promoted traffic policing, the new road safety campaigns that were being developed in the 1930s and the redrafting of the Highway Code, first issued in 1931, in 1935.

The Police Federation occasionally, though rarely, raised issues with the Home Office connected with the suitability of individuals being employed at the highest ranks within the profession. The major example of this was its opposition to the appointment of Captain Athelston N. Popkess, the Associated Provost Marshall, Aldershot Command, as Chief Constable of the Nottingham City Police Force in December 1929.[134] The Nottingham Labour Party opposed the appointment of Popkess but were defeated by 29 votes to 22 at a special meeting of the Nottingham City Council.[135] This vote arose because of Popkess's 'exclusively military experience'. He was 37 years of age, had experience with the Royal Irish Constabulary, was a member of the North Staffordshire regiment, having had 15 years service in the army, had played rugby football for England in 1913 and was a boxing referee.[136] However, the Home Office were well aware that he had exaggerated his own importance in his application form to the Nottingham Police Force, which, of course, the Home Office had to be informed of because the Home Secretary had to approve the appointment of chief constables. Popkess claimed to have been in charge of policing in 32,000 acres of land, and traffic controlling in areas in Aldershot three times as large as Nottingham, in which 42,000 troops were under his control although he was in fact the Assistant Provost, not the Provost. In the end, Popkess's appointment was approved despite Federation opposition and Labour challenge. This decision was vindicated because during the 1930s he proved to be a very effective chief constable, especially so in dealing with car crime and in promoting detective and forensic work.

It is fair to say that the Federation was feeling its way in the 1920s. It protested, in relatively mild terms, against the Geddes axe, or 'blip', that cut police pay and allowances by about 10 per cent but the Home Office had managed to keep the wage cuts to a minimum and the Federation probably lacked the confidence to do more than express dissatisfaction with the development.[137] Nevertheless, the report of the Joint Council Committee of The Police Federation of England and Wales, for the year 1924–25, reflected that successive annual reports since 1922 had made reference to the cuts imposed since 1922, which it hoped not to have to make reference to in 1925, 'and the feeling of dissatisfaction which was then created was made manifest when the Regulation giving effect to the Economy Deduction was renewed at each successive Police Council'.[138] Interestingly, the Home Office was anxious to ensure that the pay cuts had been restored on a case-by-case approach by the time the Conservative government was preparing for the events that led up to the 1926 General Strike in the spring and summer of 1925; Lt. Col. Atcherley, HM Inspector of Police, circulated a letter on the matter.[139]

Yet there were still equivocation amongst Federation delegates in the 1920s on the degree of its acceptance. Indeed, at the 24 July 1928 meeting of the Federation, held at Cambridge, Inspector E. Nichols stated that

> It has been said, and I believe, quite truly, that although we are a national body and exploited as a national body we are not a national body in spirit. [Yet there had been improvements.] Frequent reference has been made relating to the right of the citizen. Personally, I feel that no one has in the past had to fight harder for these rights of citizenship than Policemen. Only a few years ago they were absolutely denied us. Meetings similar to this council could not have been contemplated a few years ago let alone held.

PC Hardley, of the West Riding of Yorkshire Force, was rather more optimistic when he stated, a few months later, at an Open Meeting of the Federation in September 1928 that 'progress has been made in the nine years of its existence'.[140] There were four chief constables on the platform with him and he added that 'He felt that night that the ultimate dangers to the success of the Federation would not be from without, but might be from within especially if apathy predominated (Hear, hear). If they gave the public a loyal and efficient service they could look to the future with equanimity and would earn the respect of the Public Authorities of England and Wales.'

Nevertheless, the generally rising confidence of the Federation took more than a glancing blow when relations between the Federation and the national government worsened with the reduction of pay to civil servants by 10 per cent in two tranches of 5 per cent in early 1932 and in October 1932; cuts that were not restored until 1935. They included the more dramatic reduction in the starting pay of police constables from 70 shillings per week in his first year to 55 shillings per week.[141]

These cuts brought real tensions throughout the service. The Chief Constables' Committee complained bitterly about them and in October 1932 John Maxwell, the Chief Constable of Manchester, reminded the public of what 'A Bobby's Job' entailed and, noting that the reductions meant a cut of between 7 shilling and 9s 6d for many constables and were unfounded, he reminded his readers that a policeman was 'always on call'.

A police officer was a policeman for the whole 24 hours, likely to be called out at any time. He could not live where he liked – he could only live where he was told. He could not take part in any business, nor could his wife. He had to be trustworthy and honest and been of the highest character.[142]

The Federation had, by that time, already expressed its strong disapproval to the cuts. On 13 September 1932 the Joint Central Committee placed on record, through a letter to the Home Secretary signed by J. Holmes and J. Goodsell (secretaries) its 'extreme regret' at the decision of the Home Secretary to appoint a committee to examine the pay of sergeants and constables who had joined since 30 September 1931. Outlining the events affecting police pay between 1922 and 1925 it suggested that following the recommendations of the May Committee 'it can be seen at a glance that there has been a continued attack on Police pay, while at the same time, an appeal has been made to secure the services of better class applicants and numerous additional duties have been continuously imposed upon the Police.'[143]

The Federation also sent a deputation to the Home Secretary, on 15 September 1932, which asked for the continuance of the recommendations of the Desborough Committee. Sir Herbert Samuel, the Home Secretary, had received the deputation although a memorandum of 13 September stated that the last time a Home Secretary received a deputation from the Federation was on 6 March 1920 – although William Joynson-Hicks had addressed the Federation in 1924 – and that the practice was unusual, and merely responded by reminding the deputation of the 'extremely grievous financial position of the nation last year and further inform you that, much to our regret, it is not much better now'.[144] Relations between the Home Office and the Federation began to falter.

Nevertheless, within the month there was a new Home Secretary, Sir John Gilmour, and in 1932 R. R. Scott, on behalf of the Home Secretary, declared to the Joint Central Committee of the Federation an interest in restoring relations between the Home Office and the Federation.[145] Two days later the *Police Review* reflected upon the unmistakable 'signs of rift in the hitherto friendly relations between the Home Office and the Police as an organised body. This anxiety will be shared, we feel sure, by all who realise by what co-operation between Whitehall and the Federation has achieved during the last twelve years in raising the standard of Police efficiency throughout the country.'[146] Commenting about the loyalty and devotion of the police, and the 'cordially appreciative' attitude of the public, it added that

> It is with great concern that we notice in the Federation resume published this week how marked and unmistakeable are the signs of the

rift in the hitherto friendly relations between the Home Office and the Police as an organised body. This anxiety will be shared, we feel sure, by all who realise what co-operation between Whitehall and the Federation has achieved during the last 12 years in raising standards of police efficiency throughout the country. The loyalty and devotion with which the ranks of the Service have reported this interest and consideration for their welfare have been proved and toasted to the hilt. What the police have done in the past is certainly no more that they now offer for reasonable treatment. Public opinion of the Service is considerably appreciative and has on occasion expressed itself in terms of generosity of which the National Police Fund is a lasting memorial. With this in mind it would appear to be almost criminal folly to adopt the policy of the high hand and to ignore the organisation which Parliament, learning wisdom from the stupidity of the old regime, set up in order to ensure that the tragic mistakes of 1918 should never reoccur.

The mandate of the National Government is very great, but it cannot afford to ignore the teaching of history. To restore relations of friendly co-operation between the Federation and the Home Office is surely Sir John Gilmour's first duty.[147]

Gilmour was clearly mindful of his duty but had little new to say. On 7 November 1932 he met the Joint Executive Committee of the Metropolitan Police Board where he admitted that the 'confidence of the Federation was negligible' but that the pay cuts were 'a temporary measure to meet a national crisis'.[148] The message was the same when he met a deputation from the Federation on 10 November 1932, the second from the Federation to be met by a Home Secretary in a month and only the third since its formation in 1919.[149]

At this moment relations between the Federation and the Home Secretary worsened considerably. The Federation produced a book on all the decisions of the Home Office on matters the Federation had referred to it between November 1919 and October 1932.[150] Its tone was critical of the Home Office. This was followed by the even more critical *13th Annual Report* from the Federation, for 1931–32. It referred to 'Supplementary Deductions' being imposed 'without previously hearing the views of the Service', the 'delegates also decided that the members of the Police Service were being made to shoulder an unfair burden', and that they had no desire to 'shirk their responsibility as citizens but most strongly object to being selected for the drastic deductions because they are a responsible body of servants to the State'.[151] The really tendentious part was, however, when the report reported on the Home Office to their resolution condemning the cuts and stating that 'The Committee regret the terms of the reply, which when made known to the Force, caused an irritation greater than has been known in the history of the Police Federation. The Conference of 1931;... and the negative results to the representatives made, are not likely to be easily forgotten.'[152] Other sections of the report indicted the 'strong dissatisfaction' at the 'Supplementary Deductions'.[153]

The two publications together led to a tetchy relationship developing between the Federation and the Home Office. Lord Trenchard, Metropolitan Police Commissioner between 1932 and 1936, attacked the Federation's criticism in the book in a memorandum to the Home Office on 9 January 1933, and that criticism produced a trail of letters and memoranda.[154] The outcome was that R. R. Scott wrote on behalf of the Home Secretary, on 26 July 1933, to criticise the actions of the Federation. The gist was that the annual report 'contains insubordinate and improper language and passages that could only be regarded as propaganda', adding that the 'Secretary of State is bound to take strong exception to language of this kind' and 'he thinks it right to warn the [Joint Central] Committee to avoid, in any further Report they may think fit to issue'. Referring to the publication of Home Office replies he added that 'it must be on the clear understanding that its content will be wholly free from objection in tone and substance'.[155] A Home Office memorandum, produced a few days later, stressed that

> It was clearly desirable that the JEC should be warned not to repeat in Police Reports the sort of language they use in the last one; and Lord Trenchard suggested that the issue of Resume should be stopped. This does not seem necessary and desirable so long as the Resolutions are in proper order.[156]

Throughout these events the Joint Central Committee of the Federation had merely reflected that there was serious discontent amongst the ranks especially about 'an embargo on holding Open Meetings to enable members of the service to discuss their grievance', complaining bitterly that it would bring about a lower rate of pay for the new recruits who would be reluctant to apply to police forces.[157]

At the very moment that the clash between the Federation and the Home Office reached its height, as if to come back to haunt the Federation and its role, Jack Hayes, the one-time leader of NUPPO and one-time Labour MP for Edge Hill, reappeared like a spectre at the feast.

In September 1933 he wrote an article in *The Police Review and Parade Gossip*, about the problems of the Federation, attacking the way in which the rights and duties of the police had been changed without their consent. At the end of it he wrote an Open Letter to the Joint Central Committee, likening it to a ship which had initially sailed on smooth waters but now faced with a storm since 1931. He finished by writing 'To you on the bridge we look for guidance to lead us out of the present storm.... Never before in the history of our Federation has our trust in our leaders reached such a test.'[158] As already indicated earlier, he made much the same point when he addressed the Federation in Manchester at an associated meeting. In the end, despite the pressure of the Chief Constables' Association, the Federation and indeed the Police Council, the national government did not budge until it decided to restore the cuts made on public servants in 1935. Only then did the Federation and the Home Office begin to improve their relations.

There is no doubting the tension between the Federation and the Home Office in the 1930s. Yet it is difficult to see this as more than a tiff in a relationship between the state and the police which had been forged by the Police Act of 1919. To suggest that the pay crisis of the 1930s could be seen as a deep ideological division which threatened the state would be perverse.

Conclusion

The 1932 cuts in police pay place into context the whole issue of effective representation of the police. The fact is that successive governments from the First World War to the beginning of the Second World War were not prepared to entertain the idea of the police being able to strike or to negotiate on their conditions of work and pay. These were to be determined by the Desborough Committee and the decisions of government, not by the decisions of the police themselves. Indeed, governments and the authorities were shocked by the police strikes of 1918 and 1919 which saw some of the defenders of public order abrogate their responsibilities. Successive governments and local authorities were determined, by refusing to re-employ the 1919 strikers and effectively labelling them as communists, to exact the strictest punishments they could. In addition, the Coalition Government, under the premiership of David Lloyd George, passed the 1919 Police Act in order to provide the police with a forum through which to discuss their conditions of employment, if not their pay. This worked well in improving policing as a profession but faltered when serious issues of pay arose. Nevertheless, the Federation has stood the test of time and has not been replaced, with the unequivocal opposition of governments to police unionisation still conflicting with the increasing police desire to have effective negotiating powers on pay and conditions. In the end, it is doubtful whether the strike activities and the breakdown of public order in 1919 were sufficient to bring about the threatened Bolshevik revolution in Britain – neither the Labour Party, nor the British trade union movement, nor the police as a whole had ever had much compunction for that and, in any case, the Desborough Committee had ensured that the wages of policemen were effectively doubled. It is clear, however, that there were real, if exaggerated fears of a Bolshevik revolution within the political and social Establishment and that this was pressed forward with the idea of a Police Federation to provide a more professional and politically neutral police force that would be loyal to the state. Although sticky from time to time, and usually on the issue of pay, the relations between the state and the Federation remained cordial and prospered in the inter-war years. Yet their right to confer on pay was not resolved because they could be ignored. That situation did not change until the 1940s when the Federation was, as Robert Reiner suggests, given real negotiation and arbitration powers.[159]

What kept the positive relationship between the state, the police and the Federation alive in the age of the car and the rising demand for forensic detective work though was the problem of maintaining public order. Successive inter-war governments, fearing public disorder, attempted to work with the Federation and, as suggested in the next chapter, so did the chief constables who sought an even closer, often secret, relationship with the Home Office in maintaining public order.

3
Policing Public Order in the Inter-war Years

The relationship between the police and the public has often been a fraught one, dominated by mutual suspicion and sporadic conflict. This is not surprising given that the police were almost invariably used as a front-line force to maintain public order throughout the nineteenth and the twentieth centuries. This suspicion was particularly evident in the inter-war years when industrial conflict, the General Strike and violent conflict between the communists and the fascists occurred. However, there was a major difference between what happened up to 1918 and what happened afterwards since from 1919 onwards inter-war governments introduced measures to centralise the public order policies of the 183 or so police forces in England and Wales in 1919 to a degree that would have been unimaginable in Victorian and even Edwardian times.[1] What this meant was that there was relatively less violence in the maintenance of public order, given the scale of the conflict, after 1918 than before, although the police were still prone to invoke baton charges, indiscriminate arrest of people under the Emergency Powers Act (1920) and the manipulating of the law to their own advantage.

During the inter-war years the police were increasingly integrated with the military and civil forces in plans and procedures to maintain public order in the context of a newly extended democratic society. It was in an attempt to maintain public order that David Lloyd George's Coalition Government passed the Police Act of 1919. It set up the Police Federation to ensure that the police would never be subject to two rival masters – the union and the state – and would be ruled primarily by the state. It was also because of the potential public order concerns of the post-Great War years that inter-war governments stressed the need to develop the centralising aims of the second report of the Desborough Committee which advocated close co-operation between police forces since it recognised that the local watch committees, of the borough forces, and the joint standing committees, of the county forces, would block any major attempt at their unification. Establishing the balance between state control and local democratic rights has always been a central problem of policing England and Wales and one which the inter-war governments and the Home Office intended to adjust more towards state control.

In 1919 the Lloyd George Coalition Government reaffirmed its commitment to policing as a primary means of maintaining public order by reorganising its policies in the face of the widespread industrial unrest. The new plans drawn up at this stage shaped the way in which the police of England and Wales were used to control the major industrial, social and political disturbances. The Home Office policies of 1919 and the actions of the inter-war police, indeed, confirm the opinion of Richard Geary that 'At the strategic level there was centralisation of order maintenance and intelligence gathering...but at the tactical level...few changes occurred with the baton-charge remaining the stock response to disorder.'[2] Co-ordination occurred at the national level between the Home Office and police forces at a level never attempted before and achieved the preservation of public order in the most demanding of situations. Not surprisingly, chief constables, the agents of such co-ordination, were still inclined to see their districts as their personal fiefdoms where they expected their views to be accepted by the local watch committees and county boards, with consequent impact on the relations between the Home Office and local watch committees and county boards. In effect, some chief constables found themselves in long and protracted conflicts with their watch committees or their county committees who sought to remove them often against the wish of the Home Office.

The majority of recent literature on policing public order has generally agreed that policing was more co-ordinated and less violent than it might have been during the inter-war years than before, a view with which we concur. The 'Whig' historian T. A. Critchley stressed the improving quality of police and public order during the inter-war years, Richard Geary emphasised the decline of violent unrest, and Jane Morgan and Barbara Weinberger both highlighted the improved tactics of the inter-war police.[3] However, both Morgan and Weinberger also suggest that these were developments that were subject to abuse. They maintain that the law on public order was often consciously amended, ignored or flouted, and likened to the careless use of the Emergency Powers Act of 1920 in connection with other legislation, out of a desire to maintain strong centralised control in the face of the patchwork of policing in England and Wales. The policies of the Home Office frequently led the police to use, and misuse, the law against the miners and often resort to the excessive use of the law to deal with the perceived, if exaggerated threat of communism, particularly in both the 1926 General Strike and the 1926 coal lock-out. Indeed, Weinberger has concluded that, particularly in South Wales, 'The police gained immensely in prestige and authority from their role in the General Strike', adding that police-inspired violence was part of a history of continuing conflict which amounted to 'unremitting class hatred on both sides' in the South Wales coalfield.[4] Morgan added that the strengthening of centralised command over the police led to the emasculation of watch committee control in the twentieth century that ensured 'that in industrial crises the police became a central arm of the emergency and strike apparatus'.[5]

These views have been emphasised further by Keith Ewing and Conor Gearty who have highlighted the arbitrary use of police powers during the General Strike, including the suspension of civil liberties, excessive and unaccountable policing, summary justice by magistrates and judicial bias in sentencing. They conclude that the experience of the coal lock-out of 1926 demonstrates the 'fragility of legality as a governing principle of the constitution' and 'that much that was done in the name of the constitution was little better than executive lawlessness'.[6] Indeed, as will become clear, the fact is that during the General Strike chief constables were encouraged to prosecute under the Emergency Powers Act 1920 when they would have lost cases in common law, and something approaching a vendetta was conducted against Labour magistrates who were associated with the trade council, organised councils of action and workers' committees. Policing was obviously central to the integrated system that the state used to maintain social control in a more democratic inter-war Britain where its previous freedom of action was now being challenged. What we are saying is that the Home Office was complicit in an attempt to operate directly with chief constables on a scale that went far beyond the normal relationship and with a desire to bypass the authority of watch committees and county committees on a scale that has not previously been fully acknowledged.

The Home Office response to the 1919 industrial disturbances and subsequent strike action

Throughout 1919 there were many industrial disputes in Britain threatening David Lloyd George's Coalition Government. The number of days lost from strike action rose significantly from about 6 million in 1918 to about 35 million in 1919. It steadied at about 26.5 million in 1920 and peaked at nearly 86 million in 1921 before falling to fewer than 20 million in 1922.[7] This wave of industrial unrest occurred at a time when there were also other problems threatening public order. The 1918 Police Strike, discussed in the previous chapter, led to about 10,000 of the 19,000 members of the Metropolitan Police Strike at the end of August. About 2000 soldiers refused to go abroad and instead marched on Folkestone Town Hall on 3 January 1919, forming a 'Soldiers' Union'. Another 1500 soldiers marched on Whitehall on 4 January 1919. The Police Union was beginning to win wide support throughout the country and its activities culminated in the 1919 Police Strike.

The miners, the transport workers and other major groups of workers came out on strike, or at least threatened to do so, in February and March 1919. Although some of these events lapsed quickly, there was a major railway transport strike at the end of the year. There were also strikes amongst the engineers in the spring of 1919 and, at broadly the same time, the shipyard workers in Belfast and Glasgow also came out. There was a coalminers strike in Yorkshire in July and August 1919, and the government was constantly worried at the prospect of the miners, transport workers and railway servants, 'The Triple Alliance', uniting in strike action at the same time. These disturbances subsided in 1920 but culminated in the coal dispute of 1921, when the railway servants and transport workers failed to strike in their support on the infamous 'Black Friday', 15 April 1921.[8] By and large, the main issues in these strikes related to hours of work but it quickly became evident that the Coalition Government gradually convinced itself that they were caused by Bolshevik success in the Soviet Union and the revolutionary intent of the 'Triple Alliance'. The whiff of revolution seemed to be in the air.

Initially, in early 1919 the Cabinet felt the situation, in particular regarding the Glasgow disputes, could be contained easily: Winston Churchill argued for the use of the Defence of the Realm Act and Andrew Bonar Law advocated 'getting the Special Constabulary ready', a reference to the special constables attached to the police forces in wartime being made into a body of volunteers who would help preserve the public order in peacetime.[9] However, there were rising fears when the Chief Secretary for Ireland indicated that the Belfast strikers had formed 'a Soviet Committee' and the Cabinet fear that Glasgow would become unmanageable and that 12,000 troops stationed nearby would have be moved in.[10] As a result the Minister of Labour was instructed to make more definite plans for permanent organisations 'to meet civil emergencies in the future'.[11] The Home Office was inevitably central to the implementation of this decision.

Indeed, in February 1919 the government set up three major central committees to deal with food control, industrial disturbances and the protection of workers. There were, however, two main activities that the government saw as central to its public order strategy – the control of food supply and the preservation of public order. To achieve these twin objectives the government drew up integrated plans to bring the work of these committees together and to unite the armed forces, civic and citizen forces, and the police, in a co-ordinated response to the dangers to be faced. They were to be co-ordinated at both the national and the local level, civic committees being appointed at the local level to co-ordinate the municipal authorities, the local representatives of the Road Transport Boards, the Food Control Committee, the police and other bodies.[12]

The police were a major part of the secretly arranged response to the 'Bolshevik' challenge and chief constables were deeply involved in the work of this co-ordinated structure, and involved in planning at every level. However, given the 1918 Police Strike, and the emerging national Police Union, there were, inevitably, some doubts about the continued loyalty of the police force. It was said in the Protection (Sub-) Committee meeting of 3 March 1919 that the 'possibility of men sympathising with the striker in certain districts cannot be excluded' and General Sir Neville Macready, Commissioner of the Metropolitan Police, stated that 'less reliance than formerly can be placed on the Metropolitan Police'.[13] On 13 March 1919, conscious of this concern, Edward Shortt, the Home Secretary, informed the War Cabinet that 'it would be necessary for the Government to make an announcement that the Police Union would not be recognised and he desired now the authority of the War Cabinet for making such an announcement when the necessity arose.'[14]

This worry about the loyalty of the police continued to obsess the government throughout 1919. However, in February 1919 many chief constables seem to have felt that the majority of their police force would remain loyal. The Chief Constable of Newcastle-upon-Tyne felt that '90 per cent of his men would be loyal'.[15] Nevertheless, the Chief Constable of Bradford reflected that 'in the Cities the majority of men had joined the union and – at any rate in Bradford – were affiliated to the local labour party and could not be relied upon.'[16] The Chief Constable of Leeds maintained that he had 1700 'Specials' but that he could rely upon only 900 as the others were 'in the union or old'.[17] Yet the situation resolved itself towards the end of 1919 when the threat of police unionism was nipped in the bud. However, the fear of both public and police disorder shaped the thinking of the authorities between 1919 and 1921 as the government brought the police to the centre of the efforts to maintain public order and hoped that they would elide into an effective and integrated system of maintaining public control. However, one should not forget that there was already a Chief Constables' Association in existence which had been meeting in annual conferences since the 1890s to discuss their common problems of public order alongside developments in detective and scientific work and traffic control, as will become evident later in this book.

Nonetheless, 16 chief constables, mainly from the main county forces and the leading borough forces, such as the West Riding, Lancashire, Leeds, Liverpool and Manchester, met with the Home Secretary on 18 February 1919.[18] In an airing of views they were informed of the new Committee, and its three sub-committees, which were those for Supplies, Transport and Protection. They were also informed that the purpose of the new structure was to maintain public order, not to break strikes, although the fear was 'a complete stoppage of industry by a strike of the Triple Alliance miners, railway men and transport workers'.[19]

This was the meeting at which the Acting Chief Constable of the West Riding raised the question of 'borrowing troops, as without additional troops it would be impossible to protect all the 213 collieries in the Riding'.[20] The Home Secretary's response was to accept the idea and to suggest that arrangement should be made on the assumption that 'no police could be borrowed from any other Force'. In effect, this meant that soldiers might be used to aid the police and that they should look to their own forces, and particularly to the special constables, the volunteers that most forces had.[21] However, the decision was later modified and police forces were allowed to borrow men from other forces without the need for swearing in, something that occurred frequently in the General Strike of 1926.

A second similar meeting was held on 7 March 1919 and included 14 chief constables and one deputy chief constable, from Gloucestershire, representing different forces (including the ones for Monmouth, Cardiff, Swansea and Newport).[22] The Home Secretary, Sir Edward Troup, Sir Hamer Greenwood, A. L. Dixon, Sir L. Dunning, Major General Atcherley and all Home Office officials outlined to them the government policy for the emergency. They perceived the threat to be a 'Triple Alliance strike' – of coalminers, and transport workers and railwaymen – and that the duty of the police 'would be to protect the public'.[23] What emerged out of this second meeting was the decision that the maintenance of public order was primarily the responsibility of the civil authorities 'through the Police and Special Constables'. Police officers were to be demobilised from the army immediately and 'Already 100 of the 167 police in the armed forces were already back at Portsmouth', 75 out of 100 back at Plymouth, 20 of 70 back at Southampton and 40 out of 64 back at Newport.[24] The civil authorities were to be further strengthened by the War Office quickly demobilising police from the armed forces to allow them to return to their previous forces, the appointment of special constables and by civil authority appeals for further assistance. The civil authorities were to be bolstered by the main body of the army and by a mobile reserve force, the Navy and the Royal Air Force, until the demobilisation of the police who were with the armed forces.

On 17 March 1919 the Home Office held a meeting with the town clerks and mayors of a large number of county and borough authorities, with representatives from the Ministry of Food, the Road Transport Board and the General HQ of Great Britain. Only one member of the police, Lt. Col. P. R. Laurie, of the Metropolitan Police, was in attendance. Yet one of the main topics discussed was the protection of food convoys on long and short journeys, which was to become partly the responsibility of chief constables whose main function it seemed was to protect the vulnerable points en route, leaving the armed forces to provide escort.[25] The minutes of an undated meeting of the Protection Committee indicate that for long journeys the defence of a convoy was almost entirely the responsibility of the military but that on short journeys the police would have a responsibility to protect vulnerable areas along the route.[26]

On 22 March 1919 the Home Secretary also informed the 'Chief Constables of England and Wales' of a memorandum (dated 21 March) to organise local civil committees that would be circulated through them, if a miners' strike and a transport strike occurred.[27] These civil committees were to involve town clerks' representatives of the Road Transport Board, the Fuel overseers, representatives of the Food Central Committee, and the special constabulary who 'will act with their own officers under the general control of Chief Constables', although it was stated again that the military might be used on longer journeys.[28] Also on 22 March the government instructed the Post Office to ensure that telegraph and telephone messages sent by the chief constables to the Home Office or to the military authorities should be 'put through immediately' and the chief constables of industrial centres should send in a telegraph daily, submitting reports where there was nothing to declare.[29]

It was chief constables who were instructed to contact the Home Office about outbreaks of disorder, the arrival of troops and the food situation. The Home Office listed the new duties of the police in a letter, or circular letter, of 29 March 1919. And these plans evolved over the next 12 months. For instance, between July and September 1919 efforts were being made to ensure that the police were given the priority in trunk calls.[30]

The Home Office thus planned the use of the army, police and citizen's guilds as its central planks in an integrated plan to maintain public order and the protection of food convoys. Operating together, it was felt that the problem of disloyalty would be obviated. However, there were other measures contemplated by the government. The Defence of the Realm Act (DORA) continued into peacetime until the Emergency Powers Act was passed in 1920, and the Preservation of Public Order Bill introduced in 1921, allowing the powers of arrest to the police for extremist speakers or pamphlets that threatened to undermine public order. Many police forces reorganised their wartime special constables as the Special Constabulary Reserve. In Birmingham's case, there were 370 by the end of 1919 who were equipped with uniform and expected to drill six times per year 'in the case of an emergency threatening the peace of the City'.[31] There were 3000 specials in Hertfordshire and 3000 in Berkshire.[32] Thousands of special constables were organised in different forces. There were troops ready to enter Glasgow to restore order. There was to be even naval deployment off the English and Welsh coasts and near ports.[33]

In August 1919 the government turned its attention to the protection of 'electricity undertakings'. For instance, having received evidence from the Chief Constable of Dewsbury and the Chief Constable of the West Riding, it became clear that 'police protection of power stations would be of little use'.[34] The Chief Constable of the West Riding had examined the various power stations and assessed their needs: Barugh Power Station required a company of infantry, as did Thorne Power Station, whilst Penistone Power Station could be protected by the police with two reliefs and Swinton Sub-Station could be protected with a pill box and two policemen. In other words, stark assessments were made of the value of the police in specific situations.

In October and November 1919, fearful of the breakdown of communications, the Home Office drew up detailed plans to use air and road to keep the chief constables of England and Wales informed of government action by the use of the Royal Air Force to drop land despatches at many sites, including Aintree and York race courses, and for these then to be distributed by road to the local chief constables. The despatches dropped at York would be distributed to the York and the Scarborough Police by the Chief Constable of York, to the North Riding Force at Northallerton, and to Leeds, Bradford, Halifax, Huddersfield, Dewsbury and Barnsley. Those dropped or delivered at Aintree would be distributed to the chief constables at Liverpool, Wallasey, Bootle, Birkenhead, St Helens and Warrington.[35] Those delivered to Didsbury Aerodrome would be gathered by the Manchester Police and delivered to the various nearby police forces. In order to help with the distribution of despatches, some police forces were supplied with either single motorbikes or motorbikes with side cars from March 1920; 52 of the former were distributed and 19 of the latter at a cost of about £75 each.[36]

What is evident is that the government developed a systematic structure – through the Home Office, and the Labour, War and Agricultural Departments – of orders and directions for the forces of stability and control. Despite the watch committees and joint standing committees defending their own patches, and thus maintaining a patchwork of authority and control, the fact is that the police were a vital and co-ordinated part of the structure. Government planning led to a far more co-ordinated structure of planning and control than had ever previously existed. Implicit in these plans, many of which were never implemented, was the desire to use the police as the first line of defence and to hold the armed forces in reserve, except in the movement of food convoys. In effect this policy was slow to develop and in the 1921 coal dispute the Lancashire mines were more protected than oppressed by the police.[37] This was despite the fact that in the three-month coalminers' strike, or lock-out, of 1921, soldiers defended the collieries against the strikers and the police took co-ordinated action to both defend the movement of vital supplies and to protect the collieries.

By 1921 the government had a structure in place to deal with strikes and disturbances and, in addition, had the Emergency Powers Act of 1920, used in 1921, 1924 and throughout the General Strike and the coal lock-out of 1926. In 1923 the Special Constables Act and the Special Constabulary Order of 30 July were passed and introduced to formalise the system whereby many police forces had reorganised the Special Constabulary of the War into peacetime forces of special constables who figured prominently during the General Strike of 1926.[38]

Thus legislation and planning gave the government complete control of food distribution, essential services and the movement of coal and other supplies. Clause 21 of the Emergency Powers Act allowed for the prohibition of actions 'likely to cause sedition or disaffection among the civilian population' and was frequently used against speakers at industrial demonstrations even though it permitted 'peacefully persuading any other person to take part in a strike'. Regulation 22 permitted the prohibition of meetings likely to 'conduce a breach of peace and will thereby cause undue demands to be made on the police, or will cause disaffection'. Regulations 26 and 27 allowed the Home Secretary to transfer police officers without needing them to be sworn in with their new force. The Home Secretary thus gave to the police forces of England and Wales rights which would not be subject to the whims of local watch and joint standing committees.

The many plans drawn up in 1919 and 1920, along with the new legislation, gave government unprecedented powers to deal with threats to public order. The Home Affairs Committee held several meetings in the spring and summer of 1921 with Sir Basil Thomson's (M15) concerns about the 'success of the Bolsheviks outside Russia by means of propaganda' ringing in their ears.[39] The Committee discussed a bill to ensure that the police could act if violence occurred or literature likely to provoke violence and sedition was published. The Home Affairs Committee met on 25 March and again on 31 May 1921 to finalise the Public Order Bill which would strengthen police powers to act in the case of indoor and outdoor meetings, in case of violence and on the publication of literature. These measures were barely tested during the miners' strike in 1921 but seriously examined in both the General Strike and the coalminers' lock-out of 1926, where they and the degree of centralisation introduced by the government was found to be most effective.

The 1926 General Strike and the coal lock-out

The General Strike occurred between 3 and 12 May 1926 and was the largest industrial dispute in British history. It involved about 800,000 miners locked out by their employers, who were demanding wage reductions and changes in conditions, and was supported by about 1,750,000 trade unionists striking in sympathy with them. It lasted a mere nine days although the miners' dispute lasted seven months. It was probably caused by the government pushing for wage reductions against a resistance trade union movement and was seen as a time of class war in which the British government marshalled its forces effectively to defeat a hesitant and unsure trade union movement whose essential aim was to defend the miners rather than to bring about the Bolshevik-style revolution which the government of Stanley Baldwin feared. There is a mass of literature on the General Strike but the purpose of this section is not to relate or explain the events of the General Strike and the coal lock-out but to examine the central role played by the police in maintaining public order.[40]

Most historians of the General Strike discuss the reasons for the strike, the events, why it was called off and the consequences.[41] They debate the long-term causes, and the immediate and long-term consequences, of what is generally perceived to be an economic struggle between the state and the trade unions. The focus of much of the wider debate about the police and public order has already been presented: Weinberger has suggested that they exceeded their brief throughout the inter-war years whilst Morgan believes that throughout the inter-war years they were part of the process that emasculated the power of the watch committees. On the other hand, historians who have focused primarily on the General Strike and the coal lock-out have generally been more equivocal on the matter, seeing the police presence as being both a help and a hindrance. Margaret Morris, for instance, has stressed that the policing of the strike could be quite positive; according to the strikers the police at Ilkeston 'sooner assisted us rather than interfered', and that at Lincoln 'the Chief Constable was regarded "as a consistent friend of labour".'[42] The Carstairs strike committee felt that there was no need to make enemies with the police and the chief constable approached them and explained that they 'didn't want to use batons or anything like that' and suggested holding a football match.[43] Yet measured against this, Morris notes that there were troubles in Blaydon with the arrest of Will Lawther, the northern Labour leader, who had been called in to investigate a report of baton charges on pickets.[44] She also accepts that there were many instances of the police forcibly dispersing meetings. Gordon Phillips makes very much the same point, suggesting that the state was prepared to use the police to break the stoppage on vital services by *'force majeurs'* and that the forces of law became 'more aggressive and determined in their enforcement of law and order as the strike proceeded'.[45] Anne Perkins reflects upon the Chief Constable of Sunderland finding notes apportioning responsibility to revolutionaries when the red dawn arrived but also notes the varying responses of chief constables to the General Strike and coal lock-out.[46] However, such equivocation is not supported by the overwhelming evidence, presented in this chapter, which supports, and extends, the views of Morgan, Weinberger and the other historians of public order already mentioned. It suggests that the activities of the Home Office and the police were aggressive and geared towards serious police intervention in South Wales and many other parts of the country as part of a general strategy laid down by the government and the Home Office.

The maintenance of the public order role was designated by the Home Office in the summer of 1925 once the threat of a coal lock-out emerged after the coal owners demanded wage cuts from 31 July 1925. The threatened dispute did not occur because the government intervened on that day, better known as 'Red Friday', with a nine-month subsidy to allow the coal owners to continue to pay existing wage rates. Stanley Baldwin's Conservative government was then concerned to make immediate preparations, which were that it wished to both improve the relations with police, soured by the Geddes Axe cuts of 1921 and 1922 which had reduced police pay, and to bring the forces up to strength.

The Home Secretary, Sir William Joynson-Hicks, and Lt. Col. (sometimes Major General) Atcherley, an Inspector of Police, indicated the government's intention to restore the police pay cuts – just as soon as it was feasible to do so. This was discussed throughout the autumn of 1925 and, under the title 'Strengthen the Police Force', Atcherley circulated a message to the special constables and the Metropolitan Police on 16 April 1926:

> I think that you know that the line of the Home Secretary has taken with regard to the abrogation of the Geddes cut is that each case must be considered in its merits an application by the local police authority, independently of any measure it may be necessary to take to augment the force temporarily for emergency purposes.
>
> ...but when (though the 'cut' can go on in normal conditions) we ought to press the local authority to increase the force temporarily, in view of the likelihood of the emergency developing.[47]

The threat of a 'general strike' forced Baldwin's government into action in the autumn of 1925 as it reviewed public order by setting up a Cabinet Committee on Public Order which particularly focused upon the activities of communist factory groups and newspapers and the government arrangements for the dispute. The police were a fundamental part of the anti-strike activities. The Attorney General made it clear to the Home Affairs Committee and the Cabinet that communists might be prosecuted under the 1797 Incitement to Mutiny Act if they sought to influence the soldiers and sailors but that whilst violent behaviour was actionable it was legal to picket and legal to strike and that 'I should like to render illegal any strike which is directed against the State and not against the employers.'[48]

The legal position of the police in dealing with disturbances was discussed by the Committee in the Order Memorandum of the Home Secretary of 17 December 1925.[49] The Home Secretary informed the Committee that the last major discussion on the police and public order, which had taken place in 1909, had concluded that police practice regarding public meetings varied from force to force – the Manchester Police remaining outside the meeting if not invited in or where there was not going to be a breach of the peace whilst it was routine for the Birmingham Police to be inside the meetings – and that there had been little information on practice since. As a result, he was going to seek further evidence on practice from chief constables. There is no evidence that this was ever done and the government quickly looked towards the measures it had established between 1919 and 1921.

The Cabinet set up a Supply and Transport Committee which had a Protection sub-committee chaired by Sir John Anderson. Its main function was to encourage healthy citizens of 45 and under to attest their willingness to join the special constables for the duration of the emergency. In effect, this was the way in which the official police could be released to assume 'sterner' duties.[50] However, in many respects the chief constables of England and Wales (and indeed Scotland) proved more resourceful by calling upon other sources of help – the Police Reserve, Police Pensioners, the Civil Constabulary Reserve and volunteers who undertook the duties of the regular police forces to allow more highly trained permanent officers to deal with the emergency.[51]

In the General Strike of 1926, and the associated coal lock-out, three major tactical developments were implemented. First, volunteer and auxiliary reserve and Special Forces were used to release the regular police for their public order duties. Second, large numbers of police were deployed to deal with the strikers by the movement of police from one force to another. Third, great emphasis was placed upon the mobility of the police. In other words, there was a marked contrast with the Edwardian strikes where the police were used but played a more subsidiary role to that of the military although it may have been a baton of a Glamorgan police constable that led to the death of Samuel Rhys at Tonypandy on 8 November 1910 when the Somerset Light Infantry were employed.[52]

The police moved to build up reserves and special constabulary. Thousands of special reserve or special constabulary officers were recruited and used during the General Strike. About 600 specials were enrolled in

Birkenhead, 200 in Oldham, initially more than 2000 in Birmingham (although eventually 4298 and some with vehicles were recruited),[53] 800 in Stoke-on-Trent, with '300 trained', and about 3000 men in Staffordshire 'but not much needed'. Around 11,300 specials were sworn in the Northern Division of the country by 11 May 1926.[54] At least 350 reserves were deployed by the Chief Constable of Lancashire in June 1926.[55]

These recruits, particularly in industrial hotspots, allowed chief constables to release their regular officers to deal with the General Strike and the industrial disputes but also gave them the flexibility to move experienced officers from one force to another without having to be sworn in. Indeed, this latter action occurred on a significant scale. Hull, a major port area where the dockers came out, received 50 police from Leeds, 50 from Bradford, 50 from the West Riding and 13 from Halifax during the General Strike.[56] The Plymouth Force received 25 men from the Devonshire with another 75 from Lincoln. The North Midland District provided 50 police officers to Durham, and Middlesbrough borrowed, but soon returned, 50 officers from the North Riding Force.

With the continuance of the coal dispute the County Police Committee in South Wales was called upon to protect a train through Llanelly and had to draft a large number of police from the outside area and 100 Glamorgan County policemen were in readiness in the event of disturbances. The Cardiff City Police had 75 police officers in readiness to aid the Glamorgan Police in the event of trouble – the Mining Valleys and the Glamorgan Police have been called upon to assist Carmarthenshire.[57] The police forces of southern and south-western England supplied Carmarthenshire, Glamorgan and Monmouthshire with officers. The Lancashire coalfield areas drew in police from Liverpool; Durham and Gateshead supplied police for the Durham and Northumberland field.

This was also the first strike in which the police were organised in charabanc motorised units. This had been discussed in 1925 when the Home Secretary asked chief constables to make them available for the movement of troops – in case they were needed – and at the same time contracts were organised for the police themselves.[58] The result was that the large number of motorised baton-wielding police officers became a feature at coalfields. The Manchester City Police reinforced the Derbyshire and Nottinghamshire squads with motorised units based in Alfreton, Chesterfield and Mansfield.[59] Effectively there were now police 'flying squads' to reinforce police defending mines.[60]

The Baldwin government demanded daily reports from all the chief constables throughout the General Strike and they indicate that the majority of the country was peaceful. In addition, a daily report was prepared on communist activity in the General Strike.[61] This contained a regular report from the local chief constable from various regions of Britain, the vast majority of which suggests that in most areas there was relatively little disturbance throughout the General Strike.

This impression is borne out by the Home Office returns which indicate that 95 out of the 178 county and borough forces in England and Wales (down from 181 in 1919), mainly the rural counties and the small borough forces in rural areas, did not prosecute anyone during the General Strike. There were disturbances in the General Strike and in the coal lock-out but rather fewer than was expected. Many of these were of a minor nature although some led the police to baton charge the assemblies, as they did in Poplar (London) on 12 May 1926.[62] There was another famous baton charge by the police on 30 August 1926 when Alderman Jenkins led a 'deputation' of 800 men to the Quarry Level Pit, Monmouthshire, to get the men to come out: 'it was necessary for the police to make a baton charge to disperse the crowd.'[63]

The fact is that the redeployment of police, as well as the use of motorised transport, gave the police more numbers and greater flexibility than they had ever had before. It thus placed more control in the hands of the increasingly Home Office-directed chief constables, some of whom began to clash with the local authorities, local magistrates, and even watch or joint standing committees, particularly in the Labour-controlled areas where there was widespread support for the strikers. There was dramatic evidence of such disagreement.

In South Wales, a major coalmining area, Chief Constables Picton Phillips of Carmarthanshire, Lionel Lindsay of Glamorgan and Victor Bosanquet of Monmouthshire frequently clashed with local Labour groups and their watch committees whom they seem to have regarded as Soviet-inspired communists. Phillips pursued an 'anti-Communist crusade...in the Amman valley' whilst a contemporary correspondent wondered how Lindsay ever got any sleep, so incessant were his efforts against Bolshevik saboteurs in South Wales.[64] It was similarly said of Bosanquet that 'he was at war with the red peril' in the valleys of Monmouthshire.[65] These were men on a mission and Weinberger states all three chief constables 'felt that they had something of a divine right to rule'.[66]

This was particularly true of Bosanquet, who had been appointed as Chief Constable of Monmouthshire on 1 January 1894. He did not interfere with any demonstration and procession during the General Strike but subsequently led his officers in confronting and preventing a peaceful demonstration of striking miners to the offices of the Board of

Guardians in Newport on 21 May 1926 in which two miners, William Lewis and Richard Bilchrist, were arrested.[67] He was loathed by the miners who referred to him as a 'dictator', 'a man of obsolete ideas' and 'a man of overpowering ego'.[68] He tried to get the two miners prosecuted, but the magistrates refused to allow this to proceed, because there was no printed notice that the procession was illegal 'and no evidence that the police were impeded', as a result of which Bosanquet did raise the issue of biased Labour magistrates with the Home Office and in the High Court.[69] In the end the advice he received was that there was no evidence that the procession had been legally stopped on the orders of the Home Secretary, and possibly required under the Emergency Regulations, but a commitment from the Home Office that 'you could fully rely upon Home Office support'.[70] And, of course, these conflicts and tensions had first emerged in the Edwardian period.

The Standing Joint Committee (SJC) of Monmouthshire, which had 26 members – 13 from the Quarter Sessions and 13 (all Labour) from the County Council – narrowly voted for Bosanquet's resignation. In April 1926, there had already been tension between Bosanquet and the SJC when the SJC had agreed with the Home Office that the Monmouthshire force did not need to be brought up to strength with eight extra policemen but had opposed the need to provide £1000 in order that the Police Reserve, drawn up to deal with the coal lock-out and the General Strike, could be properly equipped. The General Strike and the coal lock-out made matters worse. As a result, in May 1926 the SJC passed a motion, by eight votes to seven, to remove Bosanquet. Mr J. D. Vaughan, Labour leader for Gwent, explained that under the Emergency Regulations 'the chief constable has proved himself an irritant to the peace of the county.'[71]

Whilst opposed by the Labour group, Bosanquet was strongly supported in his actions by many local magistrates, the Home Office and the press.[72] The *Western Mail* also attacked 'the attempt of the Labour majority of the Monmouthshire Standing Joint Committee to exert undue influence over the action of the Chief Constable' and argued for the creation of the whole police force along national lines and 'to be administered directly by the State', a view on local democracy which would not have found support in the localities but found much support with government.[73] The *Western Mail*, 1 December 1929, noted that extra police costs during the coal lock-out of 1926 were £20,000 for Gloucestershire, £30,000 for Glamorgan, £36,000 for Nottingham and £60,000 for Derbyshire but that 'a wicked Labour movement' in Monmouthshire only allowed £1050.

Labour members of the Standing Joint Committee who voted in favour of sacking Bosanquet found that the Home Secretary was reluctant to take action. It appeared that whilst the Home Secretary had to sanction the appointment of a chief constable it seemed as though he had no power to sack him. Vaughan stated in 1929, after three years of struggle to remove him, that Bosanquet was 'the most obstinate man on earth', adding that

> He is 65 years old this year and I was hearing that he would come into the category of compulsory retire, and then we would have a new man, but the present chief was appointed so long time ago that he comes under an Act which provides that so long as he has obtained a certain rank by a certain time he can go on until he is a hundred years old if he feels so inclined (laughter). The standing joint committee had no power to remove this obstinate official and from the beginning of our labours he has set his face against reform.
>
> 'As far as I am concerned' said Mr. Vaughan, 'I am not going to waste any more time over economics in that department. The Home Office has set its face against us. Here the whole thing is ended, and we are in for an extravagant form of police administration in this county until -- I am not anxious that any man should die; I am not in that line of business (laughter). Can I put it kindly that we are up against a wall and can make no further protest.'
>
> [A resolution was passed by] 22 to 12 vote reaffirming the present resolution advising that Government transfer control of finance of Standing Joint Committee to County Council and give the CC [County Council] power to appoint their own chief.[74]

The Home Office kept a file on Bosanquet in which it was stated in 1932, by Colonel Allen, that he 'has all his wits about him and has a general grip of things'. The 1933 report on him suggested that he had good control although he was 'v. much a cripple' and 'has great difficulty in getting in and out of his car'.[75] However, his health deteriorated and the saga ended with his death in 1934.

Thomas Pey, Chief Constable of Wigan, was also strongly opposed to the striking miners. Educated by the Jesuits he was a pugilist in all the senses of the word. During the coal lock-out he tackled those who wished to stop the miners returning to work. He frequently stood in Wigan market square with his senior officers noting every speech made by the communists.[76] He was critical of Arthur Cook on his visit to the town and personally led a raid to arrest a local communist. He also led his officers – with batons drawn – protecting those who were returning to work in the mines in October 1926.[77] His reward for public service was an OBE in June 1927. Ironically, and surprisingly, there was little opposition to Pey in Wigan, perhaps because he appealed to the moderate mining trade unions, and the Labour-dominated town council and Allen Parkinson, the town's Labour MP, suggested that he was a defender of their rights.[78] Chief Constable Ellington of St Helens was also in conflict with his watch committee, largely over his acceptance of police from Liverpool. There was no support from the Home Office for critical Labour members.[79]

In Birmingham there were further troubles as the chief constable wished to take action against the Birmingham Trades Council, one of whose officials suggested that the government had been defeated by the General Strike.[80] There was also an attempt to take action against Percy Lionel Edward Shirmen, a civil servant of the Crown employed as a fitter in the Emergency Department of the Postal Service in Birmingham, 'an agitator of the worst type', according to a detective inspector in the Birmingham Police.[81] George Francis Sawyer, a member of the Birmingham Watch Committee, referred to 'the Special Constables as nothing more than a body of terrorists' and was charged under Regulation 21 of the Emergency Regulations, 1926, with 'doing an act likely to cause disaffiliation among members of the Police Force and among the civilian population'.[82] As indicated in Table 3.1, magistrates

Table 3.1 Removed and cautioned magistrates as a result of the General Strike

A. Removed from the Bench

Name	Location	Reason
1. Mr W. Hollands	Folkestone	Threatened non-strikers
2. Mr E. T. Bird	Stoke-on-Trent	Abuse to police officer and threatening working drivers
3. Mr W. Hemingway	W.R. of Yorkshire	Intimidation at W.R. Assizes, 26 October 1926
4. Henry Bolton	Blaydon UDC	Preventing distribution of food
5. Aaron Jones	Lancashire	According to CC of Lancashire, spoke at miners' meetings

B. Removed from local advisory committees

1. Mr F. W. Rudland	Birmingham	
2. Mr J. W. Mitchell	Blackpool	

C. Cautioned

1. Mr J. W. Mitchell	Blackpool	Action in promoting the General Strike
2. Ald. Waring	St Helens	On St. Helen's Workers' Committee opposed mayor
3. Mr John McGurk	Bury	17 October at Radcliffe encouraged to get safety men out of the pits
4. Mr H. Ellison	Preston	Claimed Bench was full of capitalists when cases held

were also removed from the Bench because of what was seen as their extreme views.

The government was intent upon prosecuting agitators and law breakers under both the ordinary law and the Emergency Regulations but that was not always easy to achieve and some of the most determined government action, almost invariably supported by the action of the chief constables, was taken against magistrates, normally Labour ones, who tended to side with the strikers. Only occasionally was action taken against Conservative and right-wing magistrates who exceeded the generous boundaries of anti-trade union bias that the Home Office seemed prepared to allow.

The Attorney General indicated to the House of Commons that the Home Office had examined 68 cases of magistrates breaking the oath to keep the peace. The Home Office reflected that its files could only account for the 52 cases indicated in Table 3.2 and maintained that in all but one case, that of Dr Salter MP, had been reported to the Lord Chancellor by 24 June 1926.[83] The action taken in these cases is, as indicated in Table 3.1, even less complete in the Home Office files for whilst seven Justices were removed from the Bench, four removed from the local advisory committees set up by the Lord Chancellor, and seven Justices had been cautioned it was admitted that even these records might be incomplete.

It was the chief constables who acted as the main correspondents with the Home Office in building up cases against the magistrates. Bosanquet,

Table 3.2 Total number of magistrates named as examined in the Home Office files

Name	Location
1. Henry Bolton	Blaydon
2. Mr Egan	Birkenhead
3. Sam Filer	Tredegar
4. Frank Foster	Brighouse
5. Mr H. F. Heaviside	Doncaster
6. H. L. Trotter	Doncaster
7. Dr Salter MP	Bermondsey
8. Ald. R. Waring	St Helens
9. John Webster	Macclesfield
10. Councillor Bell	Northumberland
11. Mr F. Billington	Colchester
12. W. G. Fearnhead	Norwich
13. William Hemingway	West Riding
14. T. Andrews	Methyr Tydfil
15. J. Airey	Wallasey
16. Mrs Graham	Wallasey
17. John Roberts	Wallasey
18. H. A. Thomas	Wallasey
19. F. W. Rudland	Birmingham
20. Geo Haynes	Birmingham
21. C. F. Brett	Birmingham
22. J. Hall	Birmingham
23. H. Elison	Preston
24. John Jeffrey	Durham
25. Chris Holden	Leigh
26. John McGurk	Bury
27. E. T. Bird	Stoke-on-Trent
28. Capt. Alb. Smith	Lancashire
29. M. J. Bramall	West Riding
30. J. W. Lane	West Riding
31. George Robert	West Riding
32. Jos Smith	West Riding
33. H. M. Bunstead	West Riding
34. Harry Dyson	Workington
35. T. J. Eastland	West Sussex
36. W. Holland(s)	Folkestone
37. J. Henson Infield	Brighton
38. J. W. Mitchell	Blackpool
39. Mr Perry	Middlesex
40. Mr Ingleden	Northumberland
41. Aaron Jones	Lancashire
42. Sir Alfred Palmer	Gateshead
43. R. H. Farrah	Hull
44. A Parsee on Bench	Ipswich

45. D. Leeunfer Thomas	Pontypridd
46. Sir John Thorneycroft	Southampton
47. W. H. Taylor	Derbyshire
48. George Daley	Derbyshire
49. Ald. S. Lunn	West Riding
50. Mrs Rose Davies	Glamorgan
51. William Rees	Glamorgan
52. Mayor of Preston	Preston

of Monmouthshire, sent a letter to the Home Office on Sam Filer PBE JP from Tredegar in which he concluded that Branches of Magistrates in the Industrial District constituted 'as they are by labour men would dismiss any case brought. Abortive proceedings would have been harmful.'[84] Filer had been seen picking up copies of the *British Worker* from the railway station, had attempted to stop the distribution of other papers and was the Vice-Chairman of the Council of Action. Lionel Lindsay, Chief Constable of Glamorgan, had complained of the 'leniency' of the Labour magistrate D. Leeunfar Thomas, and on 15 December 1926 complained of Rose Davies and William Rees, Labour magistrates attempting to act as Justices, to 'hear the charges of rioting'.[85] The Chief Constable of Brighton reported upon J. Henson Infield breaking the Emergency Powers Act, and County Alderman S. Lunn, of the West Riding of Yorkshire, was complained of by the West Riding Chief Constable: Lunn was Secretary of the Maltby Miners' Branch and 'Attempted to adjudicate in a strike case in which the defendant was accused of attacking the Police'.[86] In addition he had addressed a crowd of miners on the previous evening and 'He had moreover been in connection with the accused before the case came on. The Police objected to his presence and he withdrew from the Bench.'

Adams, the Chief Constable of Doncaster, raised the case of H. F. Heaviside and F. L. Trotter, both JPs connected with the local Council of Action which had been responsible 'for all the disturbances in the districts adjoining Doncaster'. Adams felt that their conduct 'during the emergency has not been consistent with their Oath of Allegiance, and that it will be difficult in future for the police to make themselves subservient to them when acting in an official capacity'.[87] In a letter, dated 19 May, he stated that 'in my opinion the two Justices named are no longer fit and proper persons to be a member of the Magistrates Bench.'[88] Heaviside and Trotter denied the accusations in letters to the Home Office in July and August 1926. In the end the Lord Chancellor indicated, in a letter of 3 August, that he had difficulty in reconciling the evidence against the two men, asking for more detailed evidence from the chief constable.

It was the Chief Constable of Lancashire who reported upon Aaron Jones's speech 'threatening scabs'. Jones of Ashton was investigated for addressing a meeting of 400 miners at Ashton on 19 August 1926, his speech being fully recorded by DPS Littleproud, who quoted him as wishing to take action against Garwood Coal and Iron Company and suggesting that the Enginemen and Boilerermen, who were acting as safety men in the pits, should 'be cast out'. He was removed from the Bench after accusing the police of being 'always on the side of the bosses'.[89]

John McGurk (1874–1944), a Lancashire miners' agent, was reprimanded for supporting the Miners' Federation of Great Britain policy to withdraw safety men from the mines and for his denunciation of police posters stating that those interfering with the safety men were liable for prosecution: 'they could start with me as a County Magistrate, every man jack he would bring out tomorrow'.[90] Mr Albert Smith JP, the late Labour MP for Clitheroe and better known as Captain Albert Smith Secretary of the Overlookers' Society, was also accused of picketing activities on 20 May 1926.[91]

In the wake of the dispute, and throughout 1927, chief constables continued to report upon other Labour men being put forward as magistrates, often commenting upon their activities in the General Strike. Cheshire's Chief Constable condemned J. J. Eastland, and Wallasey's Chief Constable similarly reflected upon Mr Warren and Mr Larson.[92]

It was rare for Conservative or Liberal magistrates to be investigated. Nevertheless, even the Home Office could not ignore Sir Alfred Palmer, Chairman of the Justices at the Gateshead Petty Sessions, who described a group of defendants 'as a gang of hooligans' and asked them 'Why you don't go to Russia, I do not know. I am sure that the Government and I personally would subscribe willingly to get rid of the whole lot of you and let you go and live in that country where everything is so blissful and so happy. We don't want you, nobody does.' In this particular case, the Secretary of State still felt obliged to reduce the fine from £50 to £5.

In the end the magistrates were generally investigated where they were members of local Councils of Action, made inflammatory speeches or published articles and pamphlets, such as the *Birmingham Strike Bulletin* or the *Northern Light*, which might cause disaffection and be contrary to the Emergency Powers Act. They were also investigated where chief constables felt that they were lenient in their sentencing. Complaints about the leniency of the sentences made by Labour magistrates have already been mentioned for Monmouthshire, but also emerged amongst the Ipswich and Southampton magistrates referred to in Table 3.2, and in some cases, as that of George Daley of Derbyshire, there were claims that the magistrates attempted to have the case dismissed.

The chief constables were also instructed by the Home Office to report upon situations which might lead to prosecutions under the ordinary law and the Emergency Powers Act. The Chief Constable of Northampton, for instance, did report upon disturbances that occurred on 12 May 1926 but was much more concerned to report on the speech made by John Beckett, then Labour MP for Gateshead but later a prominent figure in the British Union of Fascists, on Sunday 9 May. In this speech Beckett condemned

> the Flying Squad and Special Constabulary as they have done what I have seen at Newcastle charging the peaceful crowd of people, breaking their heads with batons, also the same at Gateshead. You men and women will have to converse and fraternize with your friends in the Police, and tell of this; also we shall have to get amongst the soldiers and the Navy. If they give us twelve months, we shall do it.[93]

However, in this case the Director of Public Prosecutions advised that no action should be taken despite the fact that, under the conditions of the General Strike, Beckett's speech could be construed as constituting an attempt, under the Emergency Powers Act, to cause 'disaffection amongst the civilian population'.

The Home Office specifically asked all the chief constables of England and Wales, at that time 178, to report on disturbance during the General Strike in their districts that led to prosecutions during the nine days. What amazed the Home Office was how little violence there was.

This perhaps makes the point about the general effectiveness of the authorities in maintaining public order and the immensely regional nature of the General Strike. There were, indeed, nil returns from 23 of the 56 county forces and from 72 of the 122 borough forces.[94] In other words, well over half of the police forces of England and Wales had no prosecutions to report in respect of the General Strike. These returns also reflect the exaggerated fears of the authorities. By and large these were the predominantly rural counties, including the East Riding and North Riding of Yorkshire, and the boroughs that were barely associated with the coal dispute but and, interestingly so, Barnsley, a major coal town, also recorded no prosecutions. In summarising the situation the Home Office reflected that

> In a large number of the counties and boroughs the number of proceedings was surprisingly small; even in the City of London there were only 6 cases! In Cheshire with the great works of Messrs Lever, Brunner Mond, etc. etc., apart from one Communist who was imprisoned, only three men were fined and one discharged.[95]

The Home Office's immediate analysis of the results indicates its thinking behind the actions taken in the General Strike and its assessment of the success at maintaining public order. It was bullish about the success of its measures and strongly committed to a policy that 'loyal workmen not to be interfered with', concerned about the intimidation of lorry drivers, and content with the moderate police measures taken: 'At a few places there were baton charges by the police. In most countries much sterner measures would have been taken.'[96]

The analysis indicated that 64 communists were subject to proceedings by the county and borough forces and 68 by the Metropolitan Police and that the rest of those prosecuted, 1188 in the counties and boroughs and 572 in the Metropolitan district, were strikers, unemployed hooligans or criminals. In other words, there was only a small number of the hard left prosecuted despite the fact that more than half of the 3000 or so members of the Communist Party of Great Britain were arrested at some point during the General Strike.

In essence, government fear of the communist and revolutionary threat meant that it undoubtedly organised more force than was required to deal with the industrial threat. Despite the evidence, the Home Office report insisted on condemning the 'misguided' chief constable who had shown leniency to one person arrested who had previous convictions for assaulting policemen. It also rejected the Labour Party call for an amnesty to those arrested and convicted during the General Strike and particularly those arrested under the Emergency Powers Act: 'As regards those guilty of disorder, they were the matches that might have ignited the gunpowder; when the mass was quiescent, they set a bad example.' Of those cases dealt with by the borough forces only 154 of those arrested were sentenced to imprisonment and only 18 were given more than three months imprisonment.

The report also commented on Labour magistrates, stating that 'a few Magistrates here and there thought proper, after the collapse of the strike, to dismiss offenders, bind them over, or otherwise treat them with leniency. This course of action arose out of some confusion of ideas as lends some few persons to suggest an amnesty.' It added that 'The right course with crime is to press sentences that are adequate, and not more than adequate.' This meant that 'there is no case for amnesty, and that if it is required that the prerogative should be exercised, individual cases must be made out in the usual way.' The Home Secretary, indeed, rejected the Trades Union Congress call for an amnesty on those imprisoned as a result of their actions during the General Strike (Table 3.3).[97]

Such figures on police prosecutions connected with the General Strike, however, represent only the tip of the iceberg because there were in fact almost 7960 prosecutions under both common law and the Emergency power regulations resulting from both the General Strike and the much more protracted and bitter coal lock-out. Table 3.4 indicates that the prosecution success rates ran at about 67 per cent and that this was broadly the same under both common law and the Emergency

Table 3.3 Prosecutions arising from the General Strike[98]

	County and borough forces	Metropolitan police district	Total
Case dropped	4	0	4
Discharged	105	17	122
Bound over	122	117	239
Returned to Industrial School	3	0	3
Fined	412	226	638
Fined and to pay damages	22	2	24
Imprisoned	436	193	629
Committed for trial	1	2	3
Pending	83	15	98
Total	1188	572	1760

Source: HO 144/12050, Part 1, Chief Constables, Returns on Prosecutions arising from the General Strike.

Table 3.4 Prosecutions connected with the General Strike and coal lock-out 1 May 1926 to 19 December 1926

	Under ordinary law	Under emergency regulations
Bound over	488	297
Fined	2197	1284
Imprisoned	475	644
Sent to Borstal Inst.	2	0
Sent to Refy or Industrial School	2	2
Judgment respited		1
Total persons convicted	3158	2228
Dismissed	490	454
Withdrawn	384	146
Dealt with under Probation Acts	611	456
Adjourned *sine die*	12	18
Certified insane	0	1
Pending	1	1
Total	1498	1076
Total persons prosecuted	4656	3304
Imprisoned for failing to pay fines or find surety	35	23

regulations, although imprisonment was much more likely under the Emergency Regulations.[99]

The high level of prosecutions was partly caused by the continuing government concern to protect miners, and particularly safety men, who went back to work. Indeed, in July 1926 the Home Secretary wrote to the chief constables of

> the distinct wish and intention of H. M. Government that the utmost protection should be given to every man who desires to work in the coal mines ... ample police available are available in other parts of the country and arrangements can be made for you to have such further reinforcements as you require.[100]

Soon afterwards 380 extra police officers were sent to Glamorgan and some to the West Riding of Yorkshire. Indeed, disturbances and prosecutions connected with the protection of safety men were high in South Wales and the Home Office reflected that

> As regards South Wales, the problem of protection, like the measure safeguarding them seems to require some further consideration. The

Divisional Inspector complained at the Conference that the police arranged in Glamorganshire have not been adequate. The information he quoted was not altogether unimportant but one gathered that the police policy had been to keep the police back until actual need for intervention had arisen rather than take steps when a mine was to be opened, or other developments were expected, to ensure adequate police protection being ready on to the spot to deal with any eventuality. The SJC has now taken shape to call up 200 First Reserve to supplement and the force can be rapidly augmented by police from outside if the occasion arises, but in view of the situation in South Wales it seems desirable to discuss the whole position with the Chief Constable, and, if possible, Sir Rhys Williams, the Chairman of the Standing Joint Committee.[101]

The overall impression offered by the evidence is that public order held up very well in most parts of the country and that it was only after the General Strike and in the coalmining districts that tension between the police and the striking miners really led to serious disturbances and criminal prosecutions. Even then it was felt, perhaps with some exaggeration, that relations with the mining communities and the police had generally been good. Indeed, as the coalmining dispute came to an end in November 1926, the *Police Review and Parade Gossip*, the journal of the regular policeman, stated that

> In the House of Commons it has been said that the behaviour of England during the last six months bears great testimony to the good spirit and good feeling of the mining community. I agree, but I think it bears even greater testimony to the good feeling and the good spirit of the police community throughout the country.[102]

The General Strike and the coal lock-out reveal the extent to which the government's post-war co-ordination of the police had been a success. The improved communications, the central controls imposed by the Home Office, the mobility of the police, the flying squad tactics, and the cramping and confining of the powers of local watch committees and joint standing committees, where Labour interests were to the fore, and the blatant misuse of power, generally supported by the Home Office, did much to ensure that the most important dispute in British industrial history, involving a direct challenge to the government, would fail. There was by 1926 a greater sense of co-ordination between the police, the armed forces and the civil authorities. The police were now a more effective and efficient tool of the state than ever before. Their experience in the General Strike and the coal lock-out meant that their activities in dealing with fascist and communist clashes in the 1930s posed few serious problems, although legislation emerged as they widened the extent of their powers.

Fascism and communism in the 1930s, and the Public Order Act, 1936

The formation of Oswald Mosley's British Union of Fascists in October 1932 led to conflict with the Communist Party of Great Britain which forced both the police and the Home Office to consider new means to control public order. By the early 1930s it was clear that there was going to be no communist revolution in Britain, although there is substantial evidence that the Soviet Union was beginning to fascinate and beguile British academics and writers.[103] From 1932 onwards, however, there was conflict between British communists and British fascists and between fascists and the Jewish community.

The fascist conflict with communists became blatantly evident on 12 March 1933 when Oswald Mosley held a meeting at the Free Trade Hall, Manchester, where there was so much violence that John Maxwell, the Chief Constable of Manchester, had to use his officers to get Mosley safely out of the venue.[104] This was unusual since indoor meetings were normally guarded by the stewards of those organising the meeting. It was another such conflict at Olympia on 7 June 1934 that led to further discussions about public order. There were marches by the blackshirts to Olympia and a counter march by the Jewish community and communists. There was violence within Olympia between blackshirt stewards and communist agitators in front of an audience of about 17,000.[105] The outcry with these events was so great that the government discussed the introduction of a Public Order Bill in 1934 but it was dropped largely because 'there was weak support from Labour and the Liberals for such a measure'.[106] There were no changes in the law and the police were given the task of dealing with the threat of disturbances between the contending parties in Jewish areas such as Manchester, Leeds and the East End of London.

Ultimately, however, it was the Battle of Cable Street in October 1936, when the communists and Jews attempted to stop Mosley's fascist march through the East End of London and found themselves confronted by the police that led to the introduction of the Public Order Act of 1936 and the control and banning of public meetings and processions. Although the public order threat was different from the crises of 1919–21 and 1926 it is clear that the police were drawn further into preserving public order more through banning the meetings and processions in some areas and reporting every public meeting to Special Branch and, ultimately, the Home Secretary. Yet the events after Cable Street had committed the Metropolitan Police to draw upon its Special Constabulary, much as had occurred in 1926. On 11 October it called up 2085 special constables, 1221 on 12 October, and many fewer thereafter, although the number changed from day to day, until the call up expired on 3 November 1936 when 40 special constables were called upon. In total there were calls collectively for 7440 special constables on 18 days.[107]

The main issue was to maintain public order outdoors, since by and large indoor meetings were stewarded by the organising body. After the violence at Cable Street, however, the Cabinet Committee on Protection of Public Order met four times, the first occasion being on 10 October 1936, to discuss what became the Public Order Bill of 1936. The discussions dealt with the issue of the wearing of semi-military uniforms, which was made illegal, the retention of private armies, also made illegal, and above all the issue of banning meetings and processions.[108] It was accepted that, ordinarily, the police could not stop meetings although they could stop the displaying of 'prohibitive banners and the shouting of offensive slogans'. However, the new legislation was to allow the police to prevent processions and meetings in order to 'prevent serious disorder', permission having to be sought to hold a meeting with the police being able to suspend such a meeting or a procession for three months.[109] In urban areas throughout England and Wales the police would apply for an order of prohibition to the urban district authority in consultation with the Secretary of State. In London the Commission would have to apply to the Secretary of State, as the police authority, without first applying to the local authority.

The Public Order Act came into force at the end of December 1936 and was extensively used by the Metropolitan Police, whose district saw considerable conflict between the fascists and the local East End Jewish community. Between December 1936 and November 1937 there were in London 12,021 public meetings, 3094 held by fascists and 4364 by the anti-fascists, mainly communist groups.[110] The Metropolitan Police were concerned at the high level of violence occurring in the Jewish areas of the East End of London and, consequently, used the Act from

13 March 1937 until the Second World War to stop marches and processions taking part in the main Jewish sections of the East End of London.[111]

Philip Game, Commissioner of the Metropolitan Police, regularly, and successfully, applied to the Home Secretary from February 1937 until September 1939 for the introduction of what proved to be a succession of a three-month ban for marches and processions within the emphatically Jewish sections of the East End of London. Game's letter of 3 August 1937 stressed the need to respect the rights of all groups and to ensure that 'free speech and free expression of opinion is not made a cloak for insult and abuse of a defamatory and seditious character or of a character likely to provoke a breach of the peace.'[112] His letter of 28 February 1938 suggested that there 'has of late been lots of Jew-baiting in the district covered, and there are signs that the Communists have come to realise that violent opposition to the Fascists is not the best policy', adding that the Jewish policy was more difficult to define and that disturbances and clashes might be revived by 'militant elements'.[113] His letter to the Home Secretary on 6 June 1939 points to violence at the fascist meeting at Farrance Street, Stepney, on 16 April 1939 that resulted in ten arrests. He added that 'Following the meeting attempts were made to form processions within the prohibited area and proceedings were subsequently instituted against two persons under Section 3 of the Public Order Act, 1936.'[114]

Game's confidential letter to the Home Secretary on 3 August 1937 is particularly fascinating since it also reveals the nature of the Metropolitan Police's watching role on meetings. Practically all the 12,000 or so political demonstrations and meetings held in London each year were reported upon. Game suggested that

> At all public meetings at which Police are present, especially Fascist meetings, every endeavour is to be made that at least two members of the Forces are near enough to the speakers to hear clearly what they say, even if there is constant heckling and interruption. Whilst it is not possible to lay down specifically at what stage the police is to judge when a speaker begins to indulge in abusive remarks, the Commissioner wishes all Police Officers to err on the side of action rather than inaction.[115]

It was suggested that if speakers were warned and a conviction sought, his officers would not be reprimanded if the conviction failed as long as the action was taken in good faith.

Game was also concerned about other political events and, on 17 February 1937, called for the Home Secretary to supply him with additional police in 'view of the anticipated demonstrations' arising from the London County Council elections of 4 March 1937 where fascist leaders, such as William Joyce and Raven Thomson, of the British Union, were standing.[116] Eventually, of course, the concern subsided when Britain entered the Second World War and support for British fascism faded when it was seen to be anti-patriotic on the eve of, and during, the Second World War.

Conclusion

During the inter-war years the police became more effective agents of public order than ever before. From the end of the Great War, governments, working principally through the Home Office, ensured that there was more central co-ordination of the police of England and Wales, and chief constables became drawn increasingly into an integrated system of control which included the armed forces. The police were more mobile as they became more motorised, easily transferred from one force to another as changes in the rules removed the need for swearing in, and in some cases more effective because of the formation of 'flying squads'. The police concern to maintain public order was strongly driven by the prevailing government fears of 'Bolshevism', and this became evident in the thinking of many chief constables who were fiercely hostile to Bolshevism. The impact of Bolshevism to them was evident in many industrial disputes as it had been in the 1918 and 1919 police strikes and in police trade unionism. This led many chief constables into conflict with the Labour movement which, in some areas, was becoming established in local government, on watch committees or on joint standing committees. There was therefore clear tension between the police authorities and the rights of citizens and obvious class bias. There is clear evidence that the police flouted the law to bolster their authority in maintaining public order. In the end there was probably rather less conflict and more stability than might have been supposed in the inter-war years given the level of industrial action between 1918 and 1926, and by the 1930s the police were faced with a large number of small conflicts between generally insignificant political groups and no longer faced with applying an elaborate and integrated system of control. The elaborate structures of plans of the immediate post-war years were largely redundant and unused in the 1930s, although they were still in place and the police knew their role in a major crisis of public order. During the inter-war years the police of England and Wales were better organised and integrated with other forces than at any other time in their history and by and large their new structures were more than sufficient for the task of maintaining public control. The modernisation of the police force during the inter-war years helped in this process of accommodation to its enhanced role in public order and there were other pressing issues such as the need to adjust to the transport revolution and the transformation of detective work through scientific and forensic work.

4
Detective and Scientific Work: A New Vista

C. T. Symons, a Home Office official, reported enthusiastically, almost rapturously, on 27 March 1935 that 'In my interview with Major Kennedy I was able to point out the great usefulness of a lower power binocular microscope in police work.'[1] Major Kennedy, the Chairman of the General Purposes and Finance Committee at Taunton, Somerset, was, along with the Chief Constable (Webber), being shown the £50 Leitz microscope and the Leica camera, the latest technology of their kind. Kennedy promptly announced his intention to ask his committee for £120 to help improve police work at Taunton. Shortly afterwards police officers began to assemble at Clattersbridge, near Birkenhead, to attend a course of lectures on 'Forensic Medicine and the Blood Test' given by Dr Yeomans.[2] Many of these officers then attended a week-long course which was taught between 1 and 6 July 1935 and given by Professor F. H. Tryhorn, of the University of Hull, who reminded his audience that 'This country is very much behind in dealing scientifically with minor crimes.'[3] Nevertheless, in his efforts to raise standards and an awareness of forensic techniques, Tryhorn pioneered new scientific equipment and was the adviser for the company of Reynolds and Brown, 13 Briggate, Leeds, which produced easily usable boxes of test tubes, equipment and labels. Such initiatives, and the surge of interest in scientific and forensic techniques arose from Home Office initiatives to bring science to the aid of the detection of crime, led very much by A. L. Dixon. Like detective work, scientific aids in policing only began to be discussed in the 1920s and developed seriously in the early 1930s, and particularly from 1933 onwards. Indeed it was the 1930s that saw the most dramatic changes in both scientific and detective work in England and Wales and the dawn of a new age of forensic work which impacted greatly upon the detective work, and indeed, working life of a small but growing section of the police of England and Wales.

Nineteenth-century policing in England and Wales was essentially about preventive policing and the policeman on his beat as Clive Emsley has indicated in his recent book *The Great British Bobby*.[4] Nevertheless, detective, or plain clothes, work had began in the mid-1840s and by 1859 Bradford had three detectives and Sheffield had five, although Halifax, Huddersfield, Wakefield, York and most other forces had none.[5] Most attention at this time was focused upon the detective work at Scotland Yard with the Metropolitan Police[6] and, famously, Henry Jackson is said to be the first person to be convicted on evidence from fingerprints in 1902. Yet given the limited nature of such work it is perhaps not surprising, then, there has been little written about the detective and forensic work of the provincial borough and county forces of the late nineteenth and early twentieth centuries. Gordon Smith's book on the *Bradford City Police* is perhaps more revealing than most, suggesting that there was a detective force and indicating that, in the 1930s, the Bradford Technical College provided 'research staff and scientific equipment' which allowed the police to expose forgeries by ultraviolet and infrared rays, and that the Bradford Force was the only one in 1936 to regularly use colour photography.[7] Other works on the Leeds Police, the Shropshire Police, the Wigan Police and the individual lives of policemen have little to say.[8] The most forthcoming secondary source is Clive Emsley's book on *The English Police*, which discusses detective and forensic work in the briefest of terms, stressing the work on the classification of fingerprints undertaken by Sir Edward Henry and the Metropolitan Police Force, and the immensely regional and local nature of detective and forensic work, which focused upon the Metropolitan Force and forces such as Nottingham, Sheffield, Cardiff, Hull and Liverpool.[9] As Emsley points out, in contrast, the Chief Constable appointed by the Oxfordshire Police in 1940 found that it had no specialist sections at all, not even a CID.[10]

We support the general picture that has been presented by Clive Emsley and as evidenced in other primary and secondary works. There was, indeed, remarkably little detective and forensic work in the nineteenth and early twentieth centuries and much of what did emerge was the work of the Metropolitan and the large borough forces. However, we would go further and suggest that as a result of Home Office pressure, and the campaigning of A. L. Dixon, that there was significantly more development in detective and forensic work during the inter-war years than has hitherto been suggested, and this was particularly so in the 1930s.

It was not until the twentieth century that detective work, drawing upon scientific investigation, became more widespread and not until the 1930s that there was a concerted effort by the Home Office to impose uniformity and collaboration in detective work and to encourage training courses and central control in scientific investigation. It was only then that detective and scientific work became more truly uniform and modernised and increasingly subject to government guidelines and direction. Even then, however, there was reluctance on behalf of some chief constables to develop the detection side of police work. Indeed, in his Presidential Address to the Chief Constables' Association (CCA) at its General Conference on 16 June 1932, A. K. Mayall, the Chief Constable of Oldham, stated that

> A great many minds seem to be obsessed by the question of detection of crime. There is certainly a good deal of glamour about it, and it is certainly not dull as to the preventive scale of action yet it is obvious that if crime were prevented it would not require detection. All manner of devices have been adapted to effect the arrest of offenders, e.g. the use of wireless gradually increased use of telephones, mechanical Police, and the excellent police box system.[11]

The persistence of such conservative attitudes has to be recognised. Nevertheless, such views were being challenged and transformed, and even Mayall changed his views considerably when he joined the Departmental Committee on Detective Work for England and Wales which sat between 1933 and 1938. In 1936, T. Rawson, Chief Constable of Bradford, in his Presidential Address to the CCA, outlined the high qualities and intelligence required to be a policeman in 'modern conditions' means that they had to add to their skills expertise in fingerprinting, photography and the use of the wireless.[12] Much had happened in the 1920s and there was a sea-change of activity in the mid-1930s to inaugurate a new age of modern policing in detective work.

The Police Council, representing all police ranks and the various authorities, was formed after the deliberations of the Desborough Committee in 1919 and 1920, to advise the Home Office of police requirements from the 1920s but did little to further detective work, possibly because of the economy cuts. The Police Federation shared this lack of interest. Indeed, throughout the 1920s most police forces failed to develop their detective and scientific work.

In 1928–29 there were, apart from the Metropolitan Force, 58 county forces with 581 detectives and 121 city and borough forces with 1198 detectives.[13] With only 1780 detectives in the 35,000–36,000 strong county and borough forces in England and Wales this meant that there was an average of fewer than ten detectives per force and that detectives represented less than 5 per cent of the total national police force of England and Wales. Even these averages and proportions misrepresent the real picture for some forces had no detectives whilst others had large departments. The CID at Scotland Yard, working for the Metropolitan Force, totalled about 200 officers, 1 per cent of the force, and was weakened by 'petty jealousies'.[14] Thus, in the late 1920s, nationally for all forces in England and Wales, fewer than 2000 of the 56,000 police officers, about 3.6 per cent, were employed in detective work.

Indeed, the development of detective work was limited in both numbers and the quality of the work in the 1920s. The Liverpool Police, the largest borough force in England and Wales outside the Metropolis with an establishment of around 2200 throughout the 1920s, did not distinguish between ordinary police work and detective work until 1925, although then a Special Section was formed to be a CID 'under an Inspector freed from ordinary routine work' which 'more than justified itself'.[15] In the early part of the year the Section 'helped the Birkenhead Police in the investigation of the Rock Ferry murder, and the assistance rendered to the various divisions in which it has worked has enabled the police to deal much more effectively with outbreaks of crime, particularly those against property with violence'. In 1926 the Liverpool Police reorganised its department to ensure that all detection work came under the auspices of the Special Section and that the CID office was placed under the control of a superintendent.[16] The same report went on to suggest that the CID conferences, that had taken place monthly since 1924 'with officers from surrounding forces', were continuing and 'still prove most useful'.[17] However, throughout the rest of the inter-war years the Chief Constable of Liverpool did not focus upon the work of the CID and, in his annual report of 1926, almost went out of his way to remind his readers that 'The vigilant constable on ordinary beat duty is often able to render excellent service in the detection of crime', citing the example of where a constable had caught sight of a flicker of a light on some premises, entered them, was unable to find anyone but contacted CID who noticed some soot on the floor which led them to move a cooking range to find a man 'tightly wedged in a flue'.[18]

Much smaller forces had even less of a CID presence than the Liverpool Force. The St Helens force, of around 140 officers, had a small number of officers dealing with Scotland Yard over stolen cars and in 1936 took 102 photos at the scene of crimes, and took the fingerprints of 40 suspects which matched with nine people who had previous convictions.[19] The Preston Borough Force, which had an establishment of about 137 in the mid- and late 1920s, also had a small detective function and reported in 1931 that the prints of 17 suspects had been sent to the Criminal Records Office at New Scotland Yard and had discovered that 13 had previous convictions.[20] Although the surviving reports of many of these forces are few and far between for the inter-war years the surviving evidence suggests that detective and forensic work was of limited scale in the small boroughs of England and Wales.

In the late 1920s and the early 1930s, however, there was extraparliamentary pressure from the press to create a more effective detective force as a result of the failure of the Royal Commission on Police Powers and Procedures (1929) to make any significant comments or recommendations in connection with the detection of crime. In May 1929 the *Evening News* issued an article, under the title 'London men handicapped in the provinces', which advocated the creation of a National CID based upon London but gathering together picked officers from the important police in the country and financed by the Treasury, concluding that 'If this were done it is my view that fewer crimes would remained unsolved.'[21] The article further recognised that 'Jealousy between the local C.I.D. and Scotland Yard is an important factor' in the 'failure of collaboration' but added that 'this might be overcome by having in addition three regional headquarters in the Midlands, Lancashire, and the North.'

In July 1930, the *Daily Express* felt that the Royal Commission had 'made the crime of murder much safer than it was' adding 'but it has always been safer than it might be'.[22] The newspaper went further in criticising Scotland Yard, and the 'ludicrous' investigations conducted by even some of the modernised county forces. Its suggestion for reform was that there should be a national CID for England, that chief constables should not be drawn from the armed forces but know their police work 'from A to Z', that every police surgeon should 'have to graduate in a school of medical jurisprudence' and that there should be a national Murder Squad. These reflections were not just the meanderings of a right-wing newspaper but a genuine concern about the delays that existed in Scotland Yard officers being brought into investigation and the fragmented nature of authority in dealing with investigations.

Mindful of such criticisms, in the late 1920s and the early 1930s, the Home Office became increasingly concerned about the limited impact of detective work in a new age of scientific and technical innovation.

For this reason it sponsored the discussions which favoured the creation of a national Police College, which eventually became the Metropolitan Police College at Hendon, in the early 1930s. There was initially much opposition to this college throughout the country, one county committee seeing it as elitist and 'only for the blue-eyed boys from the Metropolitan' and the 'whipper-snappers from a City Force', although, as we have already seen, the college idea gained much support from the Police Federation.[23] However, the CCA, generally reluctant to support the idea, recognised that it should be remembered also that whilst 'it would improve the standard of the senior officers... it was prepared to go in largely for scientific research'.[24]

The Home Office was also drawn into two wider and crucial debates concerning detective work. The first, and immediate debate or concern, was the tensions that were developing between the uniformed and plain-clothed branches of the police. The second surrounded the Home Office's ill-fated attempts to create a national force using the latest scientific techniques within a climate and structure of policing for England and Wales that was resistant to centralisation.

The tensions between plain-clothed and uniformed policemen were frequently commented upon. In 1929 the Royal Commission on Police Powers and Procedures failed to advise on how to improve detective work but it noted that there was 'a tendency among this branch of the service to regard itself as a thing above and apart, to which the restrictions and limitations placed upon the ordinary police do not, or should not, apply'.[25] In fact it was rather concerned about the constant use of plain-clothed policemen but agreed that 'The extent to which they should be used in a matter which must be left to the discretion of superior officers of the Police.'[26] Chief Constable John Maxwell of Manchester also stated, of the uniformed and detective branches, in his 1934 annual report that 'co-operation between the two forces [was] capable of improvement'.[27] At this point he also appointed Superintendent Valentine, at the age of 38, as Head of the Manchester CID to effect improvements in the relations between the two branches and to modernise detective work. Valentine had gone through the uniformed and plain-clothed ranks since being appointed in 1919 and since 1921 had been attached to the special detective branch of the Manchester City Police, becoming detective sergeant in 1923 and detective inspector in 1930.[28] Also in 1934, Lord Trenchard, Metropolitan Commissioner, made it clear that he deplored 'the state of jealous rivalry... between the CID and the uniform branch'.[29] In the end this was increasingly tackled, though hardly resolved, by all police officers having to gain at least a year's experience in the uniformed branch before being transferred to plain-clothed detective work.

The second debate, relating to the creation of a national CID, was provoked by the 1929 Royal Commission on Police Procedures. As already noted, the *Daily Express*, concerned that the 1929 Royal Commission had recommended no changes, campaigned for a national CID in 1930 stating that 'Some county police forces have modernised and improved their methods and have gradually raised the standard of intelligence and education in their ranks, but the Home Office has not introduced an innovation of any real importance for years.' Eventually, however, the Home Office was driven, partly by the newspaper campaign, to set up a Departmental Committee on Detective Work, for England and Wales, under A. L. Dixon on 12 May 1933, and was later optimistically billed by the *Daily Dispatch* as the 'H. O. Plan for a National Police'[30] and by the *Daily Express* as a scheme to open 'Nine Scotland Yards'.[31] This Committee formed four sub-committees that were set up to deal with the four major issues of the selection and training of detectives, crime records, communications and the use of scientific aids in the detection of crime. Its general purpose was to establish a national scheme that would raise every force in the country to the highest level of efficiency, ensuring that modern scientific methods would be available throughout the country, and that no police force would lack the highest technical expertise. This became known as the 'agility' scheme.

Dixon chaired a 26-member committee. These included two other staff of the Home Office plus Major-General Sir Llewellyn Atcherley and Lt. Col. W. D. Allan, both Inspectors of the Constabulary, Sir Hugh Turnbull of the London City Police and R. M. Horne of the Metropolitan Police. In addition there were 18 chief constables and 1 assistant chief constable, the most prominent being John Maxwell of Manchester and F. W. Crawley of Newcastle. Given the increasing association of detective work with scientific investigation in the 1930s it is well to note that the forces directly represented on the Committee were Bedfordshire, Birmingham, Bradford, Brighton, Cardiff, Doncaster, Durham, Exeter, Flintshire, Gloucester, Kent, Lancashire, Liverpool, Manchester, Newcastle, Oldham, Oxford, Shropshire and the West Riding. As became obvious in the late 1930s, many of these became closely associated with attempts to improve the quality of forensic work in the detection of crime.

After five years of deliberations, during which detective work did improve, the Committee finally published the five-volume *Report of the Departmental Committee in Detective Work and Procedures* (hereafter, the

Report), the first comprehensive attempt to deal with detective work, on 23 September 1938, following its presentation to the Home Secretary on 21 July 1938.[32] The press announced the beginning of a revolution in detective work. The *Daily Herald*, a Labour newspaper, headlined that 'Science could help solve 10,000 crimes per year', the *Daily Mail* maintained that the *Report*'s main theme was to 'Teach PCs science', and the *Daily Mirror* announced that the *Report* advocated that 'Every PC should become a chemist'.[33] The *Manchester Guardian* and the *Police Review* were less interested in sensationalism but did suggest that the recommendations of the Committee, which they presented in some detail, would bring about the transformation of detective work in England and Wales.[34] Indeed, there was going to be a rapid transformation in how detective work was done, although the *Report* did reflect upon changes that had gone on throughout the 1930s.

The first volume of the *Report* advocated courses for detectives and substantial reform in the provision of detective work because it was felt that 'One of the first essentials of a sound police organisation is the proper machinery for making use of the eyes and ears of all members of the force for detective purpose.'[35] However, there were 181 separate police forces in England and Wales, which made for difficulties of communication, although the *Report* was at pains to stress that there was co-operation between the forces and that

> A central Record and Fingerprint system for all forces is provided by the Metropolitan Police, who also issue the *Police Gazette*, by means of which particulars of persons 'wanted', crimes committed, etc, are circulated in every force, while the West Riding Police issue to most forces of the North, another paper serving a similar but more limited purpose with respect to northern crime and criminals. In conjunction with these publications extensive records are maintained at both Scotland Yard and Wakefield and are used for the assistance of other forces in the investigation of crime. A system of inter-force communication has been worked for the country as a whole, in addition to more local systems of inter-connection with the aid of teleprinter or private telephone instillations.[36]

Summarising the work of the four sub-committees, Volume 1 stressed that a great deal had been done to improve detective training, record keeping, a system of rapid inter-communication between detective forces, the application of forensic science and to thus develop a more systematic system of working 'without reference to force boundaries';

a later reference acknowledging that 'far too much importance is still attached to the force boundaries.'[37]

Much of the *Report* dealt with the rising level of indictable crimes and reiterated the concerns of the Desborough Report (1920) of the problem of the lack of a centralised and uniform system of policing and the problem of management of 41 separate forces with establishments of fewer than 50 officers.[38] It reiterated the concerns of the Select Committee of the House of Commons (1932) about the need for merger of the non-county forces where the population was less than 30,000. Yet it set these concerns against the fact that there were Detective Conferences, Chief Constable District Conferences and similar activities that established links, even though there was more need of co-operation.[39]

The *Report* also tackled the concern about the relations between the uniformed and plain-clothed detective work previously raised by Maxwell and other chief constables in the early 1930s. Indeed, it stated that

> Our enquiries have established beyond question that positive steps to this end are necessary in many forces. In the county forces as we have pointed out the uniformed constables normally and necessarily take part in crime inquiry work, but in the Metropolitan Police and the large city and borough forces which have highly organised detective departments the general practice is for any investigation necessary for the investigation of the crime to be taken in hand by the detectives as soon as possible the crime is reported, and to be carried through by members of the CID to the exclusion of the uniformed members of the force, even where the commission of the crime has first been announced by, and reported to, a uniform constable.[40]

Elaborating upon the Metropolitan Police, the *Report* further suggested that that there was in fact very little uniformed police involvement in CID and there needed to be more co-operation.[41]

Despite accepting that there may be good reasons for the two sections of the force to be kept separate, for it had been argued by witnesses that the presence of a high-ranking uniformed officer might inhibit and compromise the work of detectives, the report felt that such inhibition was exaggerated and that it should be the policy of all chief constables to encourage the involvement of the uniformed police in detective investigations 'by associating them with detective officers in the investigation of specific cases where the circumstances render the adoption of this course possible and desirable'.[42]

The other four volumes of the *Report* made specific recommendations for the future. One main recommendation was that it should be an essential qualification that detectives should gain their initial experience through the uniformed branch in order that they got 'insight into the general work of the police and into human nature'.[43] It was also concerned that training courses should be more available, that they should be eight weeks in length and similar to the revised syllabus course at Hendon, with the Metropolitan Force, and that on trial with the West Yorkshire Police at Wakefield towards the end of 1934.[44] Volume 3 was not made available to the public but dealt with the gathering of crime statistics which, it was admitted, was not 'equally complete in all forces'.[45] The issue of improved communications was examined in Volume 4 (Chapter VI). Here it was pointed out that only London, the West Riding of Yorkshire, Glamorganshire, Hertfordshire and Buckinghamshire, of the county forces, had a private telephone system, along with four other regional centres in England and Wales, that were all of varying quality.[46] It also picked up on the existence of the *Police Report* published by the West Yorkshire Police, the only alternative to the *Police Gazette* of the Metropolitan Force, and noted that its 4400 copies were published for the northern forces, some Midland forces and one or two forces in the south, on every week day except for Saturday. In addition a monthly supplement was issued (492 copies) alongside police notes, the *Police Gazette* and other sources of information.[47]

Volume 5 of the *Report*, contained Chapters VII on forensic work, and Chapter VIII, the conclusions.[48] The main findings of the forensic sub-committee were that there needed to be new syllabuses, support for the Metropolitan Laboratory and a commitment to supporting the Home Office initiative of opening new laboratories at Nottingham, Birmingham and Cardiff for the East Midlands, West Midlands and South Wales. In particular it supported Lord Trenchard's Advisory Committee on Scientific Investigation and stated unequivocally that

> The organisation within the police service of a comprehensive laboratory system for the purpose of bringing the resources of science to bear upon the investigation of crime is, we are satisfied, a development of immense value which should be pressed forward without delay.[49]

The *Departmental Committee Report on Detective Work* thus favoured an integrated and co-ordinated system of detection of crime in England and Wales based upon highly trained officers who had risen through the uniformed ranks and had been trained to an awareness of how to record evidence for scientific and forensic examination. However, it also recognised that this was difficult to achieve because there was no national system of policing in England and Wales, since some forces were too small to develop an effective detective force, and because both the knowledge of forensic science and the availability of communications systems were flimsy and thinly spread. The Home Office, and the Committee it created, thus recognised that it had to work through the chief constables in order to make them aware of the need for improved, extended and better trained detective forces co-ordinating their expertise and knowledge on a national basis. Incidentally, this was a convenient argument for those wanting a centralised force on the sly.

The 1933 Departmental Committee that eventually published its reports in 1938 was itself the starting point for change and its message was regularly pressed forward at the CCA, a body formed in 1896 that represented 121 of the borough and county borough forces in England and Wales – though not the other 58 county forces by the mid-1930s – and which held annual meetings. At the CCA conference in 1936 A. L. Dixon, the Home Office Chairman of the Committee, lectured on 'Some aspects of co-operation within the police service' and referred to the need for more systematic detective work, stating that

> The object of the introduction of detectives as to the uses of laboratory work is not to try to turn them into scientists or to encourage them in any way to pose as scientists, or to give what purports to be scientific evidence – that would be a fatal mistake – but to make them aware of what scientists can do.[50]

Some of the larger police forces had already been making significant efforts to improve their detection work, although their efforts were encouraged much further in the 1930s by a combination of the press campaign and the formation of the Departmental Committee. The Leeds Force had a CID by 1933, though its detectives were subsumed into a force of 694 policemen and two police women without any separate recognition.[51] It was not until 1937 that the structure of the force was clearly indicated; one of its four superintendents was a detective superintendent who was responsible for four sections – the Detective Office which dealt with Correspondence, Records, Aliens and Finance; the Photography Department which dealt with Fingerprints and Printing; Police women who dealt with Enquiries, Special Offences and Shoplifting; and General CID Work.[52] The precise number of those in the detective section was not given in 1937 but the figure supplied the following year was 46 out of an establishment level of 694 policemen and two police women, about 6.7 per cent of the establishment strength of the Leeds Police.[53] By 1938 and 1939 it was clear that the Leeds CID was a vital element in the success of the force which detected 41.79 per cent of the indictable offences in 1937, 44.99 per cent in 1938 and 40.55 per cent in 1939.[54]

The West Riding Police, encouraged by the Home Office, also established a Detective Training Centre in Wakefield in 1936, to replicate that set up at Hendon by the Metropolitan Force.[55] The West Riding Police had previously established a reputation for detective work and its fingerprint department had the record cards of more than 100,000 habitual criminals in its card index and it was said that 'Almost everything done at Scotland Yard is done in Wakefield and in many cases done more efficiently', that it had a daily *West Riding Police Report*, and that its CID Chief was the brilliant Chief Inspector Blacker whose record on murder cases was 'second to none'.[56] And it was stressed that 'In real life most criminals are caught in a more prosaic way by stolid policemen who sit in an office in front of a card-index system and identify offenders by rule of thumb methods.' The 500-strong Nottingham force, led by the talented but controversial Captain Athelstone Popkess, was far more advanced and a report in the *Daily Express*, on the 'Two way radio scheme' claimed, perhaps exaggeratedly, that 'yet in almost every respect... in rapid means of communication, in economy of man power, and in the use of scientific aids in crime investigation – the force is ahead of Scotland Yard'.[57]

Chief Constable John Maxwell, whose claim to fame was creating an effective traffic police in Manchester, was also particularly innovative when it came to crime detection. His force had upwards of more than 80 detectives and in 1934 the *Daily Dispatch* reported, under the title 'Chance for young detective', that since the appointment of Superintendent Valentine as Head of Manchester CID: 'Detectives... emerge after four or five years on the beat but Maxwell is looking at appropriate people after only one year.'[58] In 1933 Maxwell was appointed, by the Home Office, to the Departmental Committee in Detective Work. As part of this responsibility he had travelled to the United States and Canada in April 1936, returning in June, on a fact-finding mission about training, records, communications and scientific work.[59] Maxwell was particularly impressed with the fact that in one city he visited there were thousands of ordinary citizens who were prepared to give their finger prints in a Finger Printing Week.

Maxwell went further and, in July 1937, when the new Police Headquarters were opened in Manchester, created a Crime Information Room to be a 'nerve centre' for the 'reception of information and a speedy control through the Radio Station vehicle equipped with wireless apparatus operating in the City of Manchester'.[60] The new Police Headquarters also housed a Finger Print Department which had over 10,000 impressions filed away, the Police Training Schools 'with facilities for criminal investigation', and a Forensic Laboratory, the *Annual Report* stating that

> The establishment of the Forensic Laboratory also marked an important advance in the scientific aspect of crime investigation. It is becoming more and more evident that this department is an essential unit, and the Laboratory has already received a number of exhibits for examination which necessitated the preparation of expert evidence on the findings to be given to the Court.[61]

Equipped with modern scientific facilities the Manchester Police expanded their work almost exponentially. By the end of 1938 the Criminal Record Office had over 150,000 complete records of conviction and the Crime File number had risen to 238,307 and it was claimed that 'In a large number of cases the records in the Department led to the identification of offenders who would not have been suspected but for the information available in the Department.'[62] The officers in the Finger Print Department 'had also received a special course of instruction at the Finger Print Board of the Metropolitan Police' and 'had classified 7460 finger prints in the year'.[63] The Photographic Department took 1695 photos in 1938 and had prepared 15,158 prints and the Laboratory was working especially well: 'Since the establishment of the Laboratory at these Headquarters the work has been carried out by the Police Surgeon, and from that time in only one or two cases has it been necessary to submit articles for examination at a Laboratory other than the Police Laboratory' resulting in a considerable saving in time.[64] Between July 1937 and 31 December 1938, 963 examinations were made in the Laboratory and the Police Surgeon had attended Court to give evidence on many occasions.

The *Report of the Departmental Report on Detective Work and Procedure* did, in 1938, point to the growing number of detectives in England and Wales, although it argues that this was based upon evidence presented to it since 1933 and it is nebulous about which point in the mid-1930s its figures refer to. Measured against the statistics for 1928, mentioned earlier, there was clear improvement in the 1930s although detectives continued to form only a small part of the total police force. The *Report* reported that there were now 1198 involved in the CID work at Scotland Yard, out of an authorised establishment of 20,000 officers. In Liverpool, there were 110 detectives (compared with an authorised establishment of 1725), in Birmingham 114 (1737), Manchester 82 (1409), Lancashire 135 (2150) and in the West Riding of Yorkshire 58 (1536).[65] On these, and other figures, it indicated that only about 5 per cent of the Metropolitan, Bristol and Cardiff Forces were detectives, 5.7 per cent were so in Manchester, 5.7 per cent in Birmingham and 6.5 per cent in Leeds and Hull, whilst the percentage was as high as 7 per cent in Liverpool, Sheffield, Bradford and Newcastle-upon-Tyne.[66] It concluded that 'At the present we are satisfied that in a good many forces the situation as regards the detective strength leaves a good deal to be desired.'[67] There were probably around 3000 detectives employed in England and Wales, out of a police establishment of 60,000 plus in the mid- and late 1930s, which meant that the detective force was just about, or just under, 5 per cent of the authorised police force for England and Wales. This represented a substantial growth since the late 1920s but came with the *Report*'s warning that all forces needed to review their position.[68]

Although financial constraints had often held back the growth of detective work throughout the inter-war years the green light to go for reform was set up in 1939 with the formation of the Common Police Service Fund, established by the Home Office in 1939 to finance crime clearing houses, laboratories and wireless depots. Half of the money was provided by the government and the other half by the forces using the facility.[69]

The development of detective work in certain progressive forces in the 1930s clearly led to a mushrooming of forensic and scientific work in police investigation. Like detective work, scientific investigation had lagged until the 1930s. The Metropolitan Police Laboratory was opened in 1875, and rebuilt and reorganised in the 1930s, and a similar one was developed at Nottingham in 1902. Chief constables in Sheffield, Cardiff, Hull and Liverpool also worked closely with local biologists and pathologists. Yet it was not until 1938 that other police laboratories were opened in Birmingham and Cardiff, and at least five others were established between 1939 and 1941. As a result most police forensic work was conducted by private laboratories up to the Second World War, except where there were police laboratories such as at Manchester, Birmingham, Cardiff, Nottingham and other centres. Nevertheless, the early twentieth century saw the rapid rise of scientific investigation.

Prior to the 1930s there were the occasional lectures on science and crime. In 1921 *The Police Review and Parade Gossip* reported upon the Royal Society of Arts lecture on criminal investigation by Charles Ainsworth Mitchell which stressed that 'secret crime' in the nineteenth century often went undetected until the onset of fingerprinting and modern scientific investigation.[70] However, the real paucity of forensic work was revealed in February 1923 when J. J. Buist, Divisional Surgeon to the Cardiff Police, addressed a medical audience about the inadequate development of forensic science. His address, later published as a pamphlet entitled 'A Plea for the Improvement in the Teaching and in Encouragement in the Study of Legal Medicine', suggested that teaching in legal medicine was defective, that there was little relevant literature on the subject, that medical experts generally made poor expert witnesses and that there was no professorial expertise on the subject in England and Wales. Buist felt that the Home Office had the powers to take action and should 'appoint experts of medical officials to devote their whole time to medico-legal work in their areas. Let these gentlemen be called into all cases except trifling ones.'[71] Little was done but by 1926 the Home Office was sending out Forensic Science Circulars such as *Scientific Acts to Criminal Investigation* (HO, 1926) to police forces. However, the matter was taken further when, in May 1930, Captain E. N. Bennet, MP, sent a letter to the Home Office informing it of the work of Mr Buist, now a lecturer, and attaching a copy of his 1923 address.[72] J. R. Clynes, Home Secretary in the second Labour government of 1929 and 1931, was thus informed of Buist's work.

It was at this time that the CCA, representing all the urban and county borough forces in England and Wales, began to take an interest in scientific investigation. In 1929 it reported upon the work of Sir Bernard Spilsbury whose 'fame as a pathologist and criminologist is world-wide', and added that 'The extraordinary skilful manner in which he proves his theories out of the most trivial and unimportant data is almost uncanny.'[73] Major Vitty, of the Scotland Yard Laboratory, also added that these scientific developments were 'proving invaluable to the Police in their own perpetual fight with the modern scientific criminal'.[74] In 1930 A. L. Dixon, of the Home Office, talked to the CCA on the Home Office commitment to a 'Police Training College', including its commitment to forensic science, and W. R. Harrison spoke on 'Science in the Police Service'.[75] Dixon asked:

> Are all our detectives, are any of us, as fully alive to the application of science as we should be? Some of you no doubt would have liked

to attend the lectures which are being given at Scotland Yard at this very time. I think that you will find from some of your colleagues that what they have heard has opened up rather a new vista in this direction. I am not in fear of much contradiction when I suggest that we have not yet realised anything like the full advantages which science can afford in the direction of crime.[76]

Harrison followed this up with a lecture outlining the history of forensic work since the eighteenth century in which he finally recommended copying the example of Cardiff Police who provided a training centre for the police at Merthyr, Hereford City and Herefordshire as well as their own force.[77]

In 1933 J. E. W. MacFall (Professor of Forensic Medicine at the University of Liverpool and examiner in Forensic Medicine at the universities of Edinburgh, Birmingham, Glasgow, Manchester, Aberdeen and Sheffield) lectured on 'The Medical Side of Criminal Investigation', and arraigned the assembled chief constables with the suggestion that it was their own fault if they, as representatives of local forces, had to bring in outside experts 'from afar, and generally after some lapse of time, to aid in your investigations' and to no effect since 'Delay in investigation is fatal to good results.'[78] His particular complaint was that samples for scientific investigation, for say sperm and blood, were sent to the public analyst, who had little knowledge of how to give evidence on the questions raised, rather than to the histologist, the biochemist or the doctor.[79]

Little came of this concern until a burst of activity and publicity occurred in 1933 and 1934. The Home Office set up a Departmental Committee on Detective Work and Procedure in May 1933, as previously mentioned, and this, in turn, set up a sub-committee with the idea of 'Formulating a national scheme to bring every force up to the highest level of efficiency; ensuring that modern scientific methods shall be available in every part of the country, and that no police force shall lack the existence of the highest technical experts.' In December 1933 Mr A. Marcan sent a letter to Lord Trenchard, Metropolitan Commissioner of Police at Scotland Yard, informing him of his forensic work in Siam, where he had worked at a government laboratory in Bangkok. His main concern was to encourage moves to 'centralise or otherwise develop the scientific side of crime detection'.[80] Marcan attached some of his own published work on 'Scientific Methods in the Detection of Crime', from the *Siam Police Journal*, December 1931. Catching the moment, Trenchard replied immediately intimating that 'the development scientific work in connection with crime detection is at present under consideration.'[81]

Within a year a momentous event occurred. On 26 October 1934 Trenchard sent what proved to be a seminal letter to the Secretary of State on Home Affairs on the subject of scientific laboratories for both the Metropolis and the nation. He argued that 'science might help them in connection with making an arrest or producing evidence which might materially assist to convict a guilty criminal.'[82] Six months previously, on 9 March 1934, the Secretary of State had agreed that the Police College at Hendon should establish laboratories and engage someone of scientific skills to take charge. Noting, in his letter, that only the universities of Edinburgh and Glasgow employed professors in Medical Jurisprudence, he asked that Dr James Davidson of the Pathological Department of the University of Edinburgh and Senior Pathologist at the Royal Infirmary, Scotland, should be appointed on £1000 per year, and that a Chair of Forensic Medicine should be set up at the University of London, with new laboratories, in association with the Post-Graduate College at Hampstead. The new Chair (possibly Davidson) would spend about three-quarters of his time in scientific work and effectively oversee both the envisaged new laboratories and those at Hendon to be run by Davidson. More generally, Trenchard advised the Home Office to set up an Advisory Committee for the whole country to overlook scientific detective work.

In 1934, after a serious public debate, the Home Office attempted, as already indicated, to develop a national force for detection. The debate on this was greatly encouraged by the journalist Leslie Randall who wrote a series of articles on detective work for the *Daily Express* in 1934. One was on detective work and fingerprinting, in the West Riding Constabulary, as already mentioned, and another on the work at Scotland Yard, and yet another about the Home Office Committee on Detective Work, appointed in 1933. Randall also wrote about F. W. Crawley, Chief Constable of Newcastle-on-Tyne who, it was felt, was 'the best debunker of antiquated police methods I have met. He had for twenty-three years been a detective at Scotland Yard and Chief Constable at Lincoln, Sunderland and Newcastle-on-Tyne. Newcastle has a crime laboratory, with camera microscopes.'[83]

Superintendent W. M. Else, of the Derbyshire Constabulary, who collaborated with Assistant Chief Constable J. M. Garrow, of Derbyshire, to publish on the CID work of the Derbyshire Force was also the subject of another article by Randall. Else and Garrow had published a handbook in 1933 that examined the way in which the Derbyshire laboratories had discovered ways of photographing fingerprints in multi-coloured objects and had developed new forensic techniques with Scotland Yard and the US Police Bureau. The Derbyshire police laboratory was 'the first police laboratory to be formed in the country, and others followed'; this was presumably other than the one at Scotland Yard. It was suggested that the subjects raised by Else and Garrow 'may find a place in the curriculum of the new Metropolitan College' at Hendon.

Else was a fascinating innovator. In 1925 he became a Fellow of the Royal Microscopical Society and in 1931 he became a Fellow of the Faculty of Science. He had written a book on scientific methods and the training of detectives, discussing the science of stains, pigments and fabrics. Randall considered him to be a 'profound student of human nature; and a master in the analysis of motives that guide human actions.... As an aid to his work he must understand all the requirements of the chemist, pathologist, toxicologist, biologist, and physicist.'[84]

Randall's publicity was pushing at an open door in promoting a policy of scientific investigation. By the mid 1930s C. T. Symons, of the Home Office, was meeting with many of those interested in scientific and forensic work. He met, with some success, the Somerset police authorities at Taunton as indicated at the beginning of this chapter. He had also met with Mr R. L. Collett, Assistant Secretary of the Institute of Chemistry, who expressed support for the idea of chemists in police laboratories but registered the Institute's concern about the impartiality of evidence: 'scientific work should definitely be separated from police control so far as results were concerned', something which Symons assured him was part of Home Office policy in the appointment of chemists in police laboratories.[85]

In the mid-1930s Professor Tryhorn's courses, already mentioned, began to draw considerable attention. The course he offered between 1 and 6 July 1935 was attended by 19 officers; 14 from the Cheshire Force, 2 from Birmingham, 1 from Gloucestershire, 1 from Somerset and 1 from Durham.[86] It was widely reported upon both by Tryhorn and those who attended. The five days of lectures and practical work included discussion about the value of the microscope, methods of removing fingerprints from linoleum, blood analysis, the analysis of positions, the matching of microscopical photographs for jemmy marks and microscopic studies of clothing for stains and a whole range of other forensic activities.[87]

Tryhorn also organised another similar five-day course at the University College, Hull between 23 and 28 September 1935. This seems to have emerged from the Home Office Committee on Detective Work which suggested a course for 14–16 police officers and that it would be 'contacting the Chief Constables of Chesterfield, Devon and Wiltshire, who are not on the Committee, as we think it is possible that they may want to send people'.[88] The Chief Constables of Shrewsbury, Manchester, Exeter and Chesterfield also declared their interest in the course. The last of these, at the last meeting of his Police Authority, had made an application to send detective officers to scientific courses being held at Nottingham and Hull. Indeed, he went to see the Nottingham scientific facilities himself and wrote to A. L. Dixon, at the Home Office, that

> I was amazed at the modern apparatus, etc., and the staff that Captain Popkess had at his headquarters. I decided that at the earliest opportunity the whole of my detective staff and the photography staff would spend a few days increasing the knowledge in respect of the modern methods of crime detection.
>
> I have also made standing arrangements with Popkess for experts in all branches when required, which I found is a simple matter having regard to the fact that he has them either upon his staff, or honorary gentlemen, who are at all time on call.
>
> I had a long talk with him respecting the cinematograph being adapted for Police work. He is very keen about it and is looking forward to making some definite strides in the near future.
>
> I am enclosing for your information the syllabus for the Nottingham Course, which I think that you will find rather interesting.[89]

In the end 22 police officers attended the September forensic week at Hull; three from the Gloucester Police, two each from the Liverpool, Manchester, Bristol and East Riding Forces, and one each from the Brighton, Bradford, West Riding, Cardiff, Oxford, Shropshire, Exeter, Devon, Chesterfield, Wiltshire and Durham Forces.[90] The participants included Inspector Lewis from Cardiff and Inspector Frederick Carter from Bristol and their programme was much as the previous course in July 1935. On the Monday, for instance, there was a lecture by Professor Tryhorn between 9.30 am and 11.00 am on scientific aids and methods of packing followed by a practical session from 11.15 am to 1.15 pm on the packing of various types of exhibits and simple methods of mounting small objects for travel. From 2.00 pm until 4.00 pm there was a lecture on searching and preservation, and simplistic methods of searching clothing and so on, the preservation of exhibits and the types of material to look out for during searches. From 4.00 pm to 6.00 pm there was a practical session on the use of the searching board, and recording of material during search and the examination of footwear.

Like the July week organised by Tryhorn the week's session was probably routinely reported upon by the participants to their chief constables. One such report, by Inspector Frederick Carter of the Bristol CID to his Chief Constable, offers an astute analysis of the value of scientific study in detective work.[91] Accepting Tryhorn's advice Carter stressed that all police officers had to know the value of scientific laboratories for

> these facilities can function satisfactorily only if the police officers attending scenes of crime are sufficiently trained to observe, and to recognise, what 'traces' are likely to afford useful results from scientific analysis. It is therefore expected that the police officers should have some detailed knowledge of the extent to which the scientists as distinct from the pathologist, can render his assistance in his work.[92]

This, it was claimed, necessitated that groups of police officers should be trained in the art of 'investigating systemically and thoroughly at scenes of crime' and reiterated that a system of police laboratories should be set up throughout the country.

The views of Tryhorn were clearly presented but Carter, interestingly, also added to the report his own separate views based upon his own experience. He had begun detective work 12 years before in Bristol and several localities, and saw the new methods of crime investigation fitting into an existing system. He was convinced that 'The methods of crime investigation employed by the general run of detective officers are not haphazard, illogical and unscientific efforts that one is sometimes asked to believe.'[93] He admitted, however, that micro-chemical analysis and micro-photographic methods 'are unknown to the great majority of police forces' but felt that the Home Office initiative was useful but that

> It is essential that a true sense of proportion should be maintained. Ordinary common-sense methods that have served so long and do well must obviously be retained and relied upon, but the knowledge of how, when, and to what extent the pathologist and the chemists can rest and supplement the work of the detective should form part of the mental equipment of every officer engaged in crime protection and detection work.[94]

The universal involvement of all police officers in an understanding of forensic and scientific technique for the detection of crime was clearly someway off by the end of the 1930s. Equally distant was the desire to set up large laboratories throughout the country, as Tryhorn had suggested. Part of the problem was that even as they were being opened in the mid- and late 1930s many police forces were reluctant to use them exclusively and preferred to use private laboratories or private individuals on the occasions they sometimes needed forensic and scientific work to be done. Indeed, the distribution of police and private laboratory usage was the subject of a preliminary Home Office survey for the years 1938 and 1939. A letter by James Webster, MA, BSc, MBChem, FRSC, Director of the West Midland Forensic Laboratory, Birmingham, dated 10 May 1940, indicated at length the continuing problems in getting police forces to use the police laboratories and was accompanied by extensive tables on the forensic work ordered by every police force in England and Wales.[95]

The total number of cases in England and Wales that involved forensic science and detection was 1168 in 1938 and had gone up to 1406 in 1939, as indicated in Table 4.1. These figures indicate the rapid growth in the number of cases dealt with through forensic science, suggesting a falling off at the beginning of the Second World War, and indicates that the majority were of a biological, chemical or physical nature. In other words, a significant proportion, more than a quarter of the forensic cases, were connected with potential sexual crimes. Indeed, 146 forensic cases were associated with rape and carnal knowledge, 145 indecent assaults, and 52 with sodomy and gross indecency, and the first two categories were the two largest numbers amongst the numerous categories of crime being investigated.[96]

In 1940, Webster dug more deeply into these figures and discovered that they reflected the ongoing problem that whilst the police were increasing their use of forensic evidence it is clear that they were still using private laboratories rather than the new police laboratories that were much more geared to specific requirements of policing. He wrote extensively on the matter in a letter to the Home Office, stating that

> Small counties such as Anglesey, Denbigh and the Isle of Ely may not have had cases where scientific aids are necessary, but when one finds a county such as Oxford with a grand total of 2 cases, Hereford with 1 case, Bedfordshire with 2 cases, the North Riding with 1 case, and industrial towns such as Barnsley with nil return, Bradford with 1, and Leeds with a total of 3 cases for the year, one feels that there is either a lack of enthusiasm or ignorance in some quarters.

Table 4.1 Returns on cases involving forensic science and detective work for 1939

	Quarter					Types of forensic work					
	1st Quarter	2nd Quarter	3rd Quarter	4th Quarter	Total	P.	B.	C.	Ph.	H.	Pho.
Counties	158	163	156	164	641	46	324	176	119	38	13
Cities and boroughs	211	215	183	154	763	46	312	281	103	60	23
City of London	1	1			2	1		1			
Total	370	379	339	318	1406	93	636	458	222	98	36

Note: P. – Pathological; B. – Biological; C. – Chemical; Ph. – Physical; H. – Handwriting; Pho. – Photographical.

Outside experts

There is a lack of uniformity of policing in many of the forces in that they mix up outside experts and the Laboratories at will....

Berkshire employed Hendon, Roche Lynch and Dr. Nellie Eales in the first quarter and all the cases could have been dealt with by Hendon. In the first quarter returns for Derbyshire it is seen that they continue to use Detective Officer Palmer for the preparation of biological specimens and elementary chemistry and photography. The more advanced chemistry is done by a man called Sutton, who is an analyst, but all cases in the first quarter, with the possible exception of an x-ray...should have been dealt with by Nottingham or Hendon. Hove employed an analytical chemist called Hudson and apparently his work could have been dealt with by Hendon. Hull, by the returns, show a preference for the local police analyst and his assistant, but in request to pregnancy tests they employ Evans Lesche and Webbs of Liverpool. It is noted that like all public analysts, nothing is refused by Tankard, and they do hair, blood, wood, and biological examinations in addition to chemistry. Portsmouth also employ a local analyst called Pope for biological work, and in Portsmouth in virtually the Home Counties these should have gone to Hendon. Middlesbrough employs a Dr. Inkster but, according to the returns given to me, he has made a most curious report in one case. From a dried swab he removed active sperms. This is quite inconceivable to me. Dorset County alternate in the main between Parker of Bristol and Hendon, but they also employ an analyst called Charles. Such duplication seems unnecessary.[97]

The letter went on, in far more detail, to outline the lack of uniform policy adopted by the police forces in England and Wales in their development of scientific and forensic investigation. Nevertheless, such analysis was in its infancy and much progress had been made since the 1920s.

Conclusion

It is clear that at the beginning of the inter-war years few English and Welsh police forces had a large or effective detective force. Many of the smaller forces did not have such a service and even some of the larger ones did not employ modern recording and scientific techniques. Detective work, despite its long history in detective literature, barely existed outside Scotland Yard and a few of the larger police forces such as Liverpool, Manchester, Derbyshire and Nottingham. Forensic science, beyond the realms of fingerprinting and poisons, was largely unused. Detection was blatantly ignored by most police forces in the 1920s, although there was undoubtedly an accumulation of skill and experience by some long-serving detective services. Police forces were invariably not in need of the fictional Poirots and the gentleman detectives who littered the detective novels of the inter-war years and who provided intellectual guidance to the blindingly ignorant plain-clothed police detectives. Nonetheless, it is clear that it was not until 1933, with the formation of the Home Office Committee, that both detective work and forensic science began to develop, and at a rapid pace even though private laboratories, with the delay involved in using them, was still a major problem up to and into the Second World War when the majority of police forces were still using inappropriate private laboratories. Such work and innovation, stimulated by the 1933 Committee and the ubiquitous A. L. Dixon, was but the tip of the iceberg. Yet, combined with changes in the national co-ordination of the police for public order, and traffic policing (Part 2), it helped to fundamentally change the character of policing in England and Wales and offered a new vista for policing during the inter-war years.

Part 2

The Prophecy of Nahum: Motor Vehicles, the Police and the Public in Inter-war Britain

One of the major formative influences of the twentieth century, in both social and economic terms, was the development of the internal combustion engine.[1] As Britain emerged from the Great War motorised transport was still something of a rarity in most parts of the country, though changes in London provided a glimpse of the coming motor age. In 1919 there were about 330,000 vehicles – comprising private cars, motorcycles, buses, coaches, taxis and goods vehicles – but a decade later there were over two million motor vehicles and by 1938 the figure had topped three million.

The tenfold increase in motor vehicles in use obscures the dramatic rise in private car ownership and, to a lesser extent, of goods vehicles. Change, unsurprisingly, was not uniform across the country. Some of the most dramatic changes were to be seen in and around London and the other great towns and cities but, slowly but surely, all but the most remote parts of Britain saw – some would say were invaded by – the car

Table P2.1 Motor vehicles in use in Britain, 1919–38 (000s)

	1919	1929	1938
Private cars	110	981	1944
Motorcycles	115	731	462
Buses & coaches	44	50	53
Taxis		48	35
Goods vehicles	62	330	495
Others (excl. trams)	0	42	96
Total (excl. trams)	331	2182	3085

Source: B. R. Mitchell and P. Deane (1962), *Abstract of British Historical Statistics* (Cambridge: Cambridge University Press), p. 230.

or the lorry as the nature of British transportation was fundamentally transformed.

There was something exciting about the freedom (and speed) of movement brought by the car in particular. The emergence of a mass market (including both new and second-hand purchases) opened new horizons for more and more individuals and families. In addition, the growth of that interlinked cluster of motor trades had a highly significant part to play in the economic development of Britain between the wars. Furthermore, there was a powerful, often high profile and influential motor lobby that ensured a positive gloss was put upon the growth of motorised transport in its various forms. But the advent of the motor age was far from unproblematic. Urban streets in particular became increasingly congested; pollution (in a variety of forms) affected town and country and the dramatic increase in traffic accidents led to emotive descriptions of a holocaust on the roads. Ensuring the smooth and efficient running of the king's highway and safeguarding the safety of road users and pedestrians alike were major problems and, after some debate, the responsibility for dealing with them fell heavily on the shoulders of the police as politicians struggled to devise legislation and regulation that was appropriate for a society rapidly leaving behind the horse-drawn age. To compound matters the seemingly narrow issue of the regulation of traffic raised wider questions of individual freedom and, much to the concern of the police, brought ordinary, working-class constables into contact (and conflict) with members of the middle classes, who previously had held a positive, if somewhat patronising, perception of the British bobby. The following chapters look at the way in which the police set about this task of motor management and the extent of success that they achieved.

5
'A Mere Traffic Signalling Device'? The Debate on Policing and Traffic Control

Introduction

In August 1927 a *Punch* cartoon famously asked 'what *did* policemen do when there weren't any motors?' The answer was simple: they arrested drunks and vagrants but such was the growth of motor traffic after the Great War that road traffic control, in its broadest sense, became a central and high-profile aspect of policing. As the British Association for the Advancement of Society noted in 1935

> The rapid development of mechanical road transport has been one of the outstanding events of the post-war period, and in a single generation it has reached a marked degree on the whole economic and social life of the country.
>
> But the very rate of change meant that H. G. Wells told his radio audience in November 1932, the country was unprepared for the car and its impact.[2]

The police agreed. Sir Philip Game, the Metropolitan Police Commissioner, was also moved to write of the enormity of the changes that had taken place in the following words in the introduction to his annual report for 1936.

> Since the time of Sir Robert Peel's reforms, no single change has had more effect on the work of the police and their relations with the public than the introduction of the motor car and the consequent revolution in methods of transport.[3]

The advent of motor-propelled vehicles, especially the car, undoubtedly had a profound effect on society in general and policing in particular.

This was more so the case for the police, faced, as they were, by considerable and contradictory pressures. Particularly following the Desborough settlement, there was a heightened expectation of the police; a desire for a more professional force which in turn generated debate about the core functions of the police and the efficiency with which they were pursued. However, at the same time, there was a keen desire by governments of all persuasions to exercise rigorous economy in times of national economic crisis. In addition to such existentialist considerations, the police were faced with the practical problem of maintaining movement and safety on the rapidly changing king's highway. Attention was often focused upon London but the problems of the capital – increasing congestion, falling transit speeds but rising accident rates – were to be found in the cities and large towns of Britain. Nor were smaller towns and rural districts exempt: indeed they had their own particular problems. Two major sets of questions need to be considered. The first, and more general, relates to the role of the police and what constituted 'proper police work'. The second, and more specific, relates to the practical responses of the police to the very real problems posed by the rapid growth of motor traffic. It will be argued that, despite concerns about the resource demands made by road traffic work, the police saw such activities as an important aspect of their work, building on their role as 'guardians of the highway' that had characterised nineteenth-century policing. In so doing they played an important role, often experimental and incremental, in developing both the physical environment and the codes of conduct required to create safety and efficiency in an increasingly motorised society and economy. Further, policing the motorist raised old problems (notably, how to ensure policing by albeit begrudging consent) in new forms. The police found themselves coming into contact and conflict with sections of society who previously had seen the police as their servants, not their masters, and who resented the restrictions upon freedom (as it was seen) that the police and the law brought. The solution – neither new nor wholly successful – was to implement the law with discretion. By the end of the 1930s much had been done to win the support of the motoring public but the victory was at best partial and many of the problems of motorist animosity to the police noted in the post-war years had their roots in the unresolved difficulties of the inter-war years.

'Proper police work': crime fighting or traffic control?

Despite the common sense view that policing is about crime fighting, there has never been agreement as to the precise role of the police and the balance of their responsibilities, as a brief consideration of nineteenth-century policing reveals.[4] From its inception, the Metropolitan Police, commonly but erroneously seen as the first 'new police' force, had its principal stated object *'the Prevention of Crime'*. The *General Regulations*, issued to all constables in the force, made clear that '[t]o this great end every effort of the Police is to be directed'. The role of the 'new police' was defined in terms of '[t]he security of person and property [and] the preservation of the public tranquillity'.[5] Similar approaches were adopted by other forces as they came into being in the second quarter of the nineteenth century. The rhetoric of the thin blue line protecting law-abiding society against criminals was useful in gaining support and masking the wider regulatory role of the new police but the drive to bring 'order and decorum' to the streets necessarily led to a broadening of the police role beyond its crime-fighting function. Irrespective of such problematic areas as working-class leisure activities, the police were quickly involved in the often contentious issue of the regulation of traffic. General Orders in the 1830s and 1840s drew attention to the importance of not allowing 'foot and carriage ways to be obstructed' and to 'inforce the law relative to persons riding or driving in their vehicles without reins'.[6] The Great Exhibition of 1851 highlighted the twin problems of traffic congestion and road safety that were only to worsen during Victoria's reign. A Select Committee of 1855 bemoaned the fact that 'traffic is constantly adding to the amount of inconvenience and loss [because] the requirements of the existing traffic of the Metropolis far exceed the present facilities provided for it.'[7] In addition to the continual growth of the capital, the advent of the bicycle in the 1880s, horseless carriages in the 1890s and the motor car, whose speed limit was raised to 20 mph by the 1903 Motor Car Act, added not simply to the volume of traffic on London's streets but also to the complexity of the problem of resolving the different and often conflicting needs of road users. The relative homogeneity of road users that had characterised the early years of Victoria's reign had been replaced by a heterogeneous mix of users with markedly different capabilities and needs. This was amply demonstrated by the witnesses who gave evidence to the 1903 Royal Commission enquiring into the problems of London's traffic.[8] Nor were such problems unique. Birmingham Council, for example, under its Corporation (Consolidation) Act of 1883, passed a range of bye-laws '[f]or regulating all traffic within the borough and preventing and removing obstructions in the street...the taking up and setting down of passengers, and the loading and unloading of goods...[and] the use in streets of bicycles, tricycles, velocipedes and other similar mechanical contrivances'.[9] Similarly, many chief constables, particularly of the larger towns and cities, increasingly felt the need to ensure that members of the force were aware of the range of their responsibilities. Robert Peacock, the Chief Constable of Manchester, delivered a series of eight lectures in December 1899 on important aspects of police duty to over 250 men of the force as part of his campaign to improve the educational standards of the police. The last of these lectures was devoted to the question of 'the regulation and control of the traffic, both vehicular and passenger – more especially the former' which he saw as '[o]ne of the most important duties' of the police.[10] Such was 'the enormous amount of traffic passing through the city' that 'special traffic constables' had been established for city-centre traffic work to ensure 'the safety and the convenience of all' road users.[11]

This overview is important as it emphasises continuity in terms of traffic problems and police responsibilities for them. This is not to deny the novel elements of inter-war traffic problems, nor the difficulties they created for the police, but rather to stress that when the police came to face these problems they had a long record of involvement in which practices and procedures had been developed.[12] There was a presumption that this was a legitimate and important part of police work. The police were, in the words of *The Times* in 1926 'our real traffic controllers'.[13] However, it was a presumption that did not go unquestioned.

The practical difficulties facing the police in the immediate post-war years were considerable. The demands of war had created serious manpower problems but these were exacerbated by new demands, particularly but not exclusively relating to traffic regulation. In the commentary to the *Judicial Statistics* for 1923 it was noted that police resources

> have been seriously weakened by the creation or expansion of other duties e.g. the control and regulation of street traffic, duties in relation to cattle disease etc. while at the same time the absolute necessity for administrative economy keeps the police forces at about five per cent under their established strength.[14]

Others argued more forcefully for an expansion of police numbers but, particularly after the improvements in pay brought about by the implementation of Desborough, it was not obvious that pre-war policing levels would be restored. Leonard Dunning, the Inspector of Police, was well aware that increased costs might lead to a reduction in numbers which could 'only be made practicable by some decrease in the demand made upon the police, possibly by the private citizen taking a larger share in his own protection'.[15] However, as Dunning noted in a later report, demand from the public was increasing rather than decreasing. In 1922 he commented that

> the duties of the police in the provinces have been largely extended in answer to the demands of the ratepayer, who is more and more ready to call for a policeman to protect him from dangers other than those of crime.[16]

Five years later he elaborated upon the problem in the following terms, which echoed the praise lavished on the Edwardian bobby by *The Times*.

> [O]ne of the reasons for the resources of the police falling short of the demands made upon them is to be found in the changing ideas of what is and what is not police duty... the man on the beat now performs acts of public service not contemplated even a few years ago – services which have made him the handy man of civil life.[17]

Dunning undoubtedly had a clear purpose: namely, to maintain or, if at all possible, expand the police establishment as a whole. The whole burden of his argument was that the police carried out a myriad of essential duties, none of which could be cut without detriment to the consumer, that is, the general public. Therefore, his argument ran, to meet public demand in its many and varied forms, police establishments should be expanded, or at least maintained at current levels. Although he enjoyed a considerable reputation as an expert on policing, his views did not go unchallenged. He was all too well aware of the arguments, which had been around for some years, that proposed the hiving off of certain 'auxillary' duties to ensure that the police were able to carry out more effectively their core crime-fighting function. This posed a dilemma for Dunning and other advocates of expansion. On the one hand, the desire (indeed the outside demand) to create a more professional force led in the direction of more modern policing, especially scientifically aided detection, and a more effective attack on crime. On the other hand, an emphasis on crime fighting alone exposed how little police time was actually spent on it which, in turn, prompted the argument that hiving off traffic duties to an auxiliary force of traffic wardens would be cheaper in itself, would allow for a greater emphasis on the 'proper' work of crime fighting and might also lead to savings on the police budget without diminishing the protection of person and property expected by the public.

It is no coincidence that Dunning spoke at length about this matter. His annual reports provided him with an opportunity to develop his views in a manner which appeared impartial but in reality was part of an ongoing debate about police establishments that was given added urgency by the straightened finances of governments in the 1920s. The implementation of Desborough's recommendations on police pay – seen as essential by the government – had a dramatic financial impact, raising annual costs some threefold from about £7,000,000 in 1914 to £20,000,000 in 1920.[18] Not surprisingly, in 1920 H. B. Simpson, an Assistant Secretary at the Home Office, told the committee on the police service that '[t]he police are always rather a luxury.'[19] More worrying was the decision in February 1925 by the Chancellor of the Exchequer, Winston Churchill, to approve consideration of a proposal 'to recruit Road Wardens for traffic duties'. Churchill was shocked that 'a large number of men (probably 2500–3000) had been detached from their proper duties' and devoted to traffic control and felt that because 'traffic duty requires less skilled personnel and involves less strain than ordinary Police work... it is unjustifiable to go on paying for this work such high rates of pay and pension as the Police enjoy.'[20] His optimism was not shared by the Home Secretary who thought that a road warden scheme 'would be extremely difficult and might not lead to economy in the long run'.[21] Churchill was unshaken in his view and in late 1927 he expressed no reservation when arguing that 'a special class of traffic controllers, described as Road Wardens... [would be a] satisfactory and economical method of dealing with the problem.'[22] The proposal met with considerable opposition and not just from chief constables, the latter drawing on their experience of a wide range of experiments to solve the problem. This debate on road wardens in the mid-1920s deserves careful analysis, not least because it has been argued that the police seized the opportunity presented by traffic control to 'find some urgent new work... to justify their new expensive semi-professional status'.[23] The picture that emerges is more complex than Howard Taylor suggests with police opinion more divided than his almost conspiratorial argument would suggest.[24] Indeed, his emphasis on self-serving obscures the extent to which leading police figures sympathised with the suggestion for an alternative body to control traffic. In his report for 1926 Dunning conceded that 'in country districts, the necessity for police control is exaggerated'. Rather the example in 'a little country town' of 'a man in plain clothes regulating the traffic at a blind corner, using the standard signals and obeyed by everybody' was proof to him that 'police powers are not essential.'[25] His fellow Inspector, Parry, conceded that 'many men are employed on [traffic] duty who might be much better employed in carrying out other police duties.' Without denying the importance of traffic work it was something, he conceded, that 'in the opinion of many people could be done quite as well and much more economically by persons other than the police'.[26] And there were chief constables who expressed similar views. Captain Mowbray Sant of Surrey, no lover of the motor car, felt 'the employment of regular police to the present extent was extravagant and absorbed a wholly unjustifiable amount of police time'. Even more forceful was the Chief Constable of Hertfordshire, Major A. L. Law, who 'did not regard traffic direction as a proper police function', though few went as far as Lieutenant Colonel H. S. Turnbull, Chief Constable of the City of London Force, who deprecated the 'tendency to employ police to a greater extent than was really necessary' in county areas and argued that 'motor drivers ought to be left to look after themselves sometimes.'[27]

Notwithstanding the broader principles, the manpower difficulties facing chief constables and the dramatic increase in road traffic created immediate practical problems that had led to a variety of small-scale experiments across the country from the early 1920s onwards. An obvious approach was to re-employ police pensioners and this was done in counties such as Denbigh, Kent and the East Riding of Yorkshire and towns as varied as Macclesfield, Penzance, Scarborough and Southend. As early as 1922 the Home Office had been requested to approve a scheme for employing men (not retired constables) for traffic duty in Exeter and Torquay. The matter was delayed because of the Geddes Committee but elsewhere innovations were made. In Cardiganshire disabled ex-servicemen (four initially, later six) were employed from Whitsun to September 'to be solely ... guides at certain busy and dangerous points in exactly the same way as the guides maintained by the AA'.[28] The Standing Joint Committee (SJC) for East Suffolk similarly sought to employ three ex-servicemen but their initial suggestion of employing them as special constables was rejected as falling outside the 1923 Special Constables Order. Instead approval was given for their employment as Police First Reserve. The scheme ran from 1 April to 30 September and the men worked from 9 am to 1 pm and 2 pm to 6 pm on six days a week (not Sunday) and were given strict instructions to confine their activities to traffic control. Ex-servicemen were also employed in small numbers in Cambridgeshire from 1926.

A further alternative explored was co-operation with motoring organisations. In Lincolnshire and Somerset, and also in Grantham, the Home Office approved schemes whereby the Royal Automobile Club (RAC) provided two men free on condition that the local police authority paid for a further three men at £150 per annum. The Chief Constable of Bedfordshire, however, rejected a similar scheme for Leighton Buzzard, even though it had been approved by his SJC. He was adamant that 'an RAC man would not be of the slightest use at the particular spot where it was absolutely essential that the man on duty must have the powers of a constable.'[29] There was also a negative response to the RAC in Hampshire, where the local press stressed the particular authority of the police.[30] The agreement in Essex was with the Automobile Association (AA) whose patrols helped at 21 points in the county, though, as the Chief Constable explained, 'it would be unreasonable for them [AA patrolmen] to be called upon to enforce the Regulations relating to speed only unaccompanied by circumstances which go to make a case of dangerous driving.' Generously, he also had no objection to 'a patrol warning a motorist that a [speed] control is in operation'.[31]

The success of such experiments was limited. Cardiganshire was often held up as an example of what could be achieved but there were real limitations to the scheme. It became apparent that the traffic guides were not needed at all times of the day, nor could they help the police with key problems such as the obstruction of roads and, largely because of their limited powers, they tended to be ignored by the motoring public. Co-operation with the AA also proved problematic, principally because of the system of dual control that it insisted upon for its patrolmen working with local police. Indeed, there was a wider concern, well articulated by a correspondent to *The Times* in 1928 who noted that

> the attitude of these associations [that is, the AA and RAC] has so long been one of general hostility to the administration of the law that it seems difficult for them... to seek to assist the police.[32]

This patchwork of responses across the country reflected divisions of opinion among chief constables and police authorities. The Conference of Chief Constables, held at the Home Office on 6 April 1927, revealed the absence of consensus. While certain districts were in favour of employing first reservists or special constables others were not; many were strongly opposed to the employment of AA and RAC personnel; and at least one district was unanimously of the opinion that 'it is not desirable that any person should be employed for the purpose [of regulating and controlling road traffic] and that if the requirements of traffic render further police necessary such Police should be defrayed out of the Road Fund.'[33] As a rather jaundiced Home Office official noted, '[t]hese minutes [of the Chief Constables' conferences held in 1927] reveal a remarkable difference of opinion but do not actually take us much forward'.[34] Opinion shifted rapidly and attitudes of chief constables hardened. At their central conference, held at the Home Office on 2 August 1927, they resolved that 'any scheme for the employment of civilians for police duties connected with the regulation of traffic was undesirable.'[35]

Police opposition to civilian road wardens was not unexpected but the argument had to be made. The case that emerged was founded on a variety of assumptions. The weakest argument was based on (alleged) public expectations. As Dunning argued, 'rightly or wrongly the general public look on traffic regulation as the duty of the police, whether its purpose be to facilitate and expedite the traffic or to make the road safer.'[36] Indeed, he claimed that 'for one complaint [from the public] about theft there are hundreds which demand safety and convenience for the ordinary user of the public road.'[37] Further, but still negative in tone, doubt was cast on the amount of saving that could be made immediately and in the longer term. In particular it was argued that longer-term savings would be impossible because it would be only a matter of time before the specially constituted traffic wardens demanded the same pay and pension rights as the police. However, a more positive argument was developed that emphasised the peculiar skills and position of the police constable. As early as 1922 in his annual report for the Liverpool City Police, the Chief Constable, F. Caldwell, put forward the 'skilled professional' defence that was to become a mainstay of police resistance to the notion of road or traffic wardens.

> It is not enough that the Constable on a control point should by signal govern the movement of vehicles in one direction or another. He must experience rare judgment in the giving of his signals, should have an elementary knowledge of the mechanics of motor car driving, as also of the legal powers conferred on him alone as a constable....

Having detailed the demands of collecting evidence and appearing in court, Caldwell concluded that

> [i]t is because of all these trained requirements, and the status given by the law to a constable, that the substitution for the police of the employees of motor associations, or of men of quasi-police standing, to direct traffic is impracticable in large cities.[38]

It was a line of argument taken up by the inspectorate. In a memo to the Home Office, in response to a request for his views on Churchill's proposals, Atcherley was clear that especially in 'populous districts... in no circumstances should they [traffic points] be entrusted to any other organization than the police'.[39] His reasons were as follows:

> Occurrences of reckless and selfish practices, incompetent management, and unlawful and dangerous conduct are frequently part of the experience [of traffic duty] and it is just in such situations that the untrained or not fully warranted individual would fall short of public requirements.[40]

The Metropolitan Police took a similar stand. When asked on their views of the proposal to entrust traffic duty to specially recruited traffic wardens, the response was blunt. The proposal from the Chancellor of the Exchequer was 'based on premises that are fundamentally unsound'; namely, that traffic duty requires less skilled (and therefore cheaper) personnel and that the work involves less physical risk and mental strain. Despite initial scepticism regarding the police argument, A. L. Dixon, the Assistant Secretary at the Home Office, recognised the range of skills required: a knowledge of the law, especially at a fatal accident when there might be a case of manslaughter to be pursued; the ability to collect evidence and present a case in court; knowledge of first aid in case of accident; and tact and discretion in handling the motoring public. In short, '[t]he officer is not, and never can be reduced to, a mere traffic signalling device.'[41] The Commissioner, Brigadier-General William Horwood, also stressed the psychological element, that is, the public recognition of the full authority of a constable on traffic duty which he felt to be of 'supreme importance' and had been overlooked by the Chancellor of the Exchequer, Winston Churchill.[42] From that it followed, in his view at least, that the use of less well-trained and authoritative figures would lead to chaos on the streets of London. The point was repeated four years later when the new Commissioner, General Julian Byng, wrote to the Home Office warning that it seemed to him that

> if the legal control of traffic is to be vested in various bodies, confusion is likely to result and the authority is likely to be lessened and the safety of the public to be imperilled rather than safeguarded.[43]

The opposition of key police personnel was augmented by that of the County Councils' Association and the Association of Municipal Corporations. The former feared that the employment of men without previous police experience might lead to 'errors of judgment' and, more seriously, 'the improper assumption of a constable's power'.[44] Although somewhat sceptical of certain arguments, the Home Office finally accepted that, regarding urban areas, 'the arguments against the introduction of traffic wardens are well nigh conclusive' while in rural areas 'it seems improbable that they would be *generally* satisfactory'. It was accepted that some schemes, such as that in Essex, had had local success but it felt that 'there can be no guarantee that if the Home Office sponsored the general adoption of such methods, difficulties would not soon arise, e.g. in the matter of pay.' Indeed, it was feared that the scheme could prove counterproductive, for 'if a police authority could secure a cheaper article they might be tempted in the course of time to make far more traffic points than are strictly necessary.'[45]

The question did not go away in the late 1920s. In the spring of 1927 *The Times* openly advocated the American solution.[46] Eighteen months later, in November 1928, the Home Secretary was pressed on the notion of recruiting a special force simply for traffic control but Joynson-Hicks prevaricated, recognising that local trials had taken place but arguing that 'the matter is in the experimental stage... [so that] no decision can be reached for some time.'[47] However, three days later he made clear to Parliament that in his view 'it was essential in the central parts of London that policemen and not scouts should be placed on points duty.'[48] Less than a year later, the SJCs put forward a scheme, based on a proposal originally from the West Sussex SJC, for the creation of a subsidiary force to deal with traffic management. Echoing the wording of the original proposal from West Sussex it argued that 'far too much time is now taken up by the police in traffic management, which is not a primary police duty' and proposed that 'the Home Secretary should be asked if a subsidiary force under the control of the police could be formed to do this work.'[49] This was rejected at a Home Office conference in February 1929 attended by representatives of the County Councils' Association, the Association of Municipal Corporations, the Magistrates' Association as well as chief constables of county and borough forces. 'It was', the Conference agreed, 'undesirable to create a sort of inferior police force with limited functions and a lower rate of pay... [rather] the police with full powers of arrest must remain in control of traffic.'[50] However, the conference did concede that 'at less important points RAC and AA men could adequately regulate the traffic.'[51] In addition, as Dixon had earlier explained, the conference rejected the idea of the 'the institution of a separate corps of "traffic wardens" solely for the control and regulation of road traffic' not least because the 'introduction of yet another body... would create an additional element of complication and "patchwork".'[52] The decisions were endorsed by the 1929 Royal Commission in its first report, on the control of traffic on roads.[53]

Tensions remained between the Home Office and the police. A. L. Dixon, of the Home Office, in a paper submitted to the Royal Commission on Transport in April 1929, stressed the cost of traffic duties but stated that 'the Home Office attitude was that the employment of a certain number of police on traffic duty was desirable' but grumbled that 'the number at present employed in most districts was probably in excess of that required for purely police purposes'; nor 'could he see a traffic function that would justify the creation of traffic wardens.' Repeating his 'patchwork' point made in 1928, he concluded that '[t]he same purpose could be served in most cases at less cost by the installation of automatic traffic signals.'[54] The case could not have been put more clearly by the police and reflected realism on the part of the Home Office in face of powerful opposition. The Home Office still longed for an experiment with auxiliary traffic police but, as Dixon informed Parliament in January 1930, representatives at another Home Office conference yet again gave 'singularly little support' for the idea of auxiliary traffic police.[55] This was not even a rearguard battle. The question had been resolved: responsibility for the regulation and control of traffic thus remained with the police. If further proof were needed it could be found in the statement of the Home Secretary, Herbert Samuel, in the 1932 debate on police costs. Playing down the scale of the problem and reassuring his audience, he informed Parliament that '[t]here were somewhat exaggerated ideas as to the number of police diverted to other duties than the detection of crime' before dismissing the notion of traffic wardens as merely 'effective up to a point, but [effecting] no great saving'.[56] Certainly by the end of the decade there was a general acceptance, summed up by the House of Lords Committee on the Prevention of Road Accidents, that the police had a responsibility for traffic control and a key role to play in improving safety.[57]

No doubt, as Howard Taylor has argued, the emphasis on the particular expertise of the police served their purposes in the sense of providing a new and growing area of work but this was not simply the product of narrow self-interest, nor was it without its problems, but before considering the practicalities of traffic policing in more detail one brief exception should be noted. The police spent considerable time on crossing duty at or near schools. This was one responsibility they were prepared to concede to civilian adult patrols. By the late 1920s the Chief Constable of Liverpool was expressing concerns about the resources he could devote to school crossings. His counterpart in Leeds was similarly concerned and by 1934 was warning that the service in the city would have to be curtailed if not abandoned and argued that there was a clear need for an alternative scheme to reduce demands on his overstretched men.[58] In similar vein the Commissioner of Police for London bemoaned the fact that the equivalent of some 250 men were engaged on school patrol duty and (somewhat later) advocated 'the wider employment of Adult Patrols, as used in America, to carry the approved "Stop – Children Crossing" sign outside schools' rather than leave the responsibility with the hard-pressed police.[59] In Manchester, the police even went as far as to train older boys (i.e., 14-year-olds) to supervise younger children crossing the road as they did not have sufficient manpower to do it themselves. The boys wore safety first armlets; an idea which they had thought of and which had been made by the girls of the school![60]

Traffic regulation and control: the problems and the general debate on responsibility for road safety

Having won the battle over the control of traffic regulation and control, the police were faced with a difficult 'war' with road users in the inter-war years. Military metaphors aside, the problem comprised two distinct, potentially contradictory but related elements: movement and safety. Ensuring the free movement of traffic on the king's highway was a major concern for a variety of very good social and economic reasons but, particularly with the growth of motorised traffic, so too was road safety. Indeed, the question of road safety rapidly gained prominence in the 1920s and remained a pressing and largely unsolved problem during the following decade, despite repeated expressions of concern about the general carnage and, in particular, the massacre of the innocents on the roads of Britain.[61]

In one sense, there was nothing new about the traffic problems of the inter-war years. Dangerous driving, congestion, collisions, fatalities and so forth were to be found in the days of exclusively horse-drawn traffic. The appearance of the bicycle in the late nineteenth century was a harbinger of troubles to come. There was a degree of homogeneity in terms of speed among road users that was disrupted by a machine capable of travelling at 15 mph, compared with the 3–5 mph of pedestrians and horse-drawn traffic. The advent of motor-driven vehicles and the increase in differential speeds that resulted from this exacerbated the old problems in no uncertain terms and brought a far greater degree of unpredictability to traffic movement than had existed beforehand. This problematic situation was further compounded by contemporary (inherited) views regarding access to roads. It is easy to overlook the fact that for many generations pedestrians had used the roads in town and country for a variety of purposes, not simply for movement from one place to another, and did not expect to have this usage subject to extensive regulation or restriction. In a very real sense, roads were (and were seen to be) part of a social space for working-class people that was to be used for economic and leisure purposes; and further, there was a widespread belief that there was an equal right of access for all road users, including pedestrians. As late as 1929 the Royal Commission on Transport was clear that

> all users of the road, whether they are drivers of motor vehicles, or of horse-drawn vehicles, or riders of horses, or pedestrians, or persons driving or leading animals, or cyclists, have equal rights on the road.[62]

This multi-usage concept of the road came under increasing threat during the nineteenth century, particularly in the burgeoning towns and cities but it was after the First World War, and within a very short space of time, that roads became predominantly the preserve of wheeled, and especially motorised, traffic. However, there was nothing inevitable about the development of patterns of road usage. *Punch*, in a cartoon, 'More Solutions of the Great Motor Problem', published on 3 October 1906, posited two scenarios. One, drawing on the segregation and demarcation of railway trains, particularly the London underground, depicted a world in which there was unfettered pedestrian access with cars restricted to underground tunnels. The other depicted a more dystopian image of pedestrians fenced off from the roads on which unrestricted motor traffic prevailed. From the perspective of the early twenty-first century the triumph of the latter is obvious; from the perspective of the early twentieth century it was less so – at least not without a fight! Unsurprisingly, the changes in the realities of road usage were not accompanied by simultaneous changes in mentalities. Indeed, these profoundly different ideas competed for much of the inter-war years while a consensus on acceptable levels of restriction upon road users and (more cynically) on acceptable levels of road deaths was thrashed out. And as this aspect of 'modern' society was being fought out, the police were responsible for striking a day-to-day balance between the demands for mobility, the requirements of trade and the safety of road users.

The inter-war years are important for the range of initiatives – automatic traffic lights, roundabouts, pedestrian crossings and differential speed limits – that took place but to establish the full significance of these developments it is important to understand the way in which traffic problems were conceptualised. Again, two different elements can be identified. First, there was the blame game in which various figures, such as the foreign chauffer, the female driver, the road hog and the foolish cyclist and pedestrian were pilloried for their contribution to road accidents in particular. *The Times*, for example, conceded that there were 'motoring morons' but castigated equally 'palsied pedestrians and suicidal cyclists'.[63] Second, more specifically but clearly related, was the conceptualisation of the problem of road deaths as a technical as well as an educational matter.

The more general debate has been well analysed elsewhere and the main points need but brief mention.[64] Although motoring was 'democratised' during the inter-war years, private (as opposed to commercial) motoring never entirely shook off its aristocratic/elitist image; further, the new drivers of post-war Britain were drawn largely from the relatively well-to-do middle classes. There was a self-image of the courteous and careful gentlemen drivers – 'the brotherhood of the road' – who were all too often wrongly accused and unfairly restricted for the shortcomings of other road users. Sefton Cummings, a prolific writer and defender of the motorist, was unequivocal when he told the readers of the *Saturday Review* in 1935 that '[t]here is no doubt whatever that the motorist is the most oppressed class in the country.'[65] This image was perpetuated in part by creating and stigmatising the selfish minority within the motoring fraternity – the real-life 'Toad of Toad Hall' besotted by his car and oblivious to others. The 'road hog' became a convenient scapegoat for the rising accident rate. *The Times* railed against 'the callousness or incompetence of drivers of fast cars' and 'the wanton eccentricities of...the comparative few [who showed] selfish disregard of the rights and security of others'.[66] The creation of such scapegoats deflected criticism from drivers as a whole. The road hog was the 'enemy not only of the public but of his fellow-users of motor-cars'.[67]

The myth of the gentlemanly driver was further enhanced by the creation of a range of threatening 'others' to be found on the road. There might be a few real-life 'Toads' but the real problem, or so it was argued, came in the form of a variety of rogue drivers who were un-English, uneducated or female! The foreign chauffeur was probably the earliest of these scapegoats. Clearly English gentlemen would not drive in a selfish and dangerous manner but could his French driver be relied upon to act in the same way? Clearly not! Similarly, as driving became more democratised it was easy to blame selfish, ungentlemanly working-class drivers. It was the 'wilful caddishness and bad manners... [of] that class of persons who now go about in motor cars and who, ten years ago, were riding in buses' who were responsible for declining standards of driving according to one writer in *Autocar* in 1926.[68] Similarly, those catering for working-class leisure, such as drivers of charabancs or of 'motor-coaches with a "bean feast" party', were castigated for their selfish behaviour on the road, which itself was seen as a product of their class and their lack of gentlemanly instincts. As early as the summer of 1920 *The Times* was incensed by 'the reckless and dangerous driving [of char a bancs] and the bad manners of their passengers'; a complaint that was to be repeated in subsequent years.[69] But worse than being a foreign or working-class motorist was to be a woman driver. The more common criticism emphasised the (alleged) incompetence of women drivers who were either 'mentally sidetracked by such burning questions, prompted by an inflated vanity, as "How do I look?"' or 'so hopelessly imbued with a sense of their own worthlessness that they become completely helpless in any traffic situation'.[70] To compound matters there was a second type of female driver who was even more threatening – at least to the male of the species. According to *The Psychologist*,

> aggressive women take a fiendish delight in weaving in and out of traffic frightening poor male drivers by their recklessness and verve. Many a woman takes out her hate of her husband, or her sexual dissatisfaction in reckless driving.

The one small consolation was that '[m]any a woman who would like to use the ax [*sic*] on her husband or boss, takes out her homicidal instincts on her car.'[71] Notwithstanding hard evidence from traffic accident data, the image of the dangerous woman driver remained firmly entrenched in the male mind.

By focusing on supposedly problematic minorities within the motoring community, the image of a reasonable and responsible majority was preserved: and it was an image that was not confined to the pages of the (partisan) motoring press. Scapegoating of minority figures in the driving community was but one element in a motorist mindset that sought to blame other road users. Omnibuses and trams, heavy lorries, motorcyclists and pedal cyclists came in for varying degrees of criticism. *The Times* was particularly incensed that long-distance motor coaches were able 'to invade the crowded districts of Central London' while the Ministry of Transport expressed concern at the dangers created by 'the presence of flocks of cyclists on the road'.[72]

Nevertheless, while it is undoubtedly the case that an image of the innocent average driver, unfairly criticised and unduly restricted in his actions, was perpetrated largely but not exclusively in the motoring press, it would be wrong to suggest that criticism of motorists in general was not to be found in the 1920s and 1930s. Not surprisingly, the Pedestrians' Association, although professing no hostility to other road users, was critical of the motor interest as well as the motorist for not ensuring that 'pedestrians had a reasonable chance of using in safety the highway'.[73] In somewhat hyperbolic terms, the anonymous author of *How Manchester is Managed* commented that 'a revolution may take place in a European state with fewer casualties that the toll which traffic takes of human life in Manchester's streets [for which] the more numerous and mobile motor car... is the principal culprit.'[74] Almost as dramatic was *The Times*' observation that 'the Frankenstein's monster of motor traffic... is a serious menace to life.'[75] It was a threat that went beyond the few 'road hogs' 'who wallow in the filth of their own conceit and practice frightfulness deliberately' to include

> drivers so incompetent that they ought to be sent back to their lessons;... drivers who know themselves so competent that they take great risks – and take them once too often, [but] a commoner source of danger than any of these is the driver who has no imagination, no power of putting himself in the place of the other users of the road.[76]

Driving brought out the worst in human nature. '[I]ndividuals of a mild and conscientious disposition become autocratic and careless when they enter a potentially dangerous machine.... Swagger, selfishness, jealousy, reckless impatience, a desire to overbear and to bully – these are the offensive qualities which cause a large number of motor accidents.'[77]

The longstanding belief in equal access to and equal rights on the road was increasingly qualified by the corollary of this argument, namely, that all road users had a responsibility to ensure safety. Motorists should not 'think the road belongs to them and that if they blow their horn everybody must get out of their way'; but equally, pedestrians and cyclists should not 'think all traffic should give way for them and that they have a right to hold it up whenever they please'.[78] This thinking lay behind the outline of a code of conduct for road users, proposed by the Royal Commission, on Transport (1929) which dealt with drivers of motor vehicles, pedal cyclists and pedestrians alike.

The rhetoric of equality (of rights and responsibilities) was modified over the course of the 1930s. Indeed, increasingly the pedestrian was demonised. Predictably the earliest and most outspoken attacks were to be found in the motoring press which ran articles on 'Suicidal pedestrians' and bemoaned the unfair targeting of the motorist 'whereas the pedestrian is almost exclusively to blame, the mental deficient who will not look where he is going when he steps on the road'.[79] The logic of the 'palsied pedestrian' argument was pursued ruthlessly by a number of contributors to the debate, not least Sefton Cummings, who condemned the notion that 'the pedestrians have the right to wonder all over the road' and railed against the fact that the 'pedestrians had been "allowed" to usurp the motorists' highway'.[80] Lt. Col. A. W. C. Richardson, who, addressing the Institute of Transport in 1935, argued that 'pedestrians must be removed from motor roads' and safely housed on a modern equivalent of the Rows of Chester.[81] Segregation in the name of safety! Perhaps the most outspoken figure was Lt. Col. Mervyn O'Gorman. Ever the forceful defender of the motorist, he castigated the foolish pedestrian for his 'act of reprehensible and suicidal – and, it may be, murderous – folly'.[82] Looking back during the war years, he lamented the fact that '[t]he pedestrians' intended movement has been allowed to remain unforeseeable with the tacit consent of the authorities concerned (the Minister of Justice and the Home Secretary)' and recommended that

> [a]ll moving units [that is, pedestrians included] must be induced, first by propaganda, then by warnings and eventually by mandatory rules, to form such habits that their movements (and their intended movement) are instinctively made and continuously disclosed to other nearby road users.[83]

One suspects that O'Gorman thought such pedestrian controls should not be limited to wartime!

Elsewhere the language was more temperate but the message of shared responsibility and pedestrian culpability not dissimilar. As late as 1929 *The Times* could still argue that 'a large proportion of the casualties caused by motor vehicles must be laid at the door, not of the heedless walker, but of the reckless driver, whose guiding principle is speed at any price.'[84] Three years later the balance had changed. In a leader entitled 'Unnecessary road accidents', it drew attention to the number of 'careless pedestrians' who contributed to accidents, though it did also concede that 'the man on foot is the under-dog'.[85] Pedestrians were seen to be, at best, 'unequipped by habit, knowledge and experience to protect themselves against the new risks' of the motor.[86] At worst he was a reckless jaywalker.[87] Such was the prevalence of these sentiments that it became accepted wisdom that it would be 'inexcusable to make motorists in general the scapegoat'.[88] Rather, there was a common belief in notions of shared responsibility that pointed to co-operation as the way forward. 'The modern townsman – driver or pedestrian – has still to learn the conditions of his safety... self-control, caution and courtesy [provide the] true protection.'[89]

Such thinking led to a position in which the problems associated with motoring, particularly road accidents, were conceived in terms which, in large measure, pointed to education, rather than legislative restriction, as the solution. Motors, especially cars, were seen as neutral or benign technologies, not as inherently problematic; they were misused and misunderstood. The solution, therefore, was to be found, first and foremost, in education.

> Not only is the motorist to be educated. The ill-mannered pedal-bicyclist, the ill-mannered pedestrian – may we not add the ill-mannered owner of unguarded dogs? – are also to be talked to for their own good.[90]

Lt. Col. Moore Brabazon, later to become Minister of Transport, expressed his confidence in the ability of mankind to learn in extravagant terms.

> It is true that 7000 people are killed in motor accidents but it is not always going on like that. People are getting used to the new conditions.... No doubt many of the old Members of the House will recall the number of chickens killed in the old days. We used to come back with our radiators stuffed with feathers. It was the same with dogs. Dogs get out of the way of motorcars nowadays and you never kill one. There is education even in the lower animals. These things will right themselves.[91]

'Education', for some at least, would lead to a situation in which accidents would be minimised because 'all movements... [will become] foreseeable' for 'all traffic units'.[92]

The transformation of the pedestrian into a traffic unit was symptomatic of another important way of thinking about road traffic in which there would be technical or planning solutions to the various problems of safety and congestion. Detailed analysis of accidents would provide objective information on the major causes of road accidents, from which would follow solutions. Improved traffic layouts, better signalling, the construction of arterial roads, the segregation of different types of road users were seen to be the way forward and not just by town planners. Alker Tripp, Assistant Commissioner of the Metropolitan Police, personified this approach. In his view 'any town so planned that its citizens are killed and injured in vast numbers is obviously an ill-planned town.'[93] In short, the evolving characterisation of the traffic problem resulted in a way of thinking in which the car (let alone speed) was not *per se* dangerous and should not be restricted or banned. Drivers could and should be educated but so should other road users while the environment should be modified to accommodate the motorist and to minimise the danger to other road users. *Punch's* dystopian future was moving closer!

Police attitudes

While the general contours of the debate are relatively well known the attitude of the police has received less detailed attention, though O'Connell sees the police (or chief constables at least) as being supportive of the motorist lobby in so far as they increasingly saw pedestrians as the major part of the problem of road accidents. Chief constables, who took a firm and public stance, for or against motorists, attracted attention at the time and have featured in later histories. The Chief Constables of Surrey and Warwickshire took a strong line against motorists while the Chief Constable of Salford (Major Godfrey) was far more sympathetic to the motorist, suggesting that in the case of certain accidents coroners should return verdicts of suicide by pedestrianism! But these were not necessarily representative of the opinion of the bulk of chief constables, let alone of ordinary policemen, whose views have scarcely been explored. In fact among senior officers there was a strong sense of pragmatism that was born of an awareness of the complexities of the motoring problem, a real concern for the social costs (i.e., injuries and fatalities) of poorly or inappropriately regulated traffic and a concern for the resource implications of traffic duty. There was also a sense of frustration that grew out of inappropriate, in some cases unenforceable, laws and the very real problems that this created in terms of winning public support at a time when the expansion of motoring brought the police – and specifically working-class constables – into contact with largely middle-class drivers who viewed the police more as servants than masters and who often resented what they saw as unwarranted restrictions on their freedom of action.

Among police officers, there was also a more sophisticated analysis of the role of the motorist that went beyond the simple scapegoating of the 'road hog'. First, there was a recognition that greater responsibility rested with motorists.

> Notwithstanding this degree of culpability in pedestrians and cyclists it must be remembered that it is incumbent upon motorists, who bring a powerful machine on to the public highway, to exercise more care than the average pedestrian, and not, as many motorists do, place the responsibility for avoiding accidents entirely upon the pedestrians.[94]

Second, several chief constables challenged the claims of the motoring organisations in particular that dangerous drivers were an atypical minority. Trenchard, albeit at times a controversial Metropolitan Police Commissioner, was forthright in his opinion.

> Too often it is assumed that the dangerous drivers are a class apart. This is not the case. No doubt there is a small proportion of drivers who are habitually dangerous, but even the well-intentioned drivers... are equally guilty of lapses and thus blunder into situations in which they are quite definitely in the wrong.[95]

His successor, Game, adopted a similar stance but added an additional dimension to the argument. In particular, he challenged the defence that motorists were guilty of nothing more than a lapse of concentration.

> Well-intentioned persons are apt to complain that they have been punished for what appears to them to be nothing worse than a moment of forgetfulness or an error of judgment. They seem to forget that moments of forgetfulness and errors of judgment account for tens of thousands of casualties every year.[96]

He also rejected the common criticism of the police for prosecuting 'mere technical offences', pointing out that 'every one is a potential source of accident'.[97] Equally outspoken was the Chief Constable of Birmingham who condemned the 'carelessness or selfishness of drivers forgetful of the safety or of the interests of other users of the road'.[98]

Police criticism of the motorist was clearest when it came to the problem of urban congestion. Across the country traffic crawled through the increasingly crowded and cluttered streets of towns and cities and was brought to a standstill at peak times. The police were all too aware that the dramatic changes in the volume and composition of road traffic had effectively overwhelmed the old, narrow streets to be found in the length and breadth of the country. In town and country, road layouts which had been adequate in an age of horse-drawn traffic were ill-suited to the new demands of the emerging motor age. Roads had to cater for 'the slow-moving units for which they were originally designed – pedestrians, horses and cattle – [and] the large mass of faster modern inventions – cars, lorries, motor-cycles and bicycles'.[99] Unfortunately, old and new continued to co-exist throughout the inter-war years. As late as 1938, the Metropolitan Commissioner of Police bemoaned the fact that the combination of horse-drawn wagons and narrow streets led to '30 or 40 motor vehicles to be reduced to a crawl for long periods by the leisurely progress of one horse-drawn vehicle'.[100] Such congestion was compounded by other factors. Trams and buses, particularly before the designation of definite stopping points, added to congestion.[101] Failing to pull into the nearside lane to discharge passengers created a safety hazard as well as congestion. Also problematic were the motor-coaches that came from out of town and dropped their passengers, tourists and others, on major thoroughfares.[102] Large-scale public events – particularly sporting events such as the Cup Final, the Grand National, the Derby or Wimbledon but also political demonstrations – added to the problem.[103] And at least one chief constable remonstrated about

> a new form of 'gutter crawling' motorist [who] have appeared in the main streets, who drive slowly along with the object of attracting the attention of, and encouraging young females to accept a lift.

No doubt the inhabitants of Preston were doubly relieved to read that such 'gutter crawling' was not yet commonplace in the town and that the police were being 'especially vigilant to prevent this undesirable and dangerous practice'.[104]

Across the country, however, the greatest problem in terms of day-to-day congestion was inappropriate and inconsiderate parking. There was a tension between the desires (even expectations) of the individual driver, seeking to exploit to the full the convenience afforded by private cars in particular, and the greater good in both social and economic terms that came from the smooth movement of road traffic, which was incompatible with unrestricted parking. The exasperation of chief constables, as they routinely condemned the ordinary motorist for his or her unwillingness to think of others and to make use of designated parking areas, was palpable. The Metropolitan Police Commissioner made some allowance for rapidly changing circumstances which rendered unacceptable 'what may have been an unobjectionable practice for years' as change transformed 'a quiet street into one of considerable traffic importance'.[105] However, he was adamant that change was required and he was not alone in warning of firmer action. '[M]ore stringent measures will have to be taken', warned the Chief Constable of Liverpool in 1928, 'as there is a considerable number of owners and drivers who have not yet appreciated how selfish and inconsiderate to other users of the highway' was their behaviour in monopolising the streets.[106] Equally frustrated was his counterpart in Leeds. '[P]promiscuous parking of cars in the public street of this city is still a cause of grave concern' he observed, not least because of the delays to fire engines and ambulances.[107] His frustration was all the more marked because considerable efforts had been made in the city to provide alternative parking. An even stronger response came from his counterpart in Manchester. Chief Constable John Maxwell slated selfish motorists who 'most unreasonably wasted [police time] by [being] thoughtless or wilfully inconsiderate people who would make laws and car parks for their individual convenience' and bemoaned the fact that his 'days are burdened by considering impracticable cures and mountains of angry correspondence'.[108] Not surprisingly, there were critics. The trade paper *The Outfitter* objected that business was being adversely affected but was firmly rebuffed by a police spokesman. 'If motorists choose to litter the streets of Manchester with their motor-cars can they blame us if we try to stop them?'[109] As a consequence of the failure to heed warnings about obstructions, the police were forced to take action – often reluctantly as they were all too aware of the friction that could be thus caused.

Congestion was a problem that strained police/public relations but more contentious still was the question of road safety and the attendant restrictions on road users. Once again there was tension between two competing expectations: speedy and unfettered travel, on the one hand, road safety, on the other. Further, the question was more complicated than road congestion as it involved a variety of sensitive issues, such as legally enforced speed limits for vehicles and codes of behaviour for road users as a whole. Unsurprisingly, there was again a strong element of police pragmatism but the police were clear that motorists held a heavy responsibility for road safety and, contrary to the motoring associations, several chief constables came to argue that speed killed.[110]

Determining and enforcing speed limits for motor-propelled vehicles was a major source of dispute in the inter-war years. Technical advances in the manufacture of cars in particular had rendered the pre-war speed limits nonsensical and yet they were enshrined in law and enforced, albeit partially and with varying degrees of enthusiasm, across the country.[111] Often seizing on atypical individuals, such as the Chief Constable of Surrey, the AA and RAC fought in the 1920s for the abolition of speed limits in a high-profile campaign, which was often simplistic and emotional – presenting drivers as a persecuted minority who merely wanted the rights of free-born Englishmen. The 'intoxicating influence of speed', which *The Times* had noted back in 1907 was even more powerful in the 1920s and 1930s as land, sea and air speed records were set by various Britons. The new-found freedom of motoring was an aspiration for many non-car owners in the lower middle and working classes. Further, charges of 'un-English' speed traps struck a chord.

The police found themselves in a difficult position and a majority of chief constables in the late 1920s expressed themselves in favour of the abolition of speed limits but a sizeable minority (a third) supported the idea of some speed limit, particularly on urban roads.[112] The 1930 Road Traffic Act abolished the speed limit for cars but the experiment was short-lived. In 1934 a further Road Traffic Act introduced a 30 mph speed limit in built-up areas, though local authorities could request de-restriction. Enforcing speed limits added to the volume and sensitivity of police work but an increasing number of chief constables, particularly in the towns and cities, were increasingly unsympathetic to the demands of motorists for unfettered travel. John Maxwell, the Chief Constable of Manchester, for example, was quite clear that 'the safety of the public generally must not be sacrificed to any attempt to obtain greater speed' and bemoaned the fact that there had been an 'increase in accidents on those thoroughfares from which the speed limit of 30 miles per hour has been removed'.[113] Similar sentiments were expressed by the Metropolitan Police Commissioner and the Chief Constables of Birmingham and Bradford.[114]

The question of an appropriate speed limit could not be divorced from the wider issue of road safety and the emotive issue of traffic accidents. The accident figures gave rise to considerable concern, not least when young children were involved, which was clearly shared by police chiefs. 'Loss of life or serious physical disability... [was] a grave problem facing the community' according to A. R. Ellington, the Chief Constable of St Helens.[115] A similar sentiment was expressed by Robert Mathews, Chief Constable of Leeds, who was convinced that the 'most appalling features [was]... not the number of fatalities but the number of accidents involving maiming [that led to] a lifetime of suffering.'[116] The demands for action in turn necessitated an analysis of their causes. Most forces collected information on the location of accidents (fatal and non-fatal), the participants in the event and, based on the report of the police officer at the scene, on responsibility. The information was much valued and used to shape the actions of many chief constables and traffic officers but such data, despite its superficially impressive detail, must be treated with care. Judgements at the scene of an accident were not easy to make, even for an experienced officer, and there is a real possibility that these reports reflected prevailing beliefs about the causes of accidents.

Although the responsibilities of the motorist were reiterated, the analysis of accident figures threw up the awkward facts of negligence by a range of road users. Or so it seemed, as the following analysis of the prime causes of fatal street accidents for the last six months of 1929, and presented to the Chief Constables' Association Conference in 1930, shows (Table 5.1).

Several senior police figures saw pedestrians and cyclists as a major cause of traffic accidents. Pedestrians allegedly stopping in the middle of the road to 'discuss the failings of their mothers-in-law or their fancy for the 2.30' were castigated at the Chief Constables' Association general conference in 1930 The Chief Constable of Salford was the most outspoken but not alone in referring to 'suicidal pedestrians'; so too, at times, did his counterparts in London, Leeds, Manchester and Preston; but there was an awareness that 'suicidal tendencies' on the part of pedestrians often reflected a failure to adjust quickly to rapidly changing circumstances and conventions on the roads.[117] Others, such as the Chief Constable of Preston, recognised that

> it will take a few years before the general public acquire the habit of using [pedestrian crossings]; it has taken several years before the citizens of Paris acquired the habit; and in this country they are only in the experimental stage.[118]

Table 5.1 Prime causes of fatal street accidents

Human failure 85%					Other 15%
Pedestrians 40%	Cyclists 9%	Motor drivers 33%			Others (animals and passengers) 3%
Adults 22%	Children 18%	Motor cycles 20%	Private motor cars 8%	Others (buses, coaches, trams and lorries) 5%	

Note: road defects, weather, vehicle defects.
Source: Compiled from returns for last six months of 1928 made by Coroners for the National 'Safety First' Association. *Chief Constables' Association, General Conference, 19 June 1930*, p. 54.

Indeed, he was not alone in stressing the generational nature of the problem but (not surprisingly) failed to appreciate that it would take more than one generation for the new road sense to become habitual thinking. His patience undoubtedly waned over time. By 1938 he was sympathising with the driver faced with a pedestrian suddenly stepping out on a crossing in front of a car only a few yards away.[119] As did that of the once sympathetic Maxwell of Manchester who felt that 'legislation governing the movement of pedestrians' was necessary to reduce further the level of accidents.[120] Nonetheless, unlike many other countries in Europe and America, jay-walking was not criminalised in Britain.

Cyclists were increasingly criticised for their irresponsibility, not least as they figured more prominently in the accident figures. 'There are cyclists who ride with hands in their pockets... and others who load themselves with cumbrous articles so that they have not proper control' and yet others rode along tramlines, caught lifts off the back of lorries and even deliberately rode to and from work without lights.[121] Frustration at the latter practice again led to sympathy for the motorist.

> Physical and moral strain on motorists driving in the dark is in itself sufficient handicap without the added fear of being suddenly confronted and endangered by cyclists riding without lights.[122]

There was a widespread concern that, particularly at night, the police were unable to keep a proper check on cyclists who were highly elusive which, in turn, gave rise to demands that 'pedal cyclists should be required to carry numbers and that they should be registered.'[123] Nonetheless, this was not translated into legislation.

Frustration with foolish pedestrians and cyclists, though clearly more evident in the late 1930s than before, did not mean that the police were blinkered to the shortcomings of others. It was not only the Metropolitan Police Commissioner, in his report for 1938, who thought that 'the class of road user with the worst record...is the motorist'.[124] Moreover, there was repeated condemnation of dangerous and careless driving as a major source of accidents. The motoring organisations argued that such figures were a small minority and some chief constables agreed; but others argued that such behaviour was more widespread. 'It is beyond question that dangerous driving is responsible for a large number of accidents', the Chief Constable of Liverpool informed his Watch Committee in 1933. Furthermore, he continued, 'it is equally beyond question that very many offenders escape detection and prosecution.'[125]

Contrary to O'Connell's claim, the police were not simply part of a wider pro-motorist consensus that scapegoated the pedestrian. A few took a simplistic stance, others became more exasperated and more critical over time; but many others were more sympathetic to the pedestrian and critical of the motorist. While recognising the right of all road users to safe access to the king's highway, the police were also well aware that the balance was shifting rapidly in favour of the motorist and against the pedestrian, the bicyclist and the horse-rider. In 1936 Metropolitan Police Commissioner Game summed up the situation well. He recognised that 'the pedestrian and the cyclist are entitled to claim that they have not created the problem' and that 'they have as much right to the use of the road as anyone else', but stressed that 'under the conditions existing today, full exercise of these rights can only lead to painful, if not fatal, results.'[126] The point was illustrated by the following piece of doggerel.

Here lies the body of Samuel Hay

Who died disputing the right of way

He was right, dead right, as he strolled along

But he's just as dead as if he'd been wrong.

To that extent, pragmatism coloured their view of the problem. Similarly, pragmatism – the recognition that they could not afford to alienate a large section of the population – influenced their 'technical' responses to the problem of road accidents and their responsibility to enforce traffic laws.

6
The Police and the Practicalities of Traffic Management

Good policing has always been dependent on prioritisation, co-operation and discretion but also innovation. Police resources have never been sufficient to meet all the demands made of them and, as a consequence, choices had to be made about police priorities. Sometimes those choices coincided with the public rhetoric of fighting serious crime; more often they reflect more mundane demands for the regulation and smooth running of everyday life. Thus, the demand for free-flowing traffic in town and country and, increasingly, for safety on the roads involved the diversion of police resources into traffic regulation and control at a time when there were increasing demands being made and when resources were constrained by governments facing difficult economic times. While some senior police figures calculatingly viewed the growth of road traffic work as an ideal opportunity to argue for the maintenance or expansion of establishments, for many chief constables and, even more so for the men under them, this new demand put considerable pressure on their forces. The pressure, however, could have a positive outcome as new technologies (including motor cars) were adopted and new practices developed to make more effective use of available manpower.

In addition, finding a satisfactory solution to the cluster of problems associated with road traffic required effective co-operation with other local and central bodies, particularly when this involved modifications to the built environment and its use. To take but one example: police proposals to improve traffic flow and reduce accidents by changing road layouts or introducing traffic lights and pedestrian crossings depended upon the support of local councils and the Ministry of Transport.

Furthermore, because the control and regulation of traffic was a highly sensitive matter and its mishandling could seriously damage police/public relations, the police – at all levels – had to be careful in exercising their discretion in the enforcement of the relevant aspects of the law. Even then, police success in reducing accidents depended in part upon the willingness of local magistrates (and indeed the Home Office) to support them particularly when dangerous or careless drivers were prosecuted.

The police response to the traffic problems of the inter-war years was threefold. First, they devised and/or adopted a series of technical solutions, ranging from increased use of manpower on point duty, the introduction of mechanical traffic controls (traffic lights and pedestrian crossings), and improved road layout (roundabouts, one-way systems) and usage (waiting restrictions). Second, they joined others in an educational programme targeted at adults but increasingly focused on the next generation of road users. Third, they used the law in a selective manner, as much to educate as to persecute those who infringed the traffic laws. The response was unco-ordinated and patchy. Police chiefs differed in their analysis of the problem and its solutions and in the urgency with which they felt such solutions should be implemented. Much depended upon local commitment. Also, there was a strong element of learning by doing. Finally, there was a very real sense in which the rapid growth of the number of motor-propelled vehicles on the roads meant that the problem of traffic control and regulation was constantly changing and requiring new solutions. C. D. Buchanan, looking back from the late 1950s, captured the essence of the problem in his book *Mixed Blessing: The Motor in Britain*, when he wrote that '[w]e are always seen to have been a lap behind the motor car: by the time we had thought of 30-feet carriage ways, it was dual that we really needed... by the time we had thought of roundabouts it was flyovers that were needed.'[1] Unsurprisingly, traffic congestion remained a major problem, road accidents remained worryingly high and many chief constables (not to mention other traffic experts) remained perplexed as the solutions they sought constantly eluded them.

The traffic problem was not uniform across the country. It was particularly acute and visible in London, but other cities and large towns suffered in a similar manner, though not all chief constables or watch committees gave it high priority. Smaller towns were not immune, especially if the level of car ownership and the volume of road traffic were relatively high. As early as 1921 the Inspector of Constabulary was drawing attention to the problems created by the growth of 'mechanical transport', especially in smaller towns such as Coventry.[2] Even more problematic was Exeter but there were other market towns, such as

Bedford, or industrial centres, such as Middlesbrough, where the volume of motor traffic was much lower and the problem less pressing. Equally county forces found the growth of road traffic problematic, especially where seaside resorts or inland beauty spots brought large numbers of tourists, particularly at Bank Holidays.[3]

The most obvious and immediate response to the problems of congestion and safety was to increase the number of officers on fixed point duty at major junctions and crossroads, though this was not without its problems. First, an element of training was required. Controlling traffic at a busy crossroad was a complex task and one that could not be learnt by doing. Drivers needed clear and comprehensible directions. 'In this connection I wish to draw attention to the increasing importance of sparing no pains to secure uniformity of traffic signals', wrote Atcherley in his 1927 annual report. There was, he felt, a 'risk of very serious accidents occurring from genuinely mistaken signals'.[4] Failure also played into the hands of critics like the AA. The police on point duty in Manchester came under attack from this organisation which claimed that 'they [the traffic police] wave their arms about as if they were the wings of a derelict windmill in a gale.'[5] Despite the element of exaggeration, there was a point to be made and police forces were alert to the need to include traffic control in their training programmes. As important as clarity was uniformity. The problems caused by misleading police hand signals were recognised early on but progress was slow.[6] As the 1929 Royal Commission on Transport noted, there was a pressing need for 'complete uniformity in the hand signals given by constables on point duty all over the country'.[7] The publication of the Highway Code played an important part in creating a commonly understood set of hand signals.[8] Equally important, though not a training issue, was the question of visibility. By the end of the 1930s it was increasingly common to see the traffic policeman in white coat and gloves and in many cities he stood in a spotlight to increase his visibility (and reduce his vulnerability) but this was a relatively recent development. In London it was only in 1928 that white gauntlets and white gloves were in general use, while white coats were merely at the experimental stage; floodlights for men on point duty were first introduced in Salford in 1929 and Liverpool in 1932.

Second, and more important, the use of more men on fixed point duty and, more generally, the creation of specialist traffic departments, necessarily meant the diversion of manpower and a reduction in some other police activity. The numbers involved on traffic duty were considerable, particularly when school and other road-crossing duties were taken into account. Nowhere was this more apparent than in London. Attempts were made to return men to beat duty – some 350 men had been moved from point duty in 1930, for example – but other demands, notably schools' crossings, offset these gains. In 1935 Commissioner Game reported that 642 constables were employed exclusively on traffic duties but, staggeringly, part-time traffic duties accounted for a further 2389 men, giving a total of 3031 officers, or the equivalent of one-sixth of the total strength of uniformed men.[9] Manchester, with a total force of some 1400, had 92 fixed traffic points in the late 1920s and an additional 103 points to help school children across the road.[10] In Liverpool some 300 men were directly used on traffic duties.[11] In the boroughs as a whole, police work accounted for some 14 per cent of manpower. The demands of traffic duty were even higher in percentage terms in county forces, where the average figure was estimated to be around 23 per cent but rising to 33 per cent in some forces.[12]

As more and more officers were diverted to road traffic duties, chief constables, particularly in larger towns and cities, found it difficult to maintain normal beats throughout each day. The Chief Constables of Preston and Leeds, in 1925 and 1926, respectively, sounded almost identical warning of this inability. The former was blunt.

> The result of the large development of motor traffic has necessitated Constables remaining on point duty at the dangerous crossings on their beats, and on that account public places and streets have been unpatrolled.[13]

The Inspector of Police for the northern division General Sir W. L. Atcherley generalised the point, telling Parliament in 1925 that such was the 'state of the streets at certain periods of the day [that it] involves the stopping of regular patrol work... to look after the traffic'.[14] Clearly there were exceptions – there was little indication that beats were being neglected in towns such as Middlesbrough and St Helens or even cities such as Bradford but there was clearly a growing problem as the volume of motorised traffic steadily increased, albeit unevenly, across the country.

One response (discussed in greater detail in Chapter 8) was to modernise the beat system which in most places had been established before the Great War. Rationalising beats, introducing police boxes, introducing cycle and motor patrols were all means of maintaining essential beat work with reduced manpower resources. However, despite arguing that responsibility for the control and regulation of traffic should remain a police function because it could not be reduced to a mechanical function, a technological answer to the manpower problem was sought in the form of automatic traffic lights. Although traffic lights, in the form of semaphore arms with red and green lamps reliant upon gas, had been briefly introduced outside Parliament in 1886, there was no serious development of the idea in Britain until the 1920s. Traffic experts were aware of usage abroad but the so-called cheeseboard system used in New York, in which the whole of one street was at red while crossroads were at green, was not felt to be easily applicable to the less than regular layouts of most British towns and cities. The Berlin system, allowing traffic moving at a fixed speed (in the region of 11 mph in practice) to encounter a succession of green lights, seemed more promising and was the basis of the system to be introduced in Leeds. The Leeds experiment, and even more so, the decision to install automated electrical traffic signals in 1927 in Princes Square, Wolverhampton sparked a debate among local authorities and the Ministry of Transport. The merits of two or three colour controls generated argument as did the advantages of automatic or vehicle-controlled lights but adoption was relatively slow. Experimentation was the order of the day in the late 1920s but implementation was stimulated when the Ministry of Transport agreed to cover 60 per cent of installation and maintenance costs.[15]

Despite the scale of its problems, London was not at the forefront of developments, despite some experimentation with portable traffic beacon lights in the Mall in 1924.[16] In 1931 the first major experiment was undertaken with the opening of a scheme of 68 fixed-cycle automatic traffic signals at 17 junctions in Oxford Street but, as Commissioner Trenchard complained, there were some 6000 in New York.[17] Trenchard's frustration was even more apparent a year later. He had recommended 487 points as suitable for traffic signals but only 20 additional sets had been installed. When the scheme was extended to Piccadilly in 1932, Trenchard claimed that 20 officers would be relieved of traffic duties thereby saving some £6000.[18] Not all were convinced. The Parliamentary Secretary to the Ministry of Transport, the Earl of Plymouth, told Parliament later that year that 'it would be a great mistake to overdo these automatic signalling systems and scatter them broadcast about London.'[19]

Progress was made: by 1935 there were 527 sets (with a further 185 proposed), rising to 860 in 1938.[20] Automatic lights were introduced into Trafalgar Square in 1933, while the scheme for Piccadilly Circus in late 1937 was heralded as a (albeit somewhat belated) triumph, comprising 'one of the most complicated systems of automatic lights in the world' and saving some £3600 per annum by releasing police from traffic duty.[21] By the late 1930s the notoriously busy and easily congested Ludgate Circus was the only major junction controlled by police-operated lights.[22] In the early years only a minority (some 30 per cent) of signals in London were 'of the vehicle-actuated type' which was seen to be superior in terms of improved traffic flow; by 1937 the figure had risen to almost 90 per cent.[23] Irrespective of the cost of installing and maintaining traffic lights, there were other problems. It took some while for drivers and cyclists to come to terms with the new system.

> The majority of road users respect the red light when it appears alone even if the road is completely clear and no-one is apparently about [but] in the case of the amber light, widespread carelessness and disregard are noticeable... the number of vehicles which are already in motion before the green light appears is in aggregate very high.[24]

Other cases of 'racing the green' worried the police. The problem worsened in the following year necessitating 'special steps... to secure enforcement'.[25] As Game complained, 'no traffic signals, however excellent, can compel obedience and experience has shown that wherever signals supersede pointsmen in any quantity, a quota of men have to be returned to carry out supervisory and enforcement duties.'[26]

And even then 'the standard of compliance with signals by drivers and cyclists [in London] still leaves much to be desired.'[27]

Similar slow progress was experienced elsewhere. In Manchester, the Chief Constable prided himself on being a progressive figure who sought to modernise all aspects of police work. With regard to specific traffic problems, John Maxwell had no doubt that there had been sufficient experimentation with traffic signals and they were a 'necessity of a progressive [traffic] policy'.[28] The introduction of traffic signals in Market Street and Cross Street in 1928 was 'most successful, and... as undoubtedly had the effect of speeding up the traffic'.[29] In the following year the new lights at Oxford Street and Whitworth Street made it 'possible to divert the services of three Constables from purely traffic control to ordinary patrol work'.[30] In fact these lights were of the one-way type and brought with them 'certain weaknesses' that led to a switch to three-way traffic lights as agreed at a recent meeting at the Ministry of Transport. Subsequent progress, however, was delayed by the need to get the support of a variety of local authorities. As he warned the Watch Committee (and the general public) in his annual report for 1932, the volume of traffic in the city continued to grow rapidly but extra traffic points controlled by Constables cannot be created without a serious effect upon the strength and efficiency of the Force. The obvious remedy, therefore, failing an increase in the strength of the Force, is the rapid introduction of signals at points where traffic control is necessary.[31]

Faced with an increasing problem of congestion, a rising number of road accidents and resource constraints, Maxwell continued to argue in the early 1930s for 'a flexible progressive system of mechanical traffic control' in central Manchester but with only limited success.[32] Indeed, from the mid-1930s onwards his emphasis shifted to other aspects of traffic control. Nonetheless, significant if slow progress continued to be made. In 1936 two of the four new sets of traffic lights installed incorporated the new 'early cut off' feature that made them 'the most up-to-date in the North of England [working] on the vehicle-actuated system which provides for a variable green period in relation to the volume of traffic'.[33]

The introduction of traffic lights was greeted in ecstatic terms in the *Manchester Evening News*. In 1928 its readers were informed

> We are becoming a mechanised nation. A flash of green light and Manchester pedestrians skip across the street with astonishing alacrity.... But amber has a mellowing effect creating a contemplative mood, in readiness for the eventual and inevitable danger associated with red. Thus was Manchester introduced to the novelty and whimsicality of automatic traffic control.[34]

In reality, as in other cities, it took time for road users to accustom themselves to the new regulations. Maxwell was disappointed that 'pedestrians have not yet taken full advantage of the protection afforded to them by crossing the streets in compliance with the [traffic] signals.'[35] A year later the situation had improved and he reported that 'the signals are being observed by drivers and pedestrians alike.'[36] Most motorists might have done so but there are still those who caused accidents by racing the lights, 'accelerating in an endeavour to cross before the change of signals, and being unsuccessful, breaking suddenly without warning' thereby causing a collision with the car behind.[37] The problem for the police was further compounded by problems in bringing prosecutions. He complained of the poorly defined provision of Section 49(b) of the 1930 Road Traffic Act and the consequent

> difficulty encountered when prosecuting drivers who proceed over an intersection thus controlled against the AMBER LIGHT. There appears

to be a divergence of opinion at the Petty Sessional Courts in this connection, and there is no doubt that definite legislation on the point is an urgent and desirable reform.[38]

Not all chief constables faced such problems. In Preston the introduction of traffic signals in 1929 was greeted in very positive terms. In his 1931 annual report the Chief Constable was effusive.

> Since the installation of this system of traffic control... a great stride has been made towards solving the problem of traffic control; by Police Officers it has always been efficient but costly.... Now road users and pedestrians alike have learned that obedience to automatic traffic signals results in the safety of the streets and an easier and regular flow of traffic with consequent reductions of delay and congestion.[39]

One of the earliest and most publicised schemes was introduced in Leeds. In 1926 the Chief Constable sounded a familiar warning. The growth of traffic

> has called for additional traffic constables in the busier thoroughfares, and in the centre of the City especially the congestion has become so acute as to render it necessary for the Police to take control of additional points, thus rendering the effective strength of the Force for actual work in connection with the detection and apprehension of offenders.[40]

The following year the Watch Committee decided to adopt his proposal for a traffic control scheme based on automatic lights using a fixed cycle. Within a year the scheme was 'operating to the general satisfaction of all road users.... Some motorists prefer the automatic signals, as being more definite and easily understood, to the signals given by some traffic constables.'[41] Such was the success of the scheme that 'deputations from about 40 different Cities and Towns' came to Leeds to see its automatic traffic control system.[42] The so-called 'Limited Progressive System' for the city centre was designed so that 'a vehicle entering the controlled area and travelling at a speed pre-determined for the system may proceed along any one street in that area without being stopped by the signals at any intersection along that street.'[43] Furthermore, 25 constables were released for normal beat duties. The scheme was subsequently modified to utilise vehicle-actuated lights but the underlying philosophy remained unchanged.⁴⁴ The Headrow system, in which 31 intersections were controlled by lights, was deemed 'an unqualified success, much of the congestion and delay previously encountered having been eliminated'.⁴⁵

Similar schemes were introduced in other, smaller towns and cities such as Brighton, Leicester, Luton, Oxford, Retford, Shrewsbury, Southampton and Portsmouth as well as in many parts of Greater London, including the major arterial roads.⁴⁶ County forces also experimented with their use, notably in Kent, Surrey and Sussex and by the end of the decade some authorities in rural areas were replacing roundabouts with traffic lights believing them to be both cheaper and more effective in terms of traffic control.⁴⁷ Initially the schemes had been only for day-time traffic but in January 1934 the Ministry of Transport circulated local authorities, asking them to consider 'the advisability of keeping traffic lights...in operation by night as well as by day'.⁴⁸ Agreement on the matter was achieved two months later. Generally speaking the police evaluation was positive. Traffic lights released men for other duties, aided the smoother flow of traffic and helped to reduce or check accident rates. For the most part the police were pleased with the behaviour of road users, though the occasional discordant note was sounded.⁴⁹

The introduction of traffic lights was but one part (maybe the most visible) of a wider range of measures to improve road safety as well as to reduce congestion. The increased volume of traffic on the roads made crossing them more hazardous, so, unsurprisingly, attention was focused on ways of reducing this danger and, once again, the police had to work closely with a variety of local authorities and their departments. The introduction of pedestrian crossings had been closely linked to the growth in traffic lights, which became crossings by default.⁵⁰ It was soon recognised that many lights had 'no interval during which pedestrians may feel that it is safe for them to cross'.⁵¹ A safer alternative was needed and in the 1920s developments were largely *ad hoc*, depending upon local initiatives, but the Road Traffic Acts of 1930 and particularly 1934, which made legal provision and funds available for pedestrian crossings, provided a major boost. Police-controlled crossing was not new but the introduction of uncontrolled crossings was not helped by an unfortunate incident involving the Minster of Transport, Hore-Belisha, in Camden Town in July 1934. Demonstrating the new, more pedestrian-focused approach, he narrowly escaped being knocked down by a motorist while on the crossing!⁵² Crossings were introduced by their thousands across the country and from late 1934 they were indicated by 'Yellow Globes on Iron Posts', quickly to be dubbed Belisha beacons.[53] Once again progress was hampered by difficulties created 'by the multiplicity of authorities who have to be persuaded to cooperate.'[54] Bermondsey Borough Council refused to introduce them as did Bournemouth and Chesham Urban District Council (UDC). Embarrassingly, the town council of Morley in the West Riding of Yorkshire refused to install pedestrian crossings despite the fact that Belisha beacons were manufactured there.[55] At least one chief constable, Captain W. J. Hutchinson of Brighton, was openly critical of the use of Belisha beacons, seeing them as a source of danger rather than safety, and argued for a system of traffic wardens to improve road safety.[56] The introduction of pedestrian crossings was an uneven process. It was estimated that in 1935 there were approximately 10,000 in the Metropolitan Police District but only a further 5000 in the rest of England, Scotland and Wales.[57]

As with the introduction of traffic lights, it took road users some time to adjust to the new. In some parts of the country pedestrians were reported to be 'too diffident', the Chief Constable and City Engineer of Sheffield railed against pedestrians 'not playing the game' and causing serious congestion while Oswald J. B. Cole, the Chief Constable of Leicester, accused pedestrians of causing accidents at crossings because of 'hovering'.[58] The greater problem, particularly in London, was the neglect of crossings by drivers. The Labour MP for Hammersmith North, Mr West, alleged that 75 per cent of motorists ignored the beacons.[59] The accuracy of the claim cannot be established but it was clear that the Metropolitan Police took an increasingly tough line to achieve 'more general observance of the regulations governing pedestrian crossings'.[60] London was not unique in this respect. The first pedestrian crossing in Manchester was opened in 1929 on London Road. It was not an immediate success as 'at the outset there was a definite lack of co-operation or mutual understanding between drivers and pedestrians... with the result that complaints of confusion and congestion were frequent.'[61] As late as 1936 Maxwell was still complaining of the need for greater mutual understanding but singling out for particular criticism 'the walking public [which] must be educated to cross very busy thoroughfares only at approved points.'[62] An even gloomier picture came from Bradford. In 1935 there were 44 accidents at pedestrian crossings, prompting the Chief Constable to conclude that 'these unfortunate happenings do much to create disregard and lack of confidence in the use of these crossings.'[63] Certainly in the early years, the presence of policemen, at both traffic lights and pedestrian crossings, was needed to ensure compliance, which negated part of their purpose.[64]

A more positive gloss was put on the situation in Leeds where over 360 crossings had been introduced by the summer of 1936. They were located at all intersections controlled by traffic lights as well as on many other uncontrolled sites. They 'undoubtedly proved their usefulness', especially in the city centre and accident statistics showed 'a very welcome decrease'.[65] The Chief Constable made two qualifications to this positive picture. First, '[t]here still seems to be some uncertainty among pedestrians as to their rights' and second, and more importantly, '[t]hese safety measures have almost reached saturation point and it now mainly rests with the general public as to whether accidents are to be reduced in any number.'[66]

The police had a part to play in other developments which were intended to improve the flow of traffic and the safety of the roads. Improved layouts – including one-way systems, roundabouts, alternate day parking, traffic islands, cycle lanes and by-passes – and improved signage were all part of the process of adaptation to the rapid growth of motor traffic. In several urban areas there were comprehensive reviews of the traffic problem and how best to cope. Salford provides a particularly good example of an attempt to provide an holistic solution. A detailed survey was carried out in February 1929 with a view to identify 'the most practical solutions to the serious traffic congestion prevailing and the minimizing of vehicular street accidents'.[67] This was followed by the introduction of a one-way system, the relocation of tram stops, the installation of traffic lights and traffic islands, improved road signage, an additional 30 constables devoted to school duty, the erection of rush barriers outside schools and the closure of some 30 streets in very congested areas to create play areas for children.[68] The Chief Constable, Major C. V. Godfrey, was one of the foremost figures in the country in this regard but men such as John Maxwell, in neighbouring Manchester, and Robert Mathews in Leeds were similarly committed to introducing new methods to solve traffic problems, though their success depended upon their ability to gain the support of and work with key figures in their local authorities.[69]

The second element in the police strategy that evolved over the interwar period reflected a wider belief that 'all the technological precautions in the world – pedestrian crossings, traffic lights, speed limits, driving tests, warning notices etc – are powerless against human carelessness' and hence a belief in the importance of education.[70] The introduction of the Highway Code in 1931 was a perfect example with its emphasis, in Herbert Morrison's words, on a gentlemanly code of 'good manners to be observed by all courteous and considerate persons' rather than legislative restraint.

The general attitude towards education was ageist. In its most negative, the old were deemed to be so wedded to their old ways and so slow in their reactions that little could be done for them whereas, at its most positive, the young offered the real possibility of creating a traffic-wise generation that would set them apart from their parents, let alone their grandparents. Unsurprisingly, considerable resources were focused on schools. Police participated in Safety Weeks, giving talks and showing slide shows and films to school children, in many parts of the country. In Leeds a 'Safety First Council' was established in 1925 which brought together various interested parties including the Education Committee and the police. Increasingly emphasis was given to the next generation of road users.[71] Similarly schemes were implemented elsewhere, usually in conjunction with the National 'Safety First' Association.[72] In Manchester a Safety First Committee was first established in 1927 but had to be revived in 1929. Thereafter, 'Safety Week' was a regular and high-profile event but, as the Chief Constable ruefully noted in 1936, 'the value of this special effort has not, unfortunately, been reflected in a satisfactory reduction in the number of accidents occurring to the children of school age.'[73] Salford quickly established a reputation for its commitment to road safety. The Traffic Office took responsibility for the 'control of road-sense propaganda' and worked closely with the City Education Office and individual schools. Determined to inculcate the '4Rs' (i.e., the conventional 3Rs plus road sense), the emphasis was on visual warnings which, according to Major C. V. Godfrey, grew out of a recognition of the effectiveness of Goebbels and Frick![74] As well as direct contact with children at school, handbills were sent to parents warning them of the dangers of the road. Safety films were shown to some 25,000 children in 1929, while the Chief Constable also took to the air locally to give a radio broadcast on 'Traffic Problems of an Industrial City'.[75] And to ensure that the message was not restricted to term times, the police kept in touch during school holidays by visiting parks and recreation grounds and 'by means of a loud-speaker van relayed gramophone records on "Safety First" by such well-known persons as Mr Hore-Belisha, Miss Gracie Fields and Sir Malcolm Campbell'.[76] The effect of such propaganda is difficult to assess but the widespread designation of play streets, pioneered in Salford, probably had a greater and more immediate impact on accident figures.

At times the educational activities of the police verged on the bizarre and ridiculous – policemen on the roofs of their cars shouting advice to pedestrians through loudspeakers – but one direct way in which the police could educate was by providing an example of good practice (and a deterrent) through their presence on the road and also by providing advice, where appropriate, to errant road users. Liverpool was the first city to introduce a motor patrol in 1920 but others were slower to follow and it was only in the 1930s, after the 1930 Road Traffic Act, that mobile squads became commonplace. Initial police responses were positive. The Chief Constable of Leeds was convinced that the 'very presence of the patrols on the road has had the effect of increasing the general standard of competency in driving and motorists have been persuaded to follow the wise suggestions of the Highway Code'.[77] Similarly, Maxwell was sure that road patrols had 'the same deterrent effect upon would-be road offenders as the uniform beat Constable has upon potential criminals'.[78] However, the most elaborate scheme to educate the motorist was the Home Office Experimental Motor Patrol Scheme introduced in 1937 which involved

> augmenting the personnel for [police patrols] not so much with a view to more frequent penal action but primarily for the purpose of inculcating a higher standard of road sense and behaviour on the part of all classes of road users, including cyclists and pedestrians.[79]

The government-funded scheme embraced the counties of Cheshire, Lancashire and Essex and the cities of London Metropolitan Police District (MPD), Liverpool, Manchester and Salford.

Given the different scale of augmentation (Table 6.1) and the different circumstances of city and county, the scheme operated in very different ways. In his evaluation of the first six months of the scheme, since 1 April 1938, the Chief Constable of Lancashire, Captain, Sir Archibald Hordern, was delighted to record a dramatic fall in road accidents of 46 per cent.[80] This had been achieved by focusing on known bad roads, mainly in the urbanised south of the county, identified from accident maps; reinforcing existing patrols and providing 'intensive supervision' where needed: 'periodic concentration...is part of the organised scheme'.[81] The county had been divided into seven motor patrol areas each under an inspector. Cars operated for at least eight hours a day, though this could be extended to 16 when required. Additional men were taken to problem areas 'where traffic conditions at the moment appear to justify control'.[82] Central intelligence regarding changing road conditions (and its rapid transmission via 'short-wave telephony') was essential to the scheme. In heavily built-up areas officers on pedal cycles

Table 6.1 Home Office Experimental Motor Patrol Scheme

	Traffic control men before scheme	Additional men	Scheme total	Total strength of Force	% Traffic control to total strength	% Increase in manpower
Lancashire	110	331	441	2166	20.4	15.4
Essex	25	80	105	707	14.9	11.3
Cheshire	35	100	135	654	20.3	15.3
Liverpool	50	50	100	2218	4.5	2.3
Manchester	50	50	100	1436	7.0	3.5
Salford	15	15	30	384	7.8	3.9
London MPD	563	70	633	18,560	3.4	0.4

Source: Chief Constables' Association, Annual Report, 1938.

and even on foot were used to supplement the motorised presence. Actions included periodic speed checks in built-up areas and brake tests, though it was stressed that the latter were not the basis for prosecution but had a high 'propaganda value'. Likewise, warning letters regarding speeding were seen to 'induce a greater degree of co-operation between the police and the motoring public'.[83] The focus on specific black spots brought dramatic results: on 'the roads that have been specially dealt with in this way during the last six months, accidents have been reduced by 73%'.[84] There were some unresolved problems, not least the continuing 'apathy of the average individual', notwithstanding a wide-ranging propaganda campaign encompassing lectures (5000 since 1 April), exhibitions, press articles, notices to schools, parents and children and, for the latter, lantern lectures during children's matinee at local cinemas.

Hordern was convinced of the importance of 'teaching drivers on the spot the very road sense which they lack' and he gave 'detailed instructions... in regard to the type of offences which should be dealt with by way of verbal caution'.[85] As a consequence prosecutions fell dramatically but, to some extent, this was a continuation of a policy adopted in 1935 whereby the law was not enforced rigidly. Nonetheless, he noted: 'Hundreds of motorists have been brought before the Courts, and many have been in honest ignorance of what they had done wrong, due to their lack of knowledge or road sense, rather than a disregard for the law.'[86] Overall, Hordern was optimistic, not least because of the 'enormous number of written and verbal expressions of appreciation

[that] have been received, not only of the Scheme, but of the helpfulness and courtesy of the officers concerned in it.'[87]

Another positive view of the scheme came from Godfrey in Salford. His intention was to ensure that his patrol men were visible on main routes, especially at peak times; 'to proceed by advice rather than admonition, and by admonition rather than prosecution'; and to give special attention to the safety of pedestrians, particularly school children.[88] The scheme was introduced in Salford in October 1937 and by June 1938 over 6500 motorists had been warned and almost 28,000 advised but prosecutions went up by 40 per cent from 201 to 336. Accident rates were reduced (fatal accidents fell by 40 per cent, from 12 to 7 in the first six months of 1938 compared with 1937 and non-fatal accidents by 20 per cent, from 209 to 166) and behaviour on the road improved.

> The great majority of road users show a ready willingness to co-operate with the Police.... Only in a few isolated cases has [police] advice been resented.... A distinct improvement is apparent...in the observance of crossings and road signs.... Pedestrians are responding by making better use of the crossings and safety islands.[89]

Lancashire and Salford, however, as well as having a previous involvement in road improvement schemes also saw the greatest reductions in accidents. The reported fall in accidents in Manchester was 8 per cent, in Liverpool and Essex 6 per cent and only 5 per cent in London. The scheme in London was handicapped by a failure to fill the 200 places that had been designated originally for the scheme. Instead a squad of 70 men, drawn from existing traffic patrols, was formed. Even more than in Lancashire or Salford, concentration was the order of the day. Four districts were selected and three 'targets' were identified: arterial roads, where the traffic was free and fast moving but included numerous cyclists and pedestrians at peak times (i.e., when factories opened and closed); some main traffic routes through built-up areas, including shopping centres, with mixed traffic; and certain roads with a heavy concentration of pedestrians and local traffic. Existing patrols were withdrawn from these roads.

Alker Tripp's evaluation was less positive. The evidence suggested that 'motor patrols are most suited to operation on open roads [but] almost useless' in built-up areas.[90] It was also the view of officers involved in the scheme that 'verbal warnings have only a transitory effect on some drivers and that summonses are the only effective way of securing compliance with the law.'[91] Although the evidence suggested a greater fall in the number of accidents on roads involved in the scheme than those that were not, this might have been due to the fact that certain motorists, especially lorry drivers, avoided roads in the scheme. Tripp was also cautious emphasising admonition rather than prosecution.

> There is everything to be said for still further fostering the practice of verbal warnings and advice, so long as this does not lead to licence on the part of road users, or create an impression of immunity from anything more serious than a word of reproof.[92]

As well as conflicting contemporary evaluations, there was one other obvious weakness with the scheme – its expense. It was by no means clear that local police budgets were sufficient to sustain the necessary intensity of police presence to make the scheme work once central funding ceased. In fact, the scheme was not renewed but was overtaken by other, more pressing events.

7
Motoring Offences and the Enforcement of the Law

Before looking at the way in which the laws relating to motoring were enforced it is necessary to examine the official statistics to gain some insight into the scale of the problem as it developed in the 1920s and 1930s. The inter-war years saw a dramatic increase (in both absolute and relative terms) in motoring offences. The Criminal Registrar was sufficiently concerned in 1924 to draw attention to the fact that 'of every three or four minor offences which occupy the attention of the police and the Courts one is committed by a motorist', but by 1931 traffic offences accounted for over 40 per cent of all criminal offences. By 1938 almost two-thirds of those found guilty of a criminal offence had been convicted for a traffic offence. Put another way, whereas the most common Edwardian criminals were guilty of a drink-related offence by the end of the 1920s they were guilty of a traffic offence – and the situation simply became starker in the following decade as the figures in Table 7.1 show.

In 1922 prosecutions for traffic offences stood at just over 82,000; following the 1930 Road Traffic Act they had reached over 200,000. Prosecutions under the 1934 Road Traffic Act are summarised in Table 7.2. Prosecutions for obstruction by all motor-propelled vehicles rose from just over 40,000 in 1934 to about 60,000 in 1938. The returns also included offences by drivers of tramcars and trolley buses, public service vehicles and motor cabs (taxis), but these have been excluded as they were numbered only in the hundreds. It is clear from these figures (which almost certainly understate the contrast) that the range of serious offences (dangerous and careless driving) are but a relatively small part of the overall figure, particularly for drivers of goods vehicles and motorcyclists. Even for car drivers (with the exception of 1934) only about one in eight offences fell into this category.

152 *The Prophecy of Nahum*

Table 7.1 Selected offences (per million of population)

	1900–09	1910–19	1920–29	1930–34	1935–38
Intoxicating liquor law	6494	3992	2109	1250	1393
Larcenies	1247	1166	1085	1140	1249
Traffic offences	1442	1989	5255	7268	11,102

Source: Judicial Statistics.

Table 7.2 Selected traffic offences, 1934–38 (by category of road user)

	1934	1935	1936	1937	1938
Goods vehicles					
Dangerous & careless driving	7,107	7,107	7,517	7,360	6,996
Other excl. obstruction	80,439	84,000	94,610	91,160	81,844
Dangerous driving, etc. as % total	8.1	7.8	7.4	7.5	7.9
Private motor cars					
Dangerous & careless driving	20,230	20,022	20,712	22,467	23,065
Other excl. obstruction	73,685	126,685	157,825	151,649	156,180
Dangerous driving, etc. as % total	21.5	13.6	11.6	12.9	12.9
Motor cycles					
Dangerous & careless driving	4,609	4,116	4,044	3,992	3,870
Other excl. obstruction	35,552	51,094	49,960	45,225	41,065
Dangerous driving, etc. as % total	11.5	7.5	7.5	8.1	8.6
Pedal cycles	52,702	66,310	70,261	79,410	76,373
Horse-drawn vehicles	3,137	2,760	2,488	2,184	1,586

Source: Judicial Statistics.

To complete the background Table 7.3 shows the percentage of guilty convictions achieved and the sentences (fine or imprisonment) handed down. Perhaps the most striking aspect of these statistics is the very small number of offenders that were actually imprisoned. Apart from the

Table 7.3 Convictions and punishments for traffic offences for selected groups, 1934–38

	1934	1935	1936	1937	1938
Goods vehicles					
Dangerous driving, etc.	7,107	7,107	7,517	7,360	6,996
% Guilty	90	85	85	84	85
% Fine	91	91	92	92	91
Other	80,439	84,001	94,610	91,160	81,844
% Guilty	96	96	96	97	97
% Fine	92	90	92	91	92
Private motor cars					
Dangerous driving, etc.	20,230	20,022	20,712	22,467	23,065
% Guilty	85	85	85	85	85
% Fine	92	92	93	92	92
Other	73,685	126,685	157,825	151,649	156,180
% Guilty	96	97	97	97	97
% Fine	90	91	92	92	93
Motor cycles					
Dangerous driving, etc.	4,609	4,116	4,044	3,992	3,870
% Guilty	89	89	89	89	89
% Fine	93	93	94	94	93
Other	35,552	51,094	49,960	45,225	41,065
% Guilty	97	98	98	98	98
% Fine	92	93	94	93	94
Pedal cycles	52,702	66,310	70,261	79,410	76,373
% Guilty	98	98	98	98	98
% Fine	89	89	90	92	93
Horse-drawn vehicles	3,137	2,760	2,488	2,184	1,586
% Guilty	96	96	95	96	97
% Fine	80	80	82	80	83

Source: Judicial Statistics.

offence of taking without the owner's consent, the numbers imprisoned never reached 1 per cent of the total found guilty in any category of road user, with the exception of taxi drivers for whom the figure was about 1 per cent (rising to 3 per cent in 1938). The other striking feature is the overall consistency of the figures.

The actual numbers imprisoned for traffic offences are shown in Table 7.4.

As the number of traffic offences grew so too did suspicion of, and hostility to, the police. The police response discussed later in this chapter

Table 7.4 Numbers imprisoned for traffic offences, 1934–38

	1934	1935	1936	1937	1938
Goods vehicles					
Dangerous driving, etc.	21	23	30	25	20
Other	18	24	27	43	28
Private motor cars					
Dangerous driving, etc.	94	109	118	133	123
Other	92	94	132	188	214
Motor cycles					
Dangerous driving, etc.	8	11	13	12	11
Other	31	32	44	71	38

Source: Judicial Statistics.

cannot be fully appreciated without an awareness of this 'motorist as victim' mentality. The thinking was summed up well, albeit in somewhat exaggerated language, in an article by 'A Motorist' which appeared in the *Saturday Review* in December 1928 under the heading 'My grouse against the police'.[1] The police were seen to be acting arbitrarily, especially with regard to spending.

> We are fined not because we are committing an offence but because we happen to be on the road at a certain time, on a certain day, when the police have decided to trap it.

The innocent motorist was, or it was alleged, in an impossible position.

> Policemen, taking their cue from their supporters, take it for granted now that motorists, like Habakkuk, are always in the wrong, and if they are not committing crime are just about to or have come fresh from its commission. We are trapped on the roads, hunted from one parking place to another, shouted at, bullied, cursed here from going too slow, fined there for going too fast, persecuted in every conceivable way.

As a consequence the motorist believes that the police

> have ceased to be peace keepers and have become our enemies with the consequence that [h]is [sic] subconscious mind responds to the injustice and persecution that he suffers and breeds in him contempt

for the law and hatred for the outward symbol of the inner tyranny that oppresses him.

Against this general background needs to be set the third element of police strategy: discretionary enforcement of the law, which overlapped with and indeed was part of the educational role. There was nothing new in this. Policemen had for long been well aware that knowing when not to enforce the law was important in maintaining popular support. Discretion became even more important with regard to motoring because of the new social dynamics that were involved. Very few middle- or upper-class Edwardians fell foul of the police. Policing was largely concerned with the regulation and disciplining of the unruly working classes. The working-class 'bobby' was, in the eyes of middle-class observers, essentially a servant. This was to change with the advent and growth of private car ownership. Even before the First World War, there were complaints that errant motorists were refusing to give their names or even stop when requested to do so by the police. Indeed, motoring organisations (RAC and AA) in the early twentieth century were quick to accuse the police of unfairly persecuting motorists. As the number of 'restrictions' on motorists increased in the inter-war years (and as car ownership itself expanded, mainly among the middle classes) the potential for conflict increased markedly. The dangers of alienating middle-class support were a source of concern for many police chiefs, even those who were critical of the selfish behaviour of many motorists. A new modus vivendi had to be created and one obvious tactic was to give motorists a period of grace in which to take on board their legal responsibilities before the full force of the law was brought to bear on them. Thus, for example, when new regulations were introduced in London in 1935, Trenchard introduced an experimental period in which 'offenders against the crossing regulations would be reminded of their obligations without being prosecuted'.[2] *The Times* supported this approach, arguing that the police in London 'are in the main more anxious to use tact and advice than abuse and punishment'.[3] Similarly the police in Sunderland were praised for their success in 'persuading the users of the road' to comply with traffic laws.[4]

Enforcement of the law was complicated by three further considerations. The first related to the inappropriateness of the law relating to road traffic and which had been largely inherited from late Victorian and Edwardian days; the second concerned the attitude and actions (some would say ambivalence) of other involved parties, notably the magistracy. The inappropriateness of the law was not something that could be easily remedied. There were strongly held and diametrically opposed views, especially on such key questions as speed limits, and there was a very real sense in which the solution that emerged in the mid-1930s was the outcome of a process of trial and error in which the principal victims were pedestrians and other vulnerable road users whose lives were lost in numbers that shocked contemporary opinion. Magisterial attitudes were similarly complex. There was nothing new in magistrates and police being at odds over the enforcement of a particular law; nor in magistrates themselves having markedly different opinions on a particular piece of legislation. However, in many parts of the country, there was a concern that magistrates showed undue sympathy with errant motorists and that this was part of a more general middle-class perception that motoring offences were not 'real' crimes. The third consideration was entirely pragmatic. Prosecuting traffic offenders was extremely time-consuming and could have a detrimental impact on working relations with the populace at large.

The law and motoring

The laws relating to motorised road traffic in the inter-war years were an uneasy amalgam of old and new. The Stage Carriage Act of 1832 established the offence of 'Wanton and Furious Driving' that endangered others, whether by intoxication or negligence. The 1835 Highways Act similarly criminalised 'furious driving' as did the widely used Town Police Clauses Act of 1847.[5] Less obviously, the 1861 Offences Against the Person Act provided for a sentence of imprisonment (not exceeding two years and with or without hard labour) for anyone found guilty of 'having the charge of any Carriage or Vehicle [who] shall, by wanton or furious Driving, or Racing, or other wilful Misconduct, or by wilful Neglect, do or cause to be done any Bodily Harm to any Person whatsoever'.[6] In addition, both Acts contained provisions for obstruction of the highway. Such legislation was directed at horse-drawn (or driven) traffic but legislation specifically focusing on mechanically powered vehicles was passed in the second half of the nineteenth century. The 1861 Locomotive Act, subsequently modified in 1865, was concerned with the problems posed by steam traction engines and was intended to set severe restrictions on their movement. The amendment of 1865 reduced maximum speeds to 2 mph in towns and 4 mph outside and added the requirement of three persons to accompany any horseless vehicle, one of whom had to walk in front of the threatening entity carrying a red flag.

By the last decade of the century there were growing criticisms of these restrictions from the small but vocal motoring interest that organised itself through such pressure groups as the Self-propelled Traffic Association and the Motor Car Club. Sympathetic MPs raised the issue in Parliament and in 1896 a new piece of legislation, the Locomotives on Highways Act (hailed by some as the Motorists' Magna Carta) was passed. Subject to certain restrictions, the speed limit was raised to 14 mph but the Act also contained a provision that prohibited driving 'at a speed that is greater than is reasonable and proper having regard to the traffic on the highways'. It was a formulation that gave rise to considerable differences in interpretation. The early twentieth century saw considerable and wider debate (indeed vitriolic argument at times) regarding the alleged absurdity of the speed limit and the alleged selfishness of the motorist. It was against this background that the Motor Car Act of 1903 was finally passed. A deliberate compromise (the inclusion of a clause limiting its life to three years was a deliberate ploy to ensure the passing of the bill), the Act contained both a speed limit of 20 mph (much to the anger of the motoring lobby) and a dangerous driving clause.[7] Despite proposals for change from the 1906 Royal Commission on Motor Cars, nothing was done to amend the 1903 Act whose life was perpetuated by a series of continuation Acts until 1930. Thus, the police in the 1920s were faced with a dilemma: should they seek to enforce a law that was seen to be increasingly unsatisfactory or should they turn a blind eye to the matter? In reality, neither option was open to them. The ever more vociferous motor lobby made it very difficult to enforce the law (particularly regarding speeding) without offending a number of high-profile and influential figures but the growing concern with the rapidly increasing incidence of traffic accidents made it equally difficult not to enforce the law, however imperfect it might be at the time.

Speeding

The 1903 Act, as well as introducing driving licences, compulsory registration and number plates, raised the speed limit to 20 mph, although local authorities could apply for a 10 mph limit in certain circumstances. Enforcement of the speed limit was a highly contentious issue in the 1920s. A number of different arguments were brought to bear by critics. Some focused on the practicalities of enforcement, highlighting the immense difficulties faced by the police in assessing the speed of a motor vehicle (especially when they were on foot) or the 'un-English' nature of 'speed traps' which (allegedly) diverted the police from general traffic regulation, let alone their proper business of dealing with real crime.[8] Others argued against the principle of a speed limit, claiming that speed in itself was not dangerous but should be moderated in light of prevailing circumstances. Further, it was argued that a speed limit had a perverse effect by encouraging motorists to drive to that limit even when circumstances dictated a slower speed for safety. Thus, speed limits increased accidents rather than reducing them – or so it was argued. Such arguments shaded into (or were a cover for) what has been termed 'automobilism': that is, the belief that motorists should have an unfettered right to road usage and to police their own behaviour.[9]

Whatever the motives behind critics of the 1903 Act, it became increasingly clear during the course of the 1920s that this law was largely a dead letter. In 1929 the Royal Commission on Transport concluded that the law 'is obsolete and most of its provisions are generally disregarded'; further, 'in many parts of the country no attempt is made to enforce [the speed limit] but it may be, and occasionally is capriciously enforced'.[10] Such 'flagrant and universal breaches of the law', it concluded, brought the law into disrepute. The Commissioners came to the conclusion that the speed limit should be abolished but only if the penalties for dangerous driving were increased. Such was the reaction against the failure of the 1903 Act (and such was the influence of the motor lobby) that the 1930 Road Traffic Act totally abolished the speed limit for motor cars, but not for lorries. It also made provision for a Highway Code – a decision that reflected the influential (though not universal) belief that a gentlemanly code for drivers was all that was required (Table 7.5).

Table 7.5 Speeding offences, 1931–38

	Exceeding speed limit	Speeding in built-up area	Passenger-carrying vehicles	Goods vehicles	Other vehicles
1931	25,555				
1932			3,912	32,504	5,580
1933			2,347	41,317	4,551
1934			2,122	44,966	3,851
1935		80,010	2,096	35,635	4,016
1936		93,050	2,240	36,565	4,907
1937		81,686	2,334	35,748	3,939
1938		83,858	2,342	33,093	4,085

Source: Annual Returns to House of Commons of Motoring Offences.

The (partial) abolition of the speed limit did not bring a reduction in accidents as some of its advocates had vociferously argued. To the contrary (though not exclusively because of unrestricted speed on the roads), accident figures soared and the carnage on the roads, the 'road holocaust' of 7000 deaths per year and hundreds of thousands of injured, became something of a national scandal. In 1934 another Road Traffic Act, among other things, reintroduced a speed limit – this time a compromise of 30 mph in built-up areas. This was welcomed by the road safety lobby and several chief constables, who were convinced that the 'speed of motor traffic is...a deadly and persistent danger'.[11] However, the reintroduction of a speed limit brought with it a range of problems, some old and some new.

The notion of a built-up area might have seemed no more than common sense to the supporters of the 1934 Act but in practice and in a rapidly sub-urbanising Britain, it proved more problematic and created tensions between police and local authorities, who wished to see speed limits introduced as a safety measure and motoring organisations who wanted to keep speed restrictions to a minimum and the Ministry of Transport which seemed all too willing to override local safety concerns and support the motor lobby.[12] The motoring organisations were certainly quick to challenge the implementation of the new law. In 1935 the AA and the RAC presented the Ministry of Transport with the results of a national survey that they had conducted. The campaign was launched in *Autocar* and invited its readers to send in the names of roads that should be de-restricted, particularly where lamp posts 'looked suspiciously new', and to threaten to boycott 'offending localities' in which there was not 'fair play' for the motorist. This may have been of little significance had not the Minister of Transport asked *Autocar* to co-operate with him in de-restriction decisions.[13] By the end of the 1930s the Ministry of Transport found itself in conflict not only with the local authorities in the major cities of Britain – Cardiff, Edinburgh and Glasgow, Birmingham, Liverpool, Manchester and London – but also a range of smaller towns and cities, including Birkenhead, Coventry, Gillingham, Reading, Stoke-on-Trent, Swindon, Wallasey and Worthing. Such was the concern with the actions of Hore-Belisha, 'gradually whittling away such safeguard as the speed limit as now administered does provide', that there was a heated debate in the House of Lords in April 1937.[14]

Enforcing the speed limit in agreed built-up areas remained difficult for more practical reasons. Determining precise speeds was difficult if not impossible in many cases, while speed traps, especially using plain-clothed police officers, were unpopular and threatened to undermine good relations between the police and the public. In an attempt to rectify matters (and also recognising a growing contempt for speed limits among motorists) many forces adopted a policy of 'persuasion rather than prosecution'.[15] Summonses for exceeding the speed limit in the Metropolitan Police District in 1937, for example, dropped by almost 30 per cent.[16] *The Times* was confident that public confidence in the police had improved as a result of the emphasis on advice and warnings.[17] Other forces similarly cut back on the level of prosecutions for traffic offences. In Manchester in 1938 prosecutions for motoring offences were down 20 per cent. As the Chief Constable of Preston explained to his Watch Committee in his annual report for 1938:

> The general policy of the police [is] to assist rather than harass the motoring public... the principal aim being the education of the motorist in his [sic] responsibilities as such, rather than the more rigid enforcement of the law.[18]

Dangerous, careless and drunken driving

Driving in a way that threatened life and limb had long been criminalised in the form of 'furious driving' but Section 1 of the 1903 Act covered reckless and negligent driving and driving at speed or in a manner dangerous to the public, the latter drawing on older notions of 'common danger'. Initially the legislation was seen to be an effective way of dealing with 'delinquent motorists' but doubts were soon raised. On two occasions in the summer of 1923 *The Times* complained that not enough was being done to deal with the danger of reckless driving and to demand more severe penalties for those convicted of dangerous driving. It had no doubt that

> the Frankenstein's monster of motor traffic... is a serious menace to life [and that it was essential] to punish with the utmost severity anyone convicted of dangerous driving, whether it is due to incompetence, to ignorance, to physical disability, or to selfish recklessness.[19]

Little changed and at the end of the 1920s doubts were again being voiced. It was felt that dangerous drivers (road hogs) had 'not been dealt with severely enough under the existing law'.[20] Some chief constables complained to the Royal Commission on Transport (1929) about the difficulties of gaining a conviction for dangerous driving, especially when there had been no accident. In particular it was felt that both magistrates and juries were reluctant to convict on more serious traffic charges, especially manslaughter but also dangerous driving.

Statistics for the most serious motoring offences in the 1930s are summarised in Table 7.6. It is evident that the number of cases brought for manslaughter or causing bodily harm was small indeed. Although significantly greater in number prosecutions for dangerous driving were three times less common than for the less serious charge of careless driving. Surprisingly low, and not just to the twenty-first-century eye, was the number of prosecutions for driving under the influence of alcohol or drugs.

That a motorist (while driving) might cause the death of another was indisputable but were they to be charged with murder, manslaughter, causing bodily harm, dangerous driving or simply careless driving. Putting aside the small and exceptional number of murders by motoring (i.e., cases of a person being deliberately knocked down and killed), it is important to start with a consideration of the most serious charge, that of manslaughter. Although relatively few in number, police forces across the country were faced with a number of fatal incidents of sufficient seriousness to warrant a charge of manslaughter. However, they found it difficult to convince the courts. Across the country judges and juries showed a reluctance to find motorists guilty of manslaughter in all but the most blatant of cases. There was anxiety that after the 1930 Road Traffic Act juries preferred to find the lesser charge of dangerous driving and even greater concern that some judges were ordering juries

Table 7.6 Serious motoring offences, 1931–38

	Manslaughter	Causing bodily harm	Dangerous driving	Careless driving	Driving under influence
1931	64	23	13,116	27,134	2,130
1932	91	37	6,888	25,505	1,952
1933	114	59	7,925	28,088	2,064
1934	130	48	10,745	33,578	2,267
1935	120	27	9,301	30,574	2,478
1936	125	20	9,039	31,955	2,849
1937	128	28	10,003	33,723	3,040
1938	130	43	9,101	34,511	2,870

Source: Annual Returns to House of Commons of Motoring Offences.

to return verdicts of not guilty for both manslaughter and dangerous driving.[21] It was a measure of police concern that E. H. Tindall Atkinson (the Director of Public Prosecutions) addressed the general conference of Chief Constables in June 1932 on 'The Law of Manslaughter in Relation to the Drivers of Motor Vehicles'. Atkinson's talk spelt out the difficulties facing the police in bringing a successful prosecution. Quoting from Hale's *Pleas of the Crown*, he made clear the situation as follows.

> A drives a cart carelessly and it runs over a child in the street. If A have seen the child and yet drives on upon him, it is murder; but if he saw not the child, yet it is manslaughter; but if the child had run across the way and the cart ran over the child before it was possible for the carter to make a stop, it is *per unfortunuum*.[22]

Referring to the 1861 Offences Against the Persons Act which dealt with injury caused by dangerous driving, and recent judgments (notably Bateman – see below), the Director of Public Prosecutions felt that such was the burden of proof required for a successful prosecution that acquittal was the likely outcome and, therefore, some change in the law was required to make it less difficult to prosecute manslaughter in motoring cases. Significantly, he did not advocate (as some had) the creation of a distinct offence of motor manslaughter but argued for change within the existing law relating to manslaughter.

Manslaughter – an umbrella term for a wide variety of homicides other than murder – was defined as unlawful killing but without the intention to kill but this was not an unproblematic formulation. In general terms, as Lord Atkin, noted in 1937

> the law... recognises murder on the one hand based mainly, though not exclusively, on an intention to kill, and manslaughter on the other hand, based mainly, though not exclusively, on the absence of intent to kill, but with the presence of an element of 'unlawfulness' which is the elusive factor.[23]

Indeed, such was the elusiveness of this element of unlawfulness that very few motorists were found guilty of manslaughter. As the figures in Table 7.7 reveal, of the small number of cases brought (on average only slightly over 100 a year) 80 per cent went to trial but almost three-quarters of those facing trial were acquitted of the manslaughter charge, though roughly half of these were found guilty of the lesser charge of dangerous driving. The high percentage of cases in which the

Table 7.7 Manslaughter (motoring) outcomes, 1930–38

	1930	1931	1932	1933	1934	1935	1936	1937	1938	Av.
Manslaughter										
Total cases	70	64	91	114	130	120	125	128	130	108
Case w/d or dismissed	12	18	18	31	30	27	20	34	28	24
Committed to trial	58	46	73	83	100	93	105	94	102	93
% Committed to trial	83	72	80	73	77	78	84	75	80	78
Of committed										
Acquitted incl. No True Bill (NTB)			51	52	62	65	77	71	88	67
% Acquitted			66	60	62	70	73	76	86	72
Convicted dangerous driving							34	39	59	44
% Acquitted convicted dangerous driving							44	55	67	55
Acquitted excl. dangerous driving							43	42	29	23
% Acquitted excl. dangerous driving							41	45	28	25
Prison > 12			15	20	31	11	18	12	7	
Prison 12–18			6	6	8	5	8	4	5	
Prison 18+						3			1	
Total local prison			21	26	39	19	26	16	13	23
% Tried to local prison			29	31	39	20	25	17	13	25
Penal servitude			1	0	0	3	0	4	0	

Source: Judicial Statistics.

prosecution for manslaughter and dangerous driving failed was seized upon by writers sympathetic to the motorist, such as Sefton Cummings. '[T]hese staggering figures', as he called them, 'must cause the greatest concern for they suggest to say the least of it, a recklessness on part of the police with regard to prosecution.'[24] The motorist as victim motif was still going strong. Equally striking is the infrequency with which a prison sentence was handed down and the highly exceptional incidence of a sentence of penal servitude. Feelings could run high. Defenders of the 'persecuted' motorist bemoaned the fact that many magistrates were 'old and bitterly prejudiced'; while 'the average witness is usually ignorant, unobservant and prejudiced'.[25] There is not yet the detailed research into the thinking of jurors and judges in such cases to come to firm conclusions. Undoubtedly some had little sympathy for the motorist and others were influenced by the potentially devastating impact a custodial sentence could have upon a person whose livelihood depended on driving, but there is also some anecdotal but clear evidence that some did not view motoring offences, even of a more serious nature that involved physical damage or even death, in the same light as 'true' serious crimes such as murder and assault.

Those who were found guilty were often exceptional, less respectable/outsider figures. For example, much publicity surrounded the trial of Luis Fontes, 'a racing motorist', who appeared before Warwick Assizes in 1935 and was sentenced to three years penal servitude. The case was stark. Fontes, who had been drunk at the time, had been racing another car and had been tracked, driving recklessly at speed, for some nine miles, before, while on the wrong side of the road, he smashed head-on into a motorcycle, killing its rider. He failed to stop at the accident but later, when held up by traffic, claimed that it 'served the motor cyclist right' as he had struck Fontes. The thoughtless, even callous, Fontes, with a string of convictions for careless and dangerous driving aroused the ire of the judge (Justice de Parcq) who condemned the 'deplorable leniency' of previous court decisions but it was easy to make a scapegoat of extreme figures such as Fontes.[26]

Such cases diverted attention away from more respectable figures who found themselves in court facing a manslaughter charge. The fact that many, including a number of members of the aristocracy, not least Lord de Clifford (who was tried and acquitted by his peers in the House of Lords), and a variety of Oxbridge undergraduates, were acquitted raised questions of the impartiality of the law. However, working-class drivers were also acquitted. Sidney Clark had killed one pedestrian and injured two others when he overtook a slow-moving vehicle and drove into three people who were returning from a Christmas shopping spree but the jury accepted his claim that the accident was unavoidable.[27] While there may have been some undue sympathy for motorists in the dock (especially if the unfortunate pedestrian could be seen to have contributed to his or her death), the real problem (which itself was part of a wider concern) was the unwillingness of the courts to return a verdict of guilty of manslaughter in all but the most extreme cases, that is, gross negligence.

Contemporary thinking about the standard of proof regarding criminal responsibility for manslaughter by gross negligence was greatly influenced by *R v Bateman* (1925) in which Lord Hewart had ruled (in a case involving a doctor whose patient had died after childbirth) that the appropriate test to be applied was that there had been 'such disregard for the life and safety of others as to amount to a crime against the state'. The case was cited in the important case of *R v Stringer* (1931) in which it was determined that evidence of careless or incompetent driving, in itself, was insufficient to warrant a manslaughter verdict.[28] The 'disregard for...life and safety' established in *R v Bateman* had to be demonstrated. In other words, it was held that though a death might occur on the road, there was a precedent for arguing that this was due to dangerous driving that was not serious enough to constitute manslaughter. This created such a problem with 'motor' manslaughter cases (though technically there was no such crime as motor manslaughter) that the government had made provision in the 1934 Road Traffic Act for juries to 'derogate the law' and convict for dangerous driving in manslaughter cases if they thought that appropriate to the circumstances of the case. The matter did not end here. Indeed, if anything the judgment increased the difficulty of determining the appropriate degree of danger, whether through negligence or recklessness, in the driving of an accused person in cases of manslaughter or dangerous driving.

These difficulties were highlighted in the 1937 case of *Andrews v DPP*. There was no doubt that the defendant had overtaken a private car in a well-lit built-up area in Leeds and, while on the wrong side of the road, had knocked down a pedestrian who was crossing the road and about to reach the pavement on the defendant's offside.[29] Andrews had been found guilty of manslaughter and sentenced to 15 months' imprisonment at Leeds Assizes. Andrews appealed to the Court of Criminal Appeal on the grounds that the jury had been misdirected and had not been informed of the option of returning a verdict of dangerous driving. The appeal was rejected and Andrews took his case to the House of Lords, where he failed once again. Lord Atkin, in his summing up, commented more generally on the present state of the law regarding deaths on the road. Referring specifically to Section 11 of the 1930 Road Traffic Act, he observed that

> [t]here can be no doubt that this section covers driving with such a high degree of negligence as that if death were caused the offender would have committed manslaughter.

However he continued.

> But the converse is not true, and it is perfectly possible that a man may drive at a speed or in a manner dangerous to the public and cause death and yet not be guilty of manslaughter.... If it were otherwise a man who killed another while driving without due care and attention would ex necessitate commit manslaughter.[30]

Undoubtedly, there were cases (such as that of Stringer mentioned above[31]) in which a verdict of dangerous driving was returned in a case of manslaughter, but the cases often involved quite extreme behaviour. James Adams was a case in point. A chauffeur, Adams had a set-to with some Jewish cyclists in a lane at South Mimms. Having pushed one from his bike, Adams drove to the top of the lane, reversed and then drove at an alleged 40 mph into another cyclist. The jury acquitted him on the charges of wanton driving and assault but, rejecting his defence that the accident had happened because one of the cyclists wobbled, forcing him up a bank, found him guilty of dangerous driving, for which he was given a six-month sentence.[32] But there were also a disturbing number of cases in which verdicts of not guilty of both manslaughter and dangerous driving were returned, notwithstanding fatalities in circumstances which offered few extenuating circumstances.[33] In one such case at Leicester Assizes in 1937 Justice Humphries was so appalled by the verdict of the jury that he made clear that he disagreed with their verdict of not guilty on a motor manslaughter charge and declared:

> I think there is a little hope that we shall ever be able to reduce the number of fatal accidents...so long as juries are terrified, as they apparently are, of the verdict of manslaughter and on clear evidence such as in this case refuse to convict a person of that offence.[34]

Dangerous driving charges, not all of which involved a fatality, were more common but could still be contentious. As early as 1931 an angry correspondent to *The Times*, signing himself 'A Justice', complained at the 'extraordinarily different sentences [for dangerous driving that] are imposed, even where all the circumstances are the same, and some are so light that they do not deter drivers'.[35] In some cases, such as that of the Cambridge undergraduate and captain of golf, Kenneth Thompson, charges of dangerous driving were dropped altogether, despite the death of the unfortunate cyclists he had hit. A fine of £10 for driving without due care and attention hardly seemed adequate. Police prosecutions were not helped by courts focusing on actual danger, especially where no accident had occurred. In one such case that appeared before the Middlewich magistrates in the late 1930s, William Seagar, a heavy-lorry driver, was charged with dangerous driving, having been recorded as travelling at speeds as high as 40 mph (and averaging 36 mph) on the Newcastle Road in Cheshire. There was no doubt that he had been travelling at speeds well in excess of the statutory limit of 20 mph for his vehicle but, as no other traffic and no member of the public had been put in danger, the magistrates acquitted him of the charge. Superintendent Kingsman, of and on behalf of the Cheshire Police, appealed against the decision and in a High Court judgment succeeded in having the verdict overturned. In delivering his judgment Justice Humphries (again) castigated the magistrates for their misplaced leniency in failing to distinguish between potential danger (which satisfied the requisite section of the Act) and actual danger. He continued:

> if justices were to be at liberty... to say that the offence of driving a motor vehicle at a dangerous speed [as in this case] was not proved, no person could ever be convicted of that offence, excepting where there had been an actual accident or the probability of one.[36]

The outcome was welcome but belated as far as the police were concerned. Even so the House of Lords Select Committee on the Prevention of Accidents were unambiguously told of the continuing difficulty of getting a successful prosecution for dangerous driving, which created a real sense of frustration among the police.[37]

To make matters worse magistrates appeared unwilling to use the full powers of the law when drivers were found guilty. In London in the early 1930s, when the maximum fine for a first offence of dangerous driving was £50, the average fine actually imposed was £4 7s 0d (£4.35). And to compound matters further, many magistrates seemed to share the view of Justice Wrothesley who, when handing down a three-month sentence for dangerous driving, consoled the defendant with the thought that 'it is no reflection on you morally to go to prison'.[38]

For much of the period magistrates and juries had shown a reluctance to find motorists guilty of the more serious traffic offences. In part this reflected the fact that the defendants were often drawn from the upper echelons of society and were seen (almost by definition) not to be criminals in the true sense of the word. However, allegations of class bias can be overstated. At least one magistrate felt that 'the time has come [1935] when defendants, regardless of their social position or circumstances, would have to be punished by a term of imprisonment, even for a first offence.'[39] Further, many working-class drivers 'escaped' because of a concern for the impact that a guilty verdict would have on the employment opportunities of the accused. Nonetheless, from a police point of view – particularly at a time when accident prevention was an important political issue – it was all very unsatisfactory.

There were similar problems – difficulties in getting successful prosecutions, inconsistencies across the country in verdicts and penalties – with regard to the less serious charge of careless driving.[40] Indeed, the creation of this offence was controversial from the outset. The proposal was presented as a solution to the problem of the unwillingness of courts to return guilty verdicts in cases of dangerous driving, that is, creating a lesser offence. The Royal Commissioners in 1929 were unimpressed with this line of argument. They could not understand how any meaningful distinction could be drawn between the two, arguing that 'careless driving could only be held to be an offence if it resulted in danger, and if it did this would clearly be dangerous driving.'[41] As well as claiming that attempting to draw a distinction between careless and dangerous driving 'would be impracticable', they warned that 'if this proposal became law it could have the effect of rendering nugatory the severe penalties which can be imposed for dangerous driving'.[42] The government chose to ignore this advice despite the difficulty of determining the precise nature of the new offence. Lord Russell, in the House of Lords debate in December 1929 on the careless driving clause of the 1930 Road Traffic Act, made a similar point to the Commissioners. 'I do not know exactly what is meant by driving without due care and attention', he informed his fellow peers. However, as government spokesman, advocating the measure, he reassured colleagues that he had 'no doubt benches of magistrates will have no difficulty in construing it'. Thus, he concluded, 'I think it will serve as an educational clause and a first offender's act for the driver who might otherwise become criminal.'[43] Others were less convinced. Lord Atkins felt that 'if you say that a motorist who drives a car negligently is only committing a minor offence, you are giving away a great deal of what you intended to do by creating the offence of dangerous driving.'[44] Sir Gervais Rentoul, in a later debate in February 1930, tried to convince the government of the folly of its position. Referring to the proposal to create the lesser offence of careless (as opposed to dangerous) driving, he maintained that he could not

> understand the object of this, nor how any real distinction can be drawn between the two. How are the police to discriminate between 'dangerous' and 'careless driving'? ... it would be impracticable. Moreover, careless driving can only be held to be an offence if it has resulted in danger and if it did this it would clearly be dangerous driving.

Like others before, he feared that 'if this proposal becomes law it would have the effect of rendering nugatory the severe penalties which can be imposed for dangerous driving.'[45] Lord Cecil was even more outspoken. In creating the 'lesser' offence of careless driving, the government was providing a 'bolt hole in a motorist's protection bill which undermines the one thing we have got out of this Act: a somewhat increased severity for dangerous driving'.[46] The government ignored such advice, the clause was passed and it had the effect that the Commissioners feared. Indeed, the 1934 Road Traffic Act made matters worse by allowing juries to convict for careless driving if they thought the facts of a case did not warrant a verdict of guilty of dangerous driving.

The implementation of the law soon led to considerable debate about magisterial interpretations. And interpretation was at the heart of the matter. An oft-quoted scenario in the debate of the 1930s was that of a driver who ignored a Halt sign. As a matter of fact they were guilty of ignoring a traffic sign but beyond that were they guilty of driving without due care and attention, driving dangerously or driving recklessly? Clearly the detailed circumstances of any case were critical but critics of the law were concerned that magistrates (and juries) took every opportunity not to find guilty of the more serious offences and even to acquit on the less serious. However, as with dangerous driving, there were signs that attitudes were changing in the late 1930s, as the judgment in *McCrone v Riding* showed. The original verdict provides an insight into the latitude allowed to motorists. The defendant was a learner driver who had knocked down two pedestrians, walking on the road, there being no footpath, at an acute bend in the road. At the trial the magistrates agreed that 'the accident was due to the inexperience and lack of skill of [the driver] who had become confused and failed to steer so as to avoid the pedestrians or slacken speed in time or to stop.' Had this not been a learner driver, the magistrates would have returned a verdict of guilty on these facts but dismissed the case because 'the respondent was exercising all the skill to be expected from a person with his short experience.'[47] An appeal in the name of Superintendent McCrone of the Lancashire Police was upheld. In his judgment Lord Hewart made clear that there was 'an objective standard, impersonal and universal, fixed in relation to the safety of other users of the highway... [and] not related to the degree of proficiency or degree of skill attained by an individual driver'. Chiding the magistrates for 'an error due to a kind of benevolence,' he concluded that 'there are not two standards, but that there is one standard only... not related to the proficiency of the driver, but governed by the essential needs of the public on the highway.'[48]

Another area that created both concern and difficulty for the police was drunken driving. The annual reports of various chief constables contained repeated references to the blight caused by the irresponsible drunken driver.[49] There was also concern that magistrates were not acting with sufficient firmness. Archibald Wilson asked 'the Justices [in Liverpool] to consider whether the penalties imposed in the past have been sufficiently heavy to act as a deterrent'.[50] However, what appeared on the surface to be straightforward proved more complex on closer examination. Under the 1925 Criminal Justice Act it was an offence to be drunk in charge of a mechanically propelled vehicle but what precisely constituted being drunk? It was a question more easily asked than answered. Police frustration was clear. 'These attempts at definition may provide the magistrate with puzzles, but the policeman in his duty of protecting the public must still be guided by his common sense.'[51] There was also anger that charges were dismissed on the advice of doctors, who had not seen the accused 'at the material time' and there was a widespread feeling, shared by some outside the police, that 'the whole thing [that is, the prosecution of drunken drivers] has been fogged by the legal and medical professions, and especially the medical profession.'[52] But the appeal to common sense ('Drunk means drunk...') or to the judgement of 'the man in the street [who] is a better judge of whether a man is drunk or sober than is a medical man' was unconvincing and unsatisfactory.

The 1930 Road Traffic Act attempted to clarify matters by making it an offence to drive in a public place 'when under the influence of drink or a drug to such an extent as to be incapable of having proper control of the vehicle' but, as no maximum consumption of alcohol was specified, this still left the problem of establishing incapability. The driver who fell from his cab or car and crawled along the pavement left little for the police to demonstrate but what of other, less clear-cut cases? Doctors were called upon but many of the tests that were used appeared somewhat arbitrary. The ability to hop on one leg or to walk along a straight line might provide an indication of drunkenness (or maybe not) but stumbling over long words or tongue twisters was not the most rigorous of tests, even of those whose education and intellectual predilections led them to use a multi-syllabic vocabulary or indulge in verbal gymnastics with ragged rascals and rocks! And what was one to make of the bow tie test? It was little wonder that defence counsels (and the press) could make fun of bumbling police and their ridiculous measures.[53]

For the police the unwillingness of courts to give them what they saw as rightfully expected support was a source of frustration but experiences did vary across the country. Some magistrates took the initiative. Perhaps the best known example came from Kingston upon Thames where, in light of the increasing number of serious accidents, particularly on the notorious Kingston by-pass, the magistrate 'had come to the conclusion... that the penalties previously imposed had not proved sufficient to act as a deterrent to selfish and impatient drivers' and decided that protection of the public required them to 'exercise more fully their power under the Road Traffic Act in an endeavour to eradicate the evil'.[54] No doubt this delighted the Surrey Police but not all forces were so fortunate. John Maxwell, Chief Constable of Manchester, referred in his report for 1932 of 'the difficulties encountered when prosecuting drivers [because of] a divergence of opinion at the Petty Sessional Courts'.[55] Somewhat exasperatedly he complained that parts of the 1930 Road Traffic Act were 'capable of too wide an interpretation'.[56] The Chief Constable of Liverpool similarly complained of the difficulties he faced, especially in the early 1930s when almost half of all the cases brought for dangerous or careless driving failed, due in part to the vigour with which such cases were defended. He took pride in the fact that 'in only 3 per cent of the total number of cases prosecuted did the police withdraw or fail to prove their case [but] it is worthy of note that of 45 cases which the police considered to warrant proceedings for dangerous driving 19 [that is, over 40 per cent] failed.'[57] Such was his concern with this situation that he commented on the matter explicitly in his annual report in no uncertain terms. The number of failed police prosecutions

> seems to indicate that either the police do not succeed in putting before the Court a proper picture of the incidents relied upon, or else that the Court and the police differ as to what constitutes dangerous driving. It is an unfortunate state of affairs as nothing more depresses

police activity than adverse decisions in Court, and there can be no doubt that there is still a good deal of dangerous driving which ought to be checked.[58]

The situation, however, was not unchanging. In 1935, and again in 1936, the number of dangerous and careless driving cases that were dismissed fell to about 20 per cent as local magistrates adopted a tougher approach. Somewhat tartly Wilson wrote 'the Justices [might] consider whether the penalties imposed in the past have been sufficiently heavy to act as a deterrent.'[59] The situation was more satisfactory elsewhere. The Chief Constable of Leeds publicly stated his satisfaction that 'the Justices support the Police by inflicting salutary punishments' on drivers convicted of serious offences.[60] Table 7.8 summarises the remarkable success with which the Leeds Police prosecuted various traffic offenders at the end of the decade. In addition, it should be noted that four manslaughter charges were brought, only one of which was dismissed.

Not all forces could claim such a record; and not all forces were as satisfied with the support they received from local courts. Indeed, the contrary was more often the case and in the evidence given to the House of Lords Select Committee on the Prevention of Accidents the chief

Table 7.8 Traffic offences, Leeds, 1937 and 1938

	1937			1938		
	No. charged	Conviction*	Conviction (%)	No. charged	Conviction	Conviction (%)
Speeding in built-up area	1677	1666	99	1272	1266	99.5
Dangerous driving	291	220	76	270	205	70
Careless driving	131	103	79	111	96	73
Driving under influence	25	22	88	28	20	80
Neglecting traffic directions	1256	1118	89	734	632	50
Obstruction	1664	1637	98	1557	1535	92
Lighting	985	796	81	726	602	61
Brakes	306	196	64	246	158	52

Note: *Excluding those dismissed under the Probationer Offenders Act.
Source: Chief Constable's Leeds Annual Reports.

constables still made a general criticism of the undue leniency of certain magistrates, the lack of consistency between magistrates and the unwillingness of juries to return guilty verdicts in manslaughter cases.[61] This was part of a growing and wider concern with the implementation (or as the critics saw it, non-implementation) of the law that could be traced back to the early 1930s. *The Times* bemoaned the fact that 'it is notorious that even the small degree of regulation imposed by the Road Traffic Act is not enforced'.[62] Very little is known of the detailed workings of the courts in dealing with road traffic offences during the inter-war years, but there are occasional insights into a system which generally downgraded motoring offences notwithstanding the intrinsic seriousness of the case. Thomas Pomeroy had killed a woman when his car ran into a group of hop-pickers in Kent; he had also fled the scene of his crime. However, he decided to appeal against his two-year sentence for dangerous driving. Reviewing the case, Justice Goddard made clear his anger, not just or even primarily with Pomeroy but with

> the magistrate who thought it proper, instead of committing the appellant to assizes on a charge of manslaughter, to commit him to quarter sessions on charges of dangerous driving and driving when disqualified. It was difficult to conceive [he continued] how any magistrate could have thought it proper to deal with the present case on a minor charge.[63]

This, however, was the problem: many magistrates (and juries) took the view that motoring offences were, for the most part, minor matters. And this was true also of summary courts as an important study of Clerkenwell court lends support to the argument that motoring offences were not viewed as 'proper crimes' and as such were more likely to be dismissed or to incur low-level penalties for those found guilty of them.[64] Despite (or perhaps because of) the rising volume of motoring offences – they accounted for two in every five cases in the late 1930s compared with less than one in ten in 1913 – the Clerkenwell magistrates showed no great willingness to use the full force of the law. In 1938 eight out of nine prosecutions for dangerous driving were dismissed and the defendant sentenced for careless driving.[65] The one case that was not treated in the same way involved a charge of reckless driving and causing grievous bodily harm and was eventually tried at quarter sessions. The fines imposed for careless driving were hardly punitive. The law provided for a maximum fine of £20; the national average fine was £2; and Clerkenwell magistrates' average fine was little more than

£1.50. Similarly with speeding offences: the statutory maximum fine was £20 but the national average was a mere £1.30 and the Clerkenwell average £1.10.

Despite claims by the motoring organisations that motorists were victims of over-zealous police and courts, the evidence from across the country does not fully support this contention. Exceptionally a bench of magistrates would make a public stand on the need to take a tougher stance and it was also the case that some judges took a firm line on offending motorists. Several chief constables also complained that many motorists were committing serious (as well as less serious) offences for which they were neither apprehended nor punished but the motoring organisations could point to the official statistics for prosecutions for motoring offences in the 1930s that suggested significant variations between both counties and boroughs.

The number of prosecutions for the most serious motoring offences, that is, a charge of manslaughter inflicting bodily harm, were relatively few in number and were to be largely found in London and the larger counties such as Lancashire and the West Riding of Yorkshire. But there were some important exceptions, particularly when prosecutions are related to population size.[66] In Norfolk, particularly, but also in Wiltshire, Derbyshire and, to a lesser extent, Cheshire, per capita prosecutions for manslaughter were significantly higher. Prosecution rates for dangerous driving also varied markedly. In the early 1930s the rate in Cheshire was almost four times that of neighbouring Lancashire. Throughout the decade prosecution rates were highest in Oxfordshire and Wiltshire, among the lowest in Leicestershire and Surrey. Prosecutions for careless driving were more common than for dangerous driving but again motorists in Oxfordshire, Wiltshire, Staffordshire and (to a slightly lesser extent) Cheshire were more likely to be prosecuted than those in Leicester, Kent and Surrey. To complicate matters further, prosecution rates (which increased in almost all counties across the decade) increased more markedly in certain counties such as Bedfordshire, Derbyshire and Warwickshire. The situation across the boroughs was very similar. Most manslaughter (or bodily harm) prosecutions came from the large cities but in the early 1930s Derby saw more manslaughter prosecutions than Manchester, Bradford more than Birmingham or Liverpool. Indeed, certain places, for example, Leicester, Macclesfield, Walsall, Wolverhampton and York, saw no motorist charged with manslaughter. Similarly the greatest number of prosecutions for dangerous and careless driving came from the great cities, but when population size is taken into account, towns such as

Derby (in the early 1930s), Blackpool, Chester, Colchester and Oxford (in the late 1930s) saw higher per capita rates of prosecution. In addition, there were marked variations between nearby towns and cities. In the Midlands per capita prosecution rates for both dangerous driving were higher in Coventry than in Birmingham or Stoke; prosecutions for careless driving more common in Wolverhampton than in Walsall. The figures for Manchester and Liverpool showed an even greater difference in prosecution rates for both dangerous and careless driving. In the West Riding of Yorkshire the police in Sheffield were much less likely to bring a prosecution for dangerous driving than their counterparts in Leeds but when it came to careless driving the situation was reversed. Tables 7.9 and 7.10 give an indication of the variations to be found in Lancashire and the West Riding of Yorkshire.

The figures throw up some striking contrasts but perhaps the most intriguing is that between Liverpool and Manchester, both with a reform-minded chief constable. In the early 1930s prosecution levels for dangerous, careless and drunken driving were appreciably lower in the former. From 1934 to 1938 there was a significantly higher prosecution rate for dangerous driving in Liverpool but not for careless or drunken driving. More striking is the contrast in the balance between dangerous and careless driving prosecutions. Before 1934 the ratio of one to three was in line with many other Lancashire towns (though not St Helens) but thereafter the ratio changed dramatically with a sharp decline in prosecutions for dangerous driving and an equally sharp increase in prosecutions for careless driving. In contrast, in Liverpool the dangerous driving/careless driving ratio was unusually low (at one to one) and remained so as prosecutions for both dangerous and careless driving rose markedly in the latter years of the 1930s. It is also worth noting the generally low level of prosecutions for driving under the influence of drink or drugs, though Bolton, Manchester and Salford were a partial exception.

In contrast to Lancashire, in the West Riding of Yorkshire there was, generally speaking and spectacularly so in the case of Halifax, a higher ratio between dangerous driving and careless driving prosecutions. But there were exceptions. The police in Wakefield (in the early 1930s), Huddersfield and particularly Leeds (in the mid- and late 1930s) were more likely to bring charges of dangerous driving. But are we to believe that the streets of Leeds were beset with significantly more dangerous drivers than Bradford or Sheffield? Or that Halifax's roads were appreciably less dangerous than those of nearby Huddersfield?

Table 7.9 Prosecution rates (per 000,000 population) for serious motoring offences in selected towns and cities in Lancashire in the 1930s

		Manslaughter	Dangerous driving (DD)	Careless driving (CD)	Ratio DD/CD	Drink driving
Blackburn	1931–33	0	57	225	1:4	30
	1934–38	65	553	1878	1:4	276
Blackpool	1931–33	7	160	353	1:2	75
	1934–38	59	1020	2245	1:2	529
Bolton	1931–33	8	90	130	1:1.5	28
	1934–38	0	333	938	1:3	249
Liverpool	1931–33	1	88	89	1:1.0	27
	1934–38	8	963	780	1:0.8	186
Manchester	1931–33	2	394	1100	1:3	92
	1934–38	12	148	3839	1:26	560
Preston	1931–33	3	204	499	1:2.5	48
	1934–38	8	664	2647	1:4	303
St Helens	1931–33	3	37	542	1:15	28
	1934–38	19	140	1664	1:12	122
Salford	1931–33	3	176	891	1:5.0	37
	1934–38	9	561	1722	1:3.0	417
Wigan	1931–33	4	94	180	1:2.0	43
	1934–38	12	553	1259	1.2.0	506

Source: Annual Returns to the House of Commons of Motoring Offences.

Table 7.10 Prosecution rates (per 000,000 population) for serious motoring offences in selected towns and cities in the West Riding of Yorkshire in the 1930s

		Manslaughter	Dangerous driving (DD)	Careless driving (CD)	Ratio DD/CD	Drink driving
Bradford	1931–33	6	31	581	1:19	88
	1934–38	30	379	2916	1:8	426
Halifax	1931–33	3	44	388	1:9	37
	1934–38	0	43	4347	1:101	286
Huddersfield	1931–33	3	83	599	1:7	32
	1934–38	18	1035	4159	1:4	230
Leeds	1931–33	0	100	320	1:3	55
	1934–38	21	2574	2139	1:0.8	323
Sheffield	1931–33	2	31	697	1:22	31
	1934–38	2	430	4654	1:11	178
Wakefield	1931–33	0	192	282	1:1.5	102
	1934–38	34	475	1966	1:4	712

Source: Annual Returns to the House of Commons of Motoring Offences.

Three general points need to be made about these figures. First, and most obviously, they gave some credence to the complaints of the AA and the RAC that the relevant laws were not enforced consistently and that, as a consequence, the unfortunate motorist who drove in Liverpool or Leeds, or in Oxfordshire or Wiltshire, was more likely to fall foul of the law than his equally innocent/guilty fellow driver in Halifax or St Helens, or in Bedfordshire or Kent. Second, and equally obvious, such perceptions created difficulties for police forces dealing (to a large extent) with a new group of offenders, many of whom were inclined to view the police as their servants, not their masters. Finally, these figures throw light on the very different ways in which the various semi-autonomous forces in the country – some led by reformist chief constables, others not – struggled to find a strategy to deal with the range of problems created by an increasingly motorised population.

Nor did the governments of the day show any great desire to intervene to ensure the rigorous and consistent application of the various laws relating to road traffic. Indeed, and probably with an eye to wider political considerations, there were repeated protestations that there was no intention to criminalise the vast bulk of drivers who were seen as upright (if not always well informed) members of society. The Highway Code, as much as the Courtesy Cops Scheme, was predicated on the likely efficacy and undoubted superiority of a 'decent chap' mentality, whereby the motorist could be educated in response to an appeal to his better self, rather than a draconian implementation of the law. However, the government did become concerned with the inconsistencies between courts in their treatment of motoring offenders. In 1936 the Home Office carried out an inquiry into the practice of summary courts in handling four traffic offences. Under the existing law, conviction for driving under the influence of drink or for failing to have third-party insurance should result in disqualification, unless there were special circumstances that made this inappropriate. Seventy per cent of all those convicted for driving under the influence of drink were disqualified. However, in some courts as many as 91 per cent were disqualified, in others as few as 36 per cent. The figures for third-party insurance were more disquieting. The national average was only 38 per cent but the range was from 4 per cent to 100 per cent. The latter court might well have been observing over-strictly the letter of the law but the former appears to have put a peculiar construction on 'special'. Courts had discretion with regard to a first offence of dangerous driving but it was worrying for the Home Office to find that little more than a third (36 per cent) of those convicted for this offence were disqualified while in some courts as few as

15 per cent lost their licences while in others as many as 65 per cent did so. Finally, figures for careless driving showed an even worse situation. In theory licences should have been endorsed on conviction unless there were special reasons for not doing so. The national average was 47 per cent endorsements with a range from 0 per cent (!) to 96 per cent across the country. The Home Office circular stressed the importance of local discretion but drew attention to the figures, indicating that 'it is undesirable that there should be wide differences in the treatment of offenders' and suggesting that many courts were not complying with the intent/spirit of the law and, in so doing, were creating a sense of injustice that brought the law into disrepute. Magistrates were reminded that it had been Parliament's intention that the suspension or endorsement of a driving licence should be the normal consequence of conviction for certain specified offences.[67]

Governmental embarrassment was increased as the motoring organisations publicised stark discrepancies from county to county. In one particularly high-profile campaign against the Warwickshire Police, Sir Stenson Cook (Secretary of the AA) highlighted the differences between the three counties of Derby, Leicester and Warwick. In the first two there were 20 and 12 motoring offences per constable, respectively; in the latter just over 40. To make matters worse road accidents (per 1000 population) were highest in Warwickshire, leading Stenson to conclude that 'merely prosecuting motorist for pin-pricking offences, instead of reducing the accident rate had apparently the effect of increasing it.'[68] The pressure on magistrates to suspend or endorse licences led to a slight increase in 1937 but the problem of variation between magistrates remained as complaints at Westminster testify.[69]

More common and for safety-minded police, equally worrying, were a range of offences that involved the neglect of traffic controls (human or mechanical), failure to stop after or report an accident or related to insurance (Tables 7.11 and 7.12). These figures (any more than those for dangerous or careless driving) do not give an accurate measure of the number of such offences actually committed, nor do they provide a reliable guide to changes over time but they are not without significance. At the very least they provide a measure of the police time devoted to such offences which, in turn, provides an indication of the scale of certain traffic problems and the seriousness with which the police viewed them. That said, the figures are somewhat problematic. Given the growth in motor traffic and the increased usage of traffic lights, what should one make of the relative stability of prosecutions for ignoring traffic signals? Or, given the rapid spread of pedestrian crossings,

Table 7.11 Failure to stop and insurance offences, 1931–38

	When required by constable	After accident	Fail. third-party insurance	Other insurance offence
1931	12,261	4,433	11,616	5,141
1932	11,228	4,090	15,456	5,268
1933	20,755	4,660	18,157	6,071
1934	43,263	5,348	19,527	7,359
1935		6,070	14,811	7,806
1936		7,014	14,692	8,919
1937		7,770	14,887	8,954
1938		8,546	15,199	9,267

Source: Annual Returns to the House of Commons of Motoring Offences.

Table 7.12 Prosecutions for neglect of traffic directions, 1935–38

	Police signal	Traffic signal	Pedestrian crossing	Others	Total
1935	4,124	31,427	7,503	5,940	48,994
1936	3,753	34,361	11,749	17,336	67,199
1937	3,587	34,144	8,675	25,349	71,755
1938	3,229	32,092	8,592	30,358	74,271

Source: Annual Returns to the House of Commons of Motoring Offences.

the decline in prosecutions for offences relating to such crossings? The figures might suggest a relatively rapid acceptance of new forms of motoring constraints among drivers but this is not consistent with the complaints made by many chief constables, as noted earlier. Alternatively, the figures may suggest an element of rationing, not so much in the Howard Taylor sense, but in terms of what the police felt was consistent with maintaining, or not alienating, public support.

Most common and most problematic for the police in terms of their relationship with the public at large were prosecutions for mechanical offences and for illegal parking. Despite considerable concern about noise pollution and road accidents, there was a widespread perception that such offences were not 'proper' crimes and that police time and effort could be put to greater effect elsewhere (Table 7.13).

It was a common complaint, highlighted and magnified by the motoring associations, that the police spent too much time creating

Table 7.13 Mechanical offences, 1931–38

	Identification	Lighting	Brakes	Noise	Emissions
1931	15,017	64,486	17,717	26,129	984
1932	12,546	49,928	19,869	17,073	724
1933	12,258	49,164	21,572	14,407	593
1934	17,963	54,369	24,628	16,600	649
1935	17,783	55,330	16,682	13,250	
1936	18,655	59,263	15,165	12,480	
1937	16,577	55,744	14,535	11,016	
1938	15,124	61,484	13,306	9,129	

Source: Annual Returns to the House of Commons of Motoring Offences.

victims out of innocent motorists while ignoring serious criminals. *The Times* spoke out on behalf of all road users in the summer of 1937.

> From lorry drivers to the users of the fastest or the costliest private cars, no motorist will ever be reconciled to seeing so many trivial offences of parking and so forth proceeded upon, while so many grave offences of bad and dangerous driving go unnoticed, or at any rate, unprosecuted.[70]

From a police perspective such offences were frustrating, time-consuming and a source of potential conflict with a growing sector of the public. And yet these seemingly 'trivial' offences were potentially (and actually) serious. A poorly maintained vehicle could be the cause of a serious accident; a selfishly parked vehicle could bring havoc to a town centre.

Conclusions

Game's observation on the impact of motor traffic on the work of the police was well made. The rapid increase in car ownership, the greater use of lorries and vans for commercial purposes and the expansion of bus and coach travel had a direct and visible impact on everyday life. In one sense, the problems were not new but the change of scale and the diversification of traffic usage in these years brought a qualitative difference that required major mental and physical changes. Old attitudes to road usage, which were deeply rooted, strongly held and not unproblematic in a world of pedestrians and horse-drawn traffic, were no longer appropriate in a world in which a wide range of motorised transport (of markedly different speeds and manoeuvrability) co-existed with horse-drawn transport, pedal cyclists and pedestrians for whom access to the road was seen as a matter of course – and of right. In the longer run, the horse disappeared from the main roads and pedestrians were concentrated on the pavements with specified crossing places on roads that were increasingly the sole monopoly of the motorist. Adjusting to this was something that took at least two generations. Reformers in the 1930s (genuinely concerned with the slaughter of the innocent and especially the young innocent on the roads) pinned their hope on the education of the next generation of road users while still in school. In fact (and putting on one side the complicating factor of the impact of wartime conditions on road safety) it was not until the 1950s that many of the lessons of road safety, for motorists and pedestrians alike, pioneered in the 1930s, were widely learned and internalised by the baby boomers of post-war Britain, the grandchildren of the 'suicidal pedestrians' of inter-war Britain.

If mental structures had to change, so too did the built environment. Towns laid out in times long past, streets and bridges constructed in an age of lighter and less traffic became increasingly unsuited to the emerging motor age. Some roads could be straightened, even widened; some town centres could be by-passed but the scale of the changes required was considerable, especially when set in the economic context of inter-war Britain. Traffic flows (and road safety) could be (and were) improved by introducing one-way systems, rationalising bus and tram routes and stopping points, providing adequate parking facilities, installing traffic lights, building roundabouts, improving road signs and road marking and imposing speed limits. Improvement was a challenge for central government, local government and a variety of public and private agencies but it brought specific challenges for the police. The responsibility for the efficient flow of traffic (and to a lesser extent the safety of the travelling public) dated back to the early days of the new police. Edwardian policemen (and police chiefs) struggled to find ways of discharging this responsibility; the pressures were greater as the problems grew (quantitatively and qualitatively) in the 1920s and 1930s. The sheer growth of road traffic and the demands this made on police manpower (in court as much as on point duty) should not be underestimated but the greater problem was developing a set of effective relationships with a new section of society which previously had had minimal and exceptional contact with the police. Crime in the nineteenth century was largely something that working-class men and women committed. With the emergence of mass motoring the middle and upper classes found themselves (potentially at least) criminalised on an unprecedented scale.

Although (as ever) constrained by wider political pressures – the stance of central or local government, most obviously – the police had a degree of autonomy and had to settle on a policy (or set of policies) that could be implemented effectively and with public opposition kept to a minimum. This was more than an old dilemma in a new guise. The growth of the regulatory state in the nineteenth century had increased the points of friction between the police and many sectors of working-class society but, for the most part, there was not the same frictional relationship with the middle and upper classes of pre-war Britain. The advent of the motor car changed this and there were signs of new tensions before the Great War. However, it was in the inter-war years that an increasing number of working-class police constables found themselves regulating the lives of their 'social superiors' who had long viewed the police as essentially their servants. Policemen found themselves in physical danger as speeding motorists failed to stop when requested; verbally and even physically abused by them when they did and subject to criticism and ridicule when they (the police) tried to enforce the law. The word of a single police constable (all too often, rightly and also wrongly enough to see a working-man found guilty) was suddenly insufficient when a man or woman of standing was in the dock. To compound matters for the police, a significant number of people did not view traffic offences as true crimes and traffic offenders as true criminals. When such people became members of juries or held influential posts as magistrates or judges the police faced even greater difficulties in enforcing laws which they believed were necessary to reduce accidents and ensure the smooth movement of traffic. Clearly, not all juries ignored clear evidence of (say) reckless and dangerous driving, but many did and in a random manner that further worried the police and government. Not all magistrates and judges took a strict line on the proof required to establish a charge of dangerous driving let alone manslaughter. Some, like Justice Humphries, were outspoken in their condemnation of certain magistrates and juries, but more were not.

Working-class mistrust (and more) of the police was nothing new and the imposition of new traffic regulations on lorry and bus drivers replicated many of the tensions that existed in pre-war Britain.[71] To the extent that a modus vivendi between the police and the working-class policed had been established before 1914 (and it would be difficult to argue that for the most part an effective balance had not been struck), these working relationships could be renegotiated to take account of changing circumstances. Middle- and upper-class mistrust and hostility was quite another matter. Never before had so many people from these strata of the social order been brought into confrontational contact with the police. The loss of the support of 'respectable' bourgeois society was not something that the police could contemplate lightly and yet there were laws to be upheld. This dilemma was never entirely resolved. Indeed, it was probably irresolvable. However, there is an interesting and important distinction between the two decades. During the 1920s the law (as it related to motoring) was inherited from the pre-war years and was known to be imperfect then, let alone in the present. Motoring organisations and their supporters in Parliament were able to make great play of the absurdity of the law and those who tried to enforce it but there was a real sense in which the police were seen as victims, in the sense that they had to enforce a law that was seen to be antiquated and inappropriate and widely held in contempt. The problem was essentially in the state of the law and the solution should properly come from the lawmakers at Westminster. This changed in the 1930s as Parliament passed two Road Traffic Acts and government played an increasingly active part, centrally and locally, in traffic affairs. Without suggesting that there was uniform support for the Road Traffic Acts (there was not), the focus switched more to police enforcement than the law itself.

The Road Traffic Acts of 1930 and 1934 greatly increased the powers of the police and, albeit with some variations across the country, the police took a firmer line against traffic offenders, as the court records clearly demonstrate. However, as the motoring organisations were so keen to point out, these variations in implementation threatened to alienate motorists and thus undermine the law. Even *The Times*, which welcomed the new powers given to the police by the Road Traffic Act of 1934, observed that 'the efficacy of the law depends upon the efficiency of the police in enforcing it' and warned that 'efficiency varies greatly in different parts of the country.'[72] Furthermore, and irrespective of variations in implementation, this strategy carried considerable risks of alienating influential sections of society and it is no coincidence that in the latter part of the decade there is a shift in emphasis from the prosecution of motorists to their education and encouragement as unselfish users of the road.[73] The success of this tactical switch is very difficult to judge as the advent of the Second World War transformed the situation that created a very different environment and a very different set of priorities for the police and the public. However, an indication of the continuing problem can be gleaned from the pages of the 1960 Royal Commission on Policing. The Commissioners, despite painting a very positive picture of the police and their relationship with the public, were sufficiently concerned with the problem of the relationship with the motoring public to devote a section of their reports specifically to this issue. Their reasonable suggestions (e.g. regarding uniformity of enforcement) masked a deeper concern about public hostility that grew out of the survey that had been conducted on public attitudes. Behind generally supportive figures lurked two problem groups: youths and motorists. The dissatisfaction of the latter had its roots in the unresolved problems of the 1930s.[74]

8
Cars, Crime and Coppers: Combating the 'Smash and Grab' Raider

On 24 March 1933 the House of Commons considered the second reading of the Banditry Bill. Its sponsor, the Conservative MP for Dorset East, Mr Hall Caine, sought to prevent 'the criminal class [taking] advantage of such a wonderful and beneficent new invention as the motor car'. The police were to see their powers of search extended and be given a new right to build barricades across roads while the courts were to be able to impose heavier fines 'upon anyone who misuses this wonderful invention in order to commit a crime' in the same way as 'the Firearms Act was passed imposing a more severe penalty on anyone who perpetrated a crime of violence by the use of a firearm than on one who used a bludgeon.'[1] The seconder, Commander Marsden, painted a lurid picture of brutal motorised bandits robbing helpless women, particularly in the countryside. The bill, he argued, would offer them protection and in so doing would encourage them to live in the country as domestic servants! Perhaps fellow members were unsympathetic to Commander Marsden's domestic servant plight for the bill failed; but this was not the first, nor the last that was heard of the new banditry. Concern about 'the new form of crime known as smash-and-grab', as Earl Beauchamp put it, was expressed on a number of occasions in Parliament in the early 1930s.[2] Indeed, Sir Herbert Samuel was forced to concede in April 1932 that there had been 'a lamentable increase in the number of what are called "smash-and-grab raids"'... the figure now [April 1932 being] about three and a half times as high as it was seven or eight years ago'.[3]

Cars had been used for criminal purposes from their earliest days in pre-war Britain, but it was in the late 1920s and early 1930s that something of a panic developed. The epicentre of the problem was London. Newspaper reports emphasised the problem in various districts of the capital but 'smash and grab' raids were also reported in other parts of the country. From Balham to Bournemouth, from Lavender Hill to Lowestoft, from Knightsbridge to Newhaven and from Tottenham to Thame motorised robbers were striking. Jewellers and furriers were commonly targeted but chemists, stocking cameras and binoculars, also fell victim as did the occasional pawnbrokers.[4] London detectives spoke of 'very large gang[s] of very desperate men' using very powerful cars in 'smash and grab' raids.[5] Private cars and, even more shocking, a motor hearse were stolen for nefarious purposes.[6] Reports in *The Times*, not among the more lurid of accounts, emphasised daring raids, large hauls and exciting car chases and (in some cases, at least) struggles between thieves and police.[7] Equally appalling were those incidents in which innocent citizens had been attacked and robbed by people pretending to be motorists in distress. The unfortunate Arthur Cunnington was one such victim. A Londoner venturing up north went to the aid of a young woman apparently pushing a car along the side of the road. Having left his car he was assaulted by two men and robbed of his wallet and papers.[8]

The fear aroused by these audacious crimes led to suggested solutions that varied from the extreme – shopkeepers shooting to kill – to the bizarre – shopkeepers to have glass 'cricket balls' filled with vermillion paint to throw at raiders.[9] Equally, the outrage at these crimes also led to demands for firm action, including flogging. One correspondent to *The Times* made a (not wholly accurate) comparison with the 'days of "garrotting"', noting that 'this pest was wiped out because the Judges made it quite clear that persons found guilty of this objectionable crime, in addition to their punishment would receive a sound flogging.'[10] He had no doubt that such a policy would be efficacious in 1931. Somewhat surprisingly, Sir Alfred Pease, a member of a distinguished Quaker family from Darlington, a former MP and an ardent fox hunter, was sufficiently incensed by 'this alarming increase of highway robberies, "smash and grab raids", and of "hold ups" in banks and post offices' also to demand more adequate punishment, namely 'a severe flogging [which] is from the humanitarian point of view far more merciful to the culprit.'[11] Pease touched a nerve. Other correspondents to *The Times* bemoaned the fact that prison was no longer a deterrent to violent criminals. For Lieutenant Colonel H. M. A. Hayes, drawing on 25 years of experience as a prison governor, the only solution was 'the cat'.[12] Likewise, Sir Henry Dickens, one time Common Serjeant in the City of London, advocated birching as the solution to this new and dastardly crime.[13]

At times the worries about the 'motor burglar' tapped into more general anxieties. Speaking in the same 1932 debate as Samuel, the Tory MP,

David Grenfell linked the emergence of this new crime to 'political doctrines [arguing that]... the growth of Socialist and Communist ideas of disregard for private property were responsible'.[14] However, unlike the street robberies of the 1850s and 1860s, these concerns with motorised robbery did not develop into a full-blown moral panic. In part this was due to the fact that senior policemen and politicians were able to play down the scale and frequency of such crimes. For example, Samuel, while conceding a large percentage increase in smash and grab raids since the mid-1920s, told the Commons that the monthly average of such crimes in London had risen from 11 in 1925 to around 20 in 1930 and reached 30 at the time of the debate. The 1932 level was on a par with that for the most serious property crime, burglary, but paled into insignificance when compared with housebreaking (over 300 reported incidents per month) and shop-breaking (just under 300 cases per month).[15] Further, the sharp increase of 1931/32 was checked in subsequent years but (and more importantly) could be used to put a very positive gloss on the response of the police. Even as the press reported daring raids on jewellers and the like, stories appeared of dramatic flying squad successes. In September 1929 three men, allegedly 'part of a very large gang of very desperate men' were sentenced to penal servitude after a 70 mph car chase which had started with Inspector Ockey leaping on to the running board of 'a fast Vauxhall car' that was being used by the would-be thieves.[16] As early as 1930 Scotland Yard's focus on 'what are known as "smash and grab" raids on shops by means of stolen motor cars' had led to the arrest of 'leaders of gangs, many of whom are now undergoing terms of imprisonment, with the result that there had been a marked reduction in the number of these outrages'.[17] The message became ever more forceful as time passed. By the summer of 1934 the public was informed of 'Scotland Yard's new campaign against motoring thieves, smash and grab robbers and other criminals who rely chiefly on surprise and speed for their success [which involved] 52 new motor cars, equipped with wireless and manned by specially trained officers'.[18] Less than a year later, Londoners were reassured that 'nearly 150 cars of various descriptions have been engaged in harrying the criminal by making it very dangerous for him to indulge in such exploits as "smash and grab raids" and armed hold-ups.'[19] Even more reassuring was the advent of the futuristically titled 'Q' or 'mystery' car which was hoodwinking professional criminals across the country and had them 'definitely "on the run"'.[20] The correspondent of *The Times*, calling on the recent experience of war, waxed eloquent.

The 'Q' cars form perhaps the most romantic section of this protective organization. Just as during the war outwardly disreputable, harmless-looking tramp steamers, specially designed to lure unsuspecting enemy submarines by their apparent helplessness but really capable of being transformed in the twinkling of an eye into miniature warships, equipped with death-dealing guns were used, so the 'Q' car is employed to hoodwink the man or woman with criminal intent. Many a desperate experienced criminal has had a shock on discovering that the car he was driving to some rendezvous has been followed by a vehicle he has judged on its face value as being of no particular consequence.[21]

The combination of new technologies gave a modern image to the traditional role of the police as crime fighters, for, in addition to the unmarked 'Q' cars, other police vehicles fitted with wireless could patrol large geographical areas, responding to information from newly created Information Rooms.[22] The Met attracted considerable attention but there were important developments elsewhere, notable in Nottingham. Chief Constable Athalstan Popkess was an indisputably controversial figure from the start to the finish of his police career. An ex-Provost Marshal of the Corps of the Military Police at Aldershot and having been involved as an intelligence officer with the Black and Tans in Ireland, he was considered to have exceptional qualifications and experience which fitted him for the post of chief constable! He was allegedly a Nazi sympathiser but it is not clear that his knowledge of Germany played a part in the reforms he initiated in the 1930s, which included the 'Uniform Cruisers' of the newly formed Mechanised Division. Equipped with two-way radios in mobile units and communicating with a central control room the Mechanised Division was seen to be at the forefront of modern policing.

Ever alert to novelty and change newspapers reported on developments across the country during the 1930s. 'Not only in London but in virtually every town and hamlet in the country police authorities are coming to rely more and more on motor-vehicles.' Or so claimed one enthusiastic correspondent of *The Times*.[23] A new paragon of policing virtue was being created: 'a new type of traffic policeman...trained to drive with the skill of the racing motorist, but at the same time to exercise the tact of a diplomat'.[24] But the new policeman also had the benefit of wireless communication through the various regional schemes centred on London, Liverpool, Manchester, Newcastle and Nottingham. A further much-publicised related development was the police telephone box which brought improved communication between a central information room and men on the beat but also enabled members of the public to make direct contact with the police, thereby creating (in theory at least) a new front line of surveillance.[25] Such was the advantage over the criminal given by modern technology that there were cases 'where men have been captured even before they could complete their entry into houses or business premises entirely as a result of the rapidity with which a police car responded to information from a member of the public'.[26] Thus a new and reassuring technological bond linked police and public in the age-old battle against that common enemy – the criminal. Or so it was argued.

Behind the flurry of publicity, however, progress was somewhat slower, much to the frustration of His Majesty's Inspectors and more progressive figures in various police forces. Looking back on the 1920s, Lionel Dunning lamented that 'progress has been extraordinarily slow' due in part to 'professional cautiousness'. Nonetheless, he felt that 'now...a spirit of enterprise prevails pretty generally'.[27] The impact of this new attitude was less obvious to his successors. L. W. Atcherley, writing only three years later, bemoaned the fact that 'the old system still lingers'.[28] Lieutenant Colonel F. Brook's comments in 1936 were even more critical. Too many senior officers failed to realise the potential of motorised officers while there were a number of places in which there was a 'decided backwardness' in the use of telephonic communication.[29] Indeed, those who were aware of developments abroad, particularly in Canada and America, were conscious of how little change had been effected.

Starting as the 'mobile patrol experiment' in 1919–20, the Met's 'flying squad' was the best known example of the modern motorised police of the inter-war years. Commissioner Sir Nevil McReady decided to experiment with 12 detectives, under Inspector Walter Hambrook, with a roving commission to maintain surveillance on known or suspected thieves. Their first vehicle was distinctly 'low-tech', a horse-drawn, canvas-covered Great Western Railway van with spy-holes cut in its side! The experiment was deemed a success and in 1920 two second-hand Crossley tenders were purchased. Somewhat surprisingly they were not replaced by faster cars until 1927 when they were replaced by Lea Francis convertibles (capable of a top speed of 75 mph) and by heavier Invictas (with a top speed of 90 mph) in 1929, by which time the unit had grown to 40 men under a detective superintendent but with only 6 specially trained drivers. The flying squad saw itself as an elite unit, set apart from the rest of the force, and enjoyed a reputation for success in its battle against serious crime.[30] While some spectacular successes were achieved and widely reported the fact remains that the flying squad was a small part of a much larger force whose methods of work still had much in common with their Edwardian predecessors. Much the same could be said of other large forces including those who were often praised for being progressive. By 1929 Liverpool had three CID cars whereas Manchester CID in 1937 had two cars for use on urgent matters while by 1938 Leeds CID had four 14 hp saloon cars and there were two other saloons linked to the city's police box system.[31] Lancashire County Police operated a force of 14 MG Magnettes, amongst the fastest cars of their day and capable of up to 100 mph, and which were first displayed and photographed in front of Lancaster Castle in 1933.[32] Traffic patrols, especially after 1930, had a dual role which supplemented CID resources in these cities. Elsewhere resources were even more limited. In the late 1930s the mobile section of the Preston Force comprised three motor cars (two of which were used for traffic supervision), a motor patrol van and nine pedal cycles.[33] The Essex Force, concerned with car-borne criminals from London, invested in two cars specially fitted with wireless in 1936 but for many forces traffic patrol men, often on relatively unstable motorcycles, some even on pedal cycles, were expected to keep an eye out for more serious criminals.

The use of cars in the fight against crime was closely linked to the introduction of the police box system, the utilisation of wireless and the development of the information or control room. Once again, progress was not always as dramatic as some press reports suggested. The police box system was a part of a wider process of adaptation to the changing environment in which the police operated – most notably suburban growth – and to the resource pressures that were a constant problem for senior police figures. The installation of what were effectively miniature police stations could bring greater flexibility and effectiveness in general police work as well as holding out the prospect of effecting economies in the delivery of the range of police services. Mundane requests for assistance could be dealt with more expeditiously but in the eyes of many the police box was part of a broader strategy of modernising the fight against crime. The need for good telephone communication had been recognised for many years but there were very real problems. Experiments with police telephone posts took place in London and Glasgow before the Great War but little progress was made. As a consequence in many parts of the country ordinary policemen on the beat had to make use of the facilities of the AA or of the telephones of private householders.[34] The police box, with its flashing light and telephone linked directly to the local sub-divisional police station, made it much easier to convey information to and from the ordinary beat constable and his superior officers. In addition, the public had access and could report suspicious or criminal behaviour as well as seek help.

The police box was developed in the north-east of England, largely due to the initiative of F. J. Crawley, Chief Constable of Sunderland and later Newcastle. In 1923 the first box appeared on the streets of Sunderland and a network of 22 boxes had been built up across the town before he left for Newcastle in 1925 where he introduced the system anew. With no centralised policy its adoption was left to the initiative of individual chief constables, such as Oswald Cole of Leicester or Percy Sillitoe (famously a later head of MI5) of Sheffield who was sufficiently impressed to introduce the system first in Sheffield and later in Glasgow. In contrast, other forces, including major cities such as Birmingham, retained their traditional system of policing. Even where the new system was adopted progress could be somewhat belated and slow. The police box system in London was started on an experimental basis in the sub-divisions of Richmond and Wood Green in 1929 but only 'after much delay due to the difficulty of obtaining the necessary authorities for the erection of the boxes on the sites selected'.[35] The system was gradually rolled out across the Metropolitan Police District, being completed in 1937 but from the outset there were concerns, partly about the rate of progress and partly by the response (or lack of) from the general public. In the early 1930s it was possible to argue that limited usage was due to lack of knowledge. As a consequence a campaign of explanatory notices and talks was instigated but with limited effect. 'The general public... still seem to be reluctant to make use of the telephones provided in the Boxes' bemoaned the Commissioner in 1931 and again in 1932.[36] In 1934 he was still lamenting the 'time it takes for people to accustom themselves to a new system'.[37] The publicity campaign continued including a high-profile appearance at the Radio Exhibition at Olympia in the summer of 1936, but in his report for the following year the Commissioner was forced to concede that 'in spite of extensive publicity there is still a noticeable reluctance to make full use of this service.'[38] Given the importance attached to the role of public information in the fight against crime this was a serious admission.

The problem was not unique to London. In Leeds, Chief Constable Robert Matthews felt 'it very noticeable that the public is very reluctant to use the telephones'.[39] Not until 1935 was he able to report 'a decided increase in the use of box telephones by the public'.[40] Even so the impact on serious crime appears to have been minimal given the absence of any comment in his reports. Other cities enjoyed greater success. Salford saw the first police boxes in 1928 and Major C. V. Godfrey in his report for that year was delighted with their success, claiming that

> in several instances where serious crimes have been committed the rapid telephonic circularisation of the districts and the despatch of officers by motor cycles has been materially responsible for the arrest of offenders who might otherwise have been afforded sufficient time to escape immediate arrest.[41]

In contrast, Preston was a relatively late adopter of the police box but its Chief Constable, John Watson, was convinced that 'rapid telephone circularisation...has resulted in the arrest of offenders who might otherwise have escaped.'[42] Furthermore, 'the general public appear to have become quite familiar with the usage of the telephone apparatus', though how much of this usage was reporting suspected criminal behaviour is not said.[43]

Manchester introduced the system at the same time as Salford but Chief Constable John Maxwell felt it necessary to mount a campaign of pamphlets and demonstrations to make known the potential of the new system.[44] In April 1928 Maxwell asked the 'public to co-operate with the police to secure the successful working of the new scheme' which was designed to change the system of the lone policeman operating a beat.[45] He added that 'the closest co-operation is essential for the preservation of the peace and the repression of crime.' He quickly had 42 boxes deployed throughout Manchester – in the B Division of Cheetham, Cheetham Hill, Crumpsall, Blackley, Moston, Harphunkey, Miles Platting and Newton Heath – all between about half a mile and three-quarters of a mile apart. Children were taught how to use the telephone facilities,[46] and it was stressed that the innovation was required because only '50 per cent of our existing beats are covered on the principle of one man per beat [because] the Superintendents have had to raid the beats to provide men for traffic control.'[47] It was claimed that the boxes would save the force having to employ men at a cost of £5500 in 1928 and it was extended throughout the C and D Divisions of Manchester and claimed that 134 of the 384 officers in those divisions could be moved to other duties once the Sunderland Box was fully introduced.[48] Within a year half of the city was policed by this method and he was able to report some limited success in combating serious crime. The public response was more positive. Over 4000 calls were received from the public but of these only 222 were to the detective department and only two were calls for arrests.[49] In comparison there were over 4000 calls to the detective department alone from policemen using the boxes.[50]

Positive public responses were noted elsewhere but the extent to which the new system improved serious crime fighting is not at all clear. For example, Henry Riches, the Chief Constable of Middlesbrough, spoke on several occasions of the 'excellent results' of the telephone box system, which had been introduced in the late 1920s, but the statistics quoted in his reports show that over two-thirds of the calls from the public related to fires or accidents requiring ambulances, doctors and hospitals. Nor did he suggest that serious crimes had been solved or reduced as a consequence of public information. While it would be wrong to judge the police box simply in terms of its impact on serious crime, in light of assertions made at the time of their introduction and later arguments that they enabled the recruitment of the general public as a first line of surveillance a word of caution is needed. As early as 1931 the *Daily Herald* suggested that crime had been made easier since the police box system was introduced, especially in the provincial cities.[51] It doubted whether the system would be further extended into towns and cities, although it was felt that it might have some merit in encouraging more efficient policing in the large and sparsely populated rural and semi-rural areas. It was evident that constables could not cover their patch and that the ring-in system was failing. Indeed, it was suggested that 'The abolition of police stations in favour of the boxes has deprived many citizens of that feeling of confidence they enjoyed when they knew in an emergency they could ring for aid to the station.'[52] The (Manchester) *Evening Chronicle* made much the same point in 1933 noting that the 'police box system has not achieved that all-embracing revolution with which its appearance was heralded.'[53] Indeed, the police box system was generally seen to be failing by the 1930s.

The police box gradually became a familiar sight on the streets of Britain but by the late 1930s it was being replaced in Manchester and several other urban forces. By January 1938 the Manchester City Police were introducing 34 Police Pillar Telephones in the B Division of Manchester, the one which had first used the Sunderland Box, and they were to operate alongside the remaining Sunderland Boxes.[54]

Indeed, for most commentators in the 1930s improved communications meant the use of wireless, rather than the police boxes and their replacements, which by 1936, 'must now be regarded as essential to the Police Service'.[55] Nonetheless, it was only in the late 1930s that progress was made across significant areas of the country.

In London wireless was used from the early 1920s onwards but elsewhere it was generally restricted to one-off special occasions such as monitoring traffic at the Derby, Wimbledon and other major sporting events. The potential in terms of crime fighting was obvious but there were technical obstacles that were not overcome for almost a decade. From the early 1930s Commissioners reported on the progress being made. 'In several instances stolen motor cars have been traced and caught by these means, the thieves being arrested in some cases whilst still in possession.' As a consequence it was decided that in 1933 the whole of the Metropolitan Police District had been divided into 52 areas by day and 30 by night to each of which would be allocated 'a car fitted with wireless ... [to] patrol continuously throughout the 24 hours'.[56] At the same time the establishment of a wireless school at Hendon to train personnel in the use of Morse was announced. Even more important was the opening of the 'Information Room' in June 1933, which could transmit information to the wireless cars (and also the 16 'Q' cars in London as well as to London telephone boxes and every chief police station). It was estimated that over 800 arrests had been made in the first six months of operation of the system centred on the Information Room.[57] In its first full year, wireless car crews and other policemen working in conjunction with them were responsible for almost 3500 arrests; this figure rose to just over 4000 in 1938. The system was further strengthened when the West Wickham Wireless Transmitting Station was opened in 1937.

Similar, if somewhat later, developments were to be found elsewhere. The appointment in 1934 of a 29-year-old civilian, Ian Douglas Auchterlonie, as a Superintendent to take full control of the Manchester Police Regional Wireless Station created something of a sensation. In fact, Auchterlonie had considerable technical skill and experience, had been trained by his father and was in possession of a licence that would allow him to set up his own radio station.[58] In the early 1930s he had worked with the Liverpool Police in developing wireless apparatus for use with all cars and motorcycles in the city's mobile squad. In Manchester the number of mobile units linked to police headquarters had increased to 25 within two years of his appointment. In addition, a wireless van, manned by two detectives and fitted with wireless transmitting and receiving equipment was brought into 24-hour duty. As Maxwell somewhat excitedly wrote: 'In effect the wireless van is really a Mobile Police Station.'[59] With the opening of the Heaton Park Wireless Station in 1935 a regional scheme was developed that included the counties of Lancashire and Cheshire, Salford, Oldham, Bolton,

Ashton-under-Lyne, Hyde, Stockport, Stalybridge, Glossop, Rochdale and Wigan.[60] The scheme was extended to include Preston, Blackburn, Bacup and Congleton in 1946, though the Preston Force had to drop out subsequently because the town was on the outer transmission limit.

After the early experiments with wireless the Liverpool Police embarked on a more ambitious scheme under licence from the Post Office and with the approval of the Home Office. By early 1934 two-way transmissions with police vehicles (including pedal cycles) over a radius of 16 miles from the Old Swan Station had been achieved. In 1936, 20 motor cars, 9 motorcycle combinations and 96 pedal cycles were equipped to receive wireless messages. Numbers grew slowly but only one car carried a transmitter, thereby making it capable of two-way communication. The initial geographical scope of the scheme was extended to cover two divisions of the Cheshire Force (Runcorn and Wirral) and the three boroughs of Birkenhead, Bootle and Wallasey. A year later St Helens was included. Further improvements followed when a new transmitting station was opened on part of the Allerton Municipal Golf Course. The impact of these developments in communication is difficult to estimate because, unlike his counterpart at the Met, the Liverpool Chief Constable gave no figures of arrest resulting from the use of wireless.

Other regional networks were developed in the West Riding of Yorkshire, the Midlands (centred on Nottingham) and the north-east (centred on Newcastle), and the Home Office played an important role in encouraging and disseminating information. The matter was discussed on a number of occasions by chief constables at their annual conferences. Three general points emerge. First, notwithstanding the pioneering work of the likes of Popkess, there was considerable ignorance about the potential of wireless among chief constables. Second, there were still considerable and ongoing technical problems (transmission ranges, wavelengths and especially problems of transmitting speech as opposed to Morse) that restricted development. And third, the enthusiasm of Home Office officials for information sharing and the development of a system of interlocking regional schemes could not be divorced from its wish to have a more centralised police force in Britain.[61]

The preoccupation with smash and grab raids and armed robberies deflected attention to the more mundane crime of car theft, although there was undoubtedly an overlap between the two. The frequency of 'larcenies of motor-cars and vans' was a source of concern in the immediate aftermath of the Great War.[62] Statistics for the whole of Great

Britain, collected at the Clearing House at New Scotland Yard, showed the problem of car theft to be dominated by London (Table 8.1).

These figures gave rise to increasing anxiety in the 1920s. The very sharp rise in thefts in 1926 led the Metropolitan Police Commissioner to bemoan the folly of owners who left their cars or cycles unattended but struck a more serious note by observing that '[s]tolen cars are used in many cases of crime, especially housebreaking and "tip and run" [that is, smash and grab] raids on jewellery shops.'[63] Such was the concern that in 1928 the Criminal Registrar devoted a section of his annual report to 'The Motor Age and the rise in the crime of "breaking in"' based, first, on figures for the Metropolitan Police District and the outer Home Counties (i.e., those areas not covered by the Metropolitan Police District). His figures showed that, while crime in the Metropolitan Police District had scarcely changed in per capita terms compared with late Edwardian times, crime in the outer Home Counties had increased more than threefold.[64] He then looked at cities and boroughs with their own police forces, while recognising that not all towns were equally affected by the coming of the car, and the surrounding county areas. Again, his figures showed that crime grew more rapidly in the county districts outside the great towns and cities. He concluded thus:

> The motor car enables the criminally-minded in the great towns to travel faster and farther afield into regions where they are not known and the chances of interference with their criminal activities before they return, or their subsequent arrest, are less.[65]

The car also increased the likelihood of theft (in his view) because the wealthy, thanks to the mobility afforded by the car, lived in 'isolated big houses... or in scattered bungalows' which were left unoccupied and unattended for long periods of time.

The crime statistics for London for the 1930s reinforced these concerns. As can be seen from Table 8.2 car thefts (and to a lesser extent motorcycle thefts) increased dramatically in the early 1930s and again in the later years of the decade. Successive Commissioners highlighted the problems that stemmed from carelessness on the part of owners. While 'in many cases [motor vehicles] are only taken for pleasure rides, the ease with which, burglars, housebreakers and other criminals can obtain the assistance of a motor car by simply appropriating one left standing in the street greatly facilitates their operations.'[66] The situation was not helped by the fact that it was only on 11 May 1932 that the Minister of Transport issued an order that allowed an unattended motor car

Table 8.1 Motor vehicle thefts reported to the police, 1921–27

	GB (Great Britain)			MPD (Metropolitan Police District)			% MPD	% GB
	Motor cars	Motorcycles	Total	Motor cars	Motorcycles	Total	Motor cars	Motorcycles
1921	380	636	1016					
1922	258	340	598					
1923	208	258	466					
1924	278	243	521	204	105	309	73.4	43.2
1925	438	220	658	331	92	423	75.6	41.8
1926	1092	376	1468	809	86	895	74.1	22.9
1927	1515	417	1932	1197	224	1421	79.0	53.7

Source: Reports of the Commissioner of Police of the Metropolis.

Table 8.2 Motor vehicle thefts and recoveries in London, 1924–38

	Thefts Motor cars	Thefts Motor-cycles	Recoveries Motor cars	Recoveries Motor-cycles	% Recoveries Motor cars	% Recoveries Motorcycles
1924	204	105	150	49	73.5	46.7
1925	331	92	246	38	74.3	41.3
1926	809	193	698	86	86.3	44.6
1927	1197	224	1131	125	94.5	55.8
1928						
1929	3265	377	3168	253	97.0	67.1
1930	4941	505	4759	407	96.3	80.6
1931	5086	304	4869	236	95.7	77.6
1932	5880	458	5714	332	97.2	72.5
1933	4486	438	4329	325	96.5	74.2
1934	3622	395	3477	304	96.0	77.0
1935	3835	329	3805	247	99.2	75.1
1936	5040	373	4965	298	98.5	79.9
1937	7203	541	7094	459	98.5	84.8
1938	9735	662	9577	579	98.4	87.5

Source: Reports of the Commissioner of Police of the Metropolis.

to be locked.[67] This helped reduce not simply the number of cars taken but also the incidence of thefts from cars of various portable items, such as cases, parcels and rugs.

The situation in the 1920s was further complicated by the fact that it was difficult to prosecute for cars that had been 'borrowed' as technically they had not been stolen. This situation was clarified by Section 28 of the 1930 Road Traffic Act which introduced the offence of TWOCing (taking away without the consent of the owner). The scale of this problem as revealed by these figures is shown below. To put these figures into some perspective it is worth noting that in London in 1931 (the first full year in which this section of the 1930 Road Traffic Act was in force) only 355 people (of whom 186 were convicted) were charged with this offence. In the same year just under 5400 motor cars and cycles were reported as stolen to the Metropolitan Police District (Table 8.3).

However, there is a danger of being blinded by Metropolitan preoccupations. Perusing the annual reports and public statements of various chief constables in many of the major cities and towns, the striking fact is the almost total absence of comment on the problem of thefts from cars, car thefts and the possible link with serious crime. Henry Riches in Middlesbrough, not entirely unsurprisingly, did not mention car thefts but repeatedly bemoaned the problems caused by bicycle thieves in the

Table 8.3 Taking motor vehicles without owner's consent, 1931–34

	1931	1932	1933	1934
Total offences	1469	1507	1400	1513
Total prosecutions	1446	1490	1382	1485
Prosecutions as % total	98.4	98.9	98.7	98.1
Total convictions	851	808	760	850
Conviction as % prosecutions	58.9	54.2	55.0	57.2
Imprisonment	162	198	168	159
Fines	661	583	582	671
Imprisonment as % convictions	19.0	24.5	22.1	18.7

Source: Annual Returns of Motoring Offences.

town. Bicycle thefts were a greater preoccupation than car thefts for Joseph Farndale in Bradford, John Maxwell in Manchester and for Lionel Everitt in Liverpool.[68] References to the threat of 'smash and grab' raids were few and far between. Indeed, such were their rarity in Leeds that Matthews made special mention in his 1936 report of a spectacular raid in which hammer-wielding thieves, using a stolen car, stole £2000 worth of rings from a jeweller's shop in the city.[69] Elsewhere Farndale made but one passing and largely dismissive comment as did Watson of Preston.[70] Meanwhile, Everitt was quite clear that joy-riding was a far more important factor in car thefts and juvenile delinquency an undoubtedly more pressing problem. In 1932 of a total of 176 reported thefts, 154 were cases of joy-riding.[71] Nonetheless, he conceded that some borrowed or stolen cars were used in such robberies which meant that the police had to take seriously all vehicle thefts.[72] There were also passing references to thefts from unattended cars, especially from the mid-1930s onwards but, generally speaking, the low key response to car-related crimes among provincial police chiefs contrasts strikingly with London fears.

Patrolling the motorist

The police became more motorised only in part in response to the growth of new crimes – or at least, old crimes in new form. There were other pressures that pushed the policemen off his feet and on to his seat. The most obvious was the growth of ordinary motor traffic. As well as men on point duty, patrols were needed to ensure the smooth movement of traffic and the apprehension of offenders, notably those who exceeded the various speed limits. Indeed, in most cases the initial decision to develop motorised policing stemmed from this concern with traffic management. Motor patrols for this purpose were introduced in some but not all forces during the 1920s. However, it was the 1930 Road Traffic Act that led to the creation of a nationwide system.

From the early 1920s there was a clear awareness of 'the advisability of improving the mobility of the police... [especially] in connection with traffic supervision'.[73] Atcherley expressed satisfaction with the progress made in the following year. 'Motor bicycles and cars have been more widely used for special periods and specific duties, with excellent results. Thus, "he concluded", the general state of efficiency so far as numbers and mobility are concerned, has been greatly improved.'[74] Atcherley's early optimism was not shared by other inspectors. For some progress was frustratingly slow, not least because the demands made on the police by their responsibility for ensuring smooth and safe passage on the roads were increasing rapidly. As late as 1933 Lieutenant Colonel F. Brook was still looking forward modestly to 'the day when certain areas of Counties, Cities and Boroughs will be supervised by Motor Police'.[75] Despite undoubted changes in quantitative terms, the traffic problem grew more rapidly. Brook was unambiguous that there was 'considerable variation in the effectiveness' with which motor vehicles were used and there remained 'much to be done' to exploit their potential to the full.[76] In addition, the growing numbers of vehicles on the road and the new demands imposed by recent legislation meant that 'the numbers of [police] vehicles in operation... are quite inadequate for this work [the enforcement of the Road Traffic Act] to be carried out even moderately effectively.'[77] In a subsequent report he struck a less pessimistic note but there was still a sense of 'work in progress' about his comments. 'Motor patrols', he conceded, 'have now become part of the ordinary organisation of police forces and can no longer be considered supplementary to, or a thing apart from, ordinary police duty. [But] there is... a widely different standard in the real value obtained from the motor patrols, both in respect to highway patrol and to their use for ordinary police duties.'[78] Unsurprisingly, Brook was enthusiastic about the experimental special motor patrol scheme (though he disliked the term 'courtesy cops') but it was a measure of the limited change made in the previous decade that it was only in 1938 that he felt confident enough to conclude that 'the real value of police officers equipped with vehicles is now more fully understood, and better use is being made of them.'[79]

Traffic control had been a major problem in London for many years but the growth and diversification of its traffic in the inter-war years greatly exacerbated matters and brought additional pressures on the Metropolitan Police. It might be expected that the Met would be in the forefront of exploiting new technologies to deal with these new pressures but the reality was somewhat different. Despite noting in 1919 the need for 'a considerable further increase of motor cars... in the near future to meet up-to-date requirements' progress was slow.[80] Motorcycles were largely confined to divisional detective inspectors and sub-divisional inspectors for supervisory purposes, though this was not without its problems because 'the solo machine is not well adapted for the use of officers of the age which enables them to attain the rank of Sub-Divisional Inspector.'[81] It was only after the 1930 Road Traffic Act that the use of motor patrols by the Met took off. The Act provided for a total of 950 vehicles of which 125 were allocated to the Met. The full allocation was not taken up immediately. After initial purchases of machines the Met motor patrol comprised 45 cars (mainly Morris Cowley 11.9 hp two-seaters), 51 solo motorcycles (BSA 4.93 hp machines), 8 motorcycle combinations and 8 tri-cars: a total of 112 vehicles.[82] The motor patrols started in December 1930 and general satisfaction was expressed at their work during the first months but it soon became apparent that there were a variety of problems. The ratio of cars to motorcycles was unsatisfactory and there were too many accidents associated with solo motorcycles and tri-cars. The latter were removed in their entirety and the former reduced in number as five MG Midget sports cars were purchased in late 1931.[83] The fleet was further enhanced early in 1932 when four second-hand 'high speed saloon cars' were purchased to tackle the problem of speeding coaches and vans. The older Morris Cowley cars were also deficient in terms of both speed and acceleration and more suitable replacements (Ford Tudor saloons and Hillman Wizard '65' tourers) purchased in 1933. At the same time the Home Office increased the Met's allocation to 140 vehicles of which 75 per cent could be cars of 10 hp or more.[84] There was a dramatic fall in the number of motorcycles as all motorcycle combinations used by the (renamed) Traffic Patrols were sold at the end of 1933. The late 1930s saw a reversal of policy with regard to the composition of the motor fleet. Improvements in road surfaces and technological developments meant that motorcycles became a more viable option. There was also anecdotal evidence that ordinary motorists reacted more favourably to police on motorcycles rather than in cars.

The search for efficient machines was but one problem. A second, and closely related, was the search for efficient drivers. In his report for 1934 Trenchard stressed that it was 'clearly of the greatest importance that the standard of driving of police cars should be the highest possible'.[85] To this end he called upon the expertise of Sir Malcolm Campbell to test existing drivers. Campbell's report, 'although on the whole favourable and in some points distinctly laudatory, made it clear that there was ample room for improvement'.[86] A driving school was accordingly established at Hendon in January 1935 which offered both elementary and advanced courses, developed with the assistance of another well-known motoring figure, Lord Cottenham. In 1937 a training course for motor cyclists was introduced as the solo motorcycle came back into vogue.

The problems, relating to both machines and men, experienced in London were to be found elsewhere but there were some striking variations in the timing of change. At one extreme was the Liverpool Force, which from 1920 onwards had a motor patrol. Initially introduced to improve traffic management in the city, it took on wider responsibilities for crime control but never lost its prime, founding function. The Edinburgh Force under Roderick Ross was another pioneer, starting its mobile unit in 1926, but for many forces the critical event was the passing of the 1930 Road Traffic Act; and even then the response was cautious. Leeds, for example, was using two motorcycles, purchased in 1928, to patrol outlying districts of the city but it did not create a dedicated motor patrol section until 1932 and even then the approach was cautious. The city was to receive funding for 'a provisional complement of eight vehicles, not more than two of which may be motor-cars' but only five – one motor car, one three-wheeler, two motorcycle combinations and one solo motorcycle – were in use in the early 1930s despite positive comments about the section from the Chief Constable.[87] The only significant change in the first five years was the replacement of the tri-car and the two motorcycle combinations with cars, albeit of less than 10 hp. The 1934 Road Traffic Act increased police responsibilities for traffic control and as a consequence 3 more cars (2 over 10 hp) were purchased and the strength of the section increased threefold, from 9 to 27.[88] A similar situation was to be found in Manchester, which had a road motor patrol, comprising six cars and ten motorcycles in 1931.[89] By the late 1930s the reorganised and renamed Mechanical Transport Department was divided into three sections: the experimental road patrol, the ordinary road patrol and general police work.[90] The first comprised 50 men (10 of whom were on foot!) and 10 cars and was part of the Home Office experiment. As in London a special motor school was set up to train all men in this section. The ordinary road patrol was responsible for the enforcement of traffic laws and comprised 16 vehicles. At the same time the force had 81 pedal cycles and 20 horses for patrol purposes in the city.[91] Elsewhere the new motor patrols were small in size. Preston in 1932 boasted one motor car, a motorcycle combination and a solo motorcycle, the latter two being used for road traffic supervision. Nonetheless the Chief Constable, John Watson, was also convinced that the three vehicles were 'an effective step in dealing with present-day methods of the modern criminal'.[92] Of the four cars in use in 1935, two were paid through the Road Fund under the provision of the 1930 Road Traffic Act. The rest of the section comprised nine bicycles. St Helens similarly had two motorcycle combinations and a Morris Oxford car for traffic patrol duties.[93] Nor was this confined to the towns of northern England. Luton had a one-vehicle motor patrol, funded under the 1930 Road Traffic Act while Southend-on-Sea had one solo motorcycle and six pedal cycles in 1930, though two Norton motorcycle combinations, funded by the Ministry of Transport, were acquired in 1931.[94]

Traffic problems were not confined to urban areas and, in addition, there was an emerging view among the police that motor patrols were more effective in suburban and rural areas rather than in congested town and city centres. Developments were also patchy across the country. The Lancashire Force was among the pioneers introducing a motorcycle patrol in 1919 – on the A6 south of Lancaster – but this was unusual. The force also had one of the largest traffic patrol sections in the country. On the eve of the Home Office experiment, the section comprised 110 men, though this was to increase dramatically to 441 after the introduction of the scheme. In many forces the few cars that there were in use were for senior officers. The West Suffolk Force was not unique in having divisional cars for the use of superintendents only.[95] Two motorcycles had been purchased by the Bedfordshire Police as early as 1924 but their use was confined to despatching documents from headquarters. However the rising crime rate of the late 1920s persuaded Chief Constable Major Frank Stevens that something needed to be done.[96] The purchase of 12 motor vehicles was approved but again the greatest stimulus to change came from the 1930 Road Traffic Act. So too in Kent where 19 BSA motorcycles were purchased for traffic patrol duty in 1931.[97] In East and West Suffolk six and three motorcycles, respectively, were used initially.[98] And so in Essex where ten solo Triumph motorcycles were purchased for patrol work.[99] By the late 1930s the traffic patrol section had grown to 25 but (as in Lancashire) the additional men under the Home Office experimental scheme brought a dramatic increase to 105 men.

There was also a more mundane aspect to the gradual motorisation of the police. Police work had for decades involved such things as dealing with a range of street accidents and illnesses in public and the conveying of prisoners to and from court and/or prison. An indication of the range (and the balance) of work undertaken by a police motor transport department in the late 1930s can be gained from the figures for the city of Leeds. In total there were nine saloon cars and three vans. Four 14-hp Vauxhall saloons were for general transport use, including the transport of CID; two of the same type were used as stand-by cars in connection with the police box system; a 10-hp Ford was used for the service of summonses in outlying districts while the most powerful car, a 15-hp Morris, was a reserve car for the use of the brake mechanic called to test brakes and so on. An 8-seater Ford van was used for conveying prisoners, police and light articles; a 14-seater Bedford van was used for conveying dead bodies, medium-sized groups of prisoners (with a facility to take male and female prisoners in separate sections), police and property. The third van (a 20-seater Commer) was for the conveyance of heavy loads, bulky property and large contingents of police and prisoners.[100]

Conclusion

The impact on policing of the rapid growth of motor transport in the inter-war years was profound. At its most spectacular it involved a new and dramatic form of crime fighting – high-speed chases were the stuff of melodrama! More mundanely, considerable amounts of police time were spent on traffic control, including the preparation and presentation in court of an ever-increasing volume of cases of law-breaking. These demands had a knock-on effect on the modification of existing police practices and the adaptation of new technologies. In addition, though there is not space to examine this in detail, the licensing of various other road users, such as taxis, made further demands on the police. However, in his recent survey of British policing, *The Great British Bobby*, Clive Emsley has stressed the continuities between policing before and after the Great War. '[T]he principal task of the uniformed Bobby of the inter-war years remained that of patrolling a carefully designated beat' particularly in the smaller towns and rural areas.[101] New and major challenges, not least the advent of mass motoring, are recognised but played down.[102] There is much force in this argument and it is important not to exaggerate the impact of the (over-reported) novel nor to underestimate the importance of the (under-reported) mundane. However, in emphasising the centrality of the beat, there is a danger of losing sight of the significance of a major socio-economic development that created major problems for the police which in turn led to significant developments in policing that in qualitative terms mark out the inter-war years from previous eras.

Take the example of London. The growth of road traffic created a range of problems – an unacceptable level of accidents, especially among the young; increasing congestion; and the rise of various motorised crimes – that put the force under considerable stress as manpower levels were, by and large, maintained but not increased. In response to this the Met devised a range of strategies – a more flexible beat system and greater use of technology including motor vehicles and wireless – that represented a break with past practice. Many bobbies were still on their feet but an increasing number were on their seats. In qualitative terms this modernisation of policing deserves emphasis. However, the quantitative limits of these changes must be recognised. Significant progress had been made, especially in the later part of the 1930s. The Traffic Patrol, expanded under the Home Office scheme of 1938, comprised 200 vehicles in an overall motor fleet of less than 600 vehicles. In a written reply to a request from Commander Locker-Lampson, the Home Secretary informed Parliament that the strength of the Metropolitan Police traffic patrols had risen from 522 in 1933 to 686 in 1937 but, and reflecting the congested nature of much of the Metropolitan Police District, foot patrols remained an essential part of the policing of London.[103] Indeed, commenting in 1938, the Commissioner, Philip Game, made abundantly clear that 'if there is to be any further augmentation of police strength for the purpose of accident prevention in London, I should propose to employ a good proportion of the additional men on foot.'[104]

London cannot be taken as typical but similar developments can be seen most clearly in the large cities such as Birmingham, Leeds, Liverpool, Nottingham and Manchester as well as in some of the larger county forces, such as Lancashire and the West Riding of Yorkshire. Furthermore, smaller borough and county forces were not unchanging. The stimulus to reform could be both internal and external. In some cases, such as Sunderland and Wolverhampton, an able individual was able to inspire change from within; in other cases, the growth of regional networks brought access to new technologies and new ideas from outside to forces that were less dynamic and innovative. In quantitative terms the bobby plodding along his beat was the experience of the majority but the number of those involved in traffic control – whether on bicycles and motorcycles or in cars – or involved in fighting motor crime was increasing. Undoubtedly, there were geographical variations between police forces at any point in time. Similarly, progress fluctuated over time but the trends in society generally and in policing specifically were clear and irreversible. The balance was shifting, slowly at times but inexorably. Great change would take place after the Second World War but the inter-war years witnessed the early shoots of these developments and the significance of this should not be underestimated.

Police traffic work, taken as a whole, had three major consequences. First, and in addition to increasing the work load, it changed the relationship between police and public in a critical manner by bringing the police into direct contact (even conflict) with a middle- and upper-class public that was used to considering the police as servants, not masters. Second, it encouraged specialisation, whether in the form of new units such as flying squads and motor patrols, or new internal departments dealing with specific issues, such as the licensing of public vehicles, let alone new collaborative committees dealing with, for example, road safety and traffic congestion, which involved the police and other local bodies. Finally, it started the process whereby the police were taken off their feet and put on their seats. Z cars were yet to come but Q cars had arrived.

9
Conclusion

In this book we have started to tackle two historiographical problems: first, the relative neglect of the inter-war years in the history of modern policing; and, second, the generally negative view of policing in these years among the few historians who have written about them. As a consequence of the general problem of neglect, we have deliberately adopted a partial approach to the history of policing between the two world wars. Important issues, such as the role of women police and the policing of working-class leisure, are not covered here except in brief passing references but will appear in later publications. Other key questions, notably the relationship between the police and the public, are dealt with in a selective, rather than a comprehensive, fashion. Nonetheless, there is a coherence to the main themes we have explored in detail and this feeds into our narrower purpose, namely, to offer a more positive interpretation of the development of policing in the inter-war years.

The responsibilities and expectations of the police as they developed in the nineteenth century ensured that the police were a workforce unlike any other. The need to be seen as impartial led, for example, to members of police forces being denied the vote until the Police Disabilities Removal Act of 1887. Even more contentious was the question of police organisation to improve work conditions. This was particularly true when police agitation coincided with wider upsurges of trade unionism such as the 1880s and the years immediately before the Great War. At such times police trade unionism was viewed with grave mistrust at best, horror at worst. The fear of the spread of communism after the Great War amplified pre-existing fears. The police strikes of 1918 and 1919 were dealt with severely. The 1919 Police Act was a deliberate attempt to provide an alternative (but safe) forum, the Police Federation, through which to discuss some but not all employment issues. Politicians of all parties were agreed that the police should not have the right to strike. Further, they were agreed that conditions of work and remuneration were, ultimately, the responsibility of government. This was clearly demonstrated both in 1921–22 and in 1932 when police pay was cut in line with national targets. In addition, there were many politicians who (in a tradition that dates back to Edwin Chadwick in the mid-nineteenth century) wanted to see policing controlled from the centre, rather than having control dispersed to watch committees and standing joint committees. Centralist sentiments, however, met stout resistance; in part from local politicians who believed strongly in their right to control their local police force but also in part from chief constables who increasingly saw themselves as a powerful professional force which should not be restricted by political dictat both local and national. The very limited reduction in the number of forces during the inter-war years, despite powerful arguments for rationalisation and amalgamation of forces throughout the period, is evidence of the success of resistance from the localities. However, the extent of resistance from chief constables should not be overstated as there was a sense in which central government and police chiefs had a common interest in reducing or by-passing local control. Watch committees and standing joint committees found it difficult to assert their authority over police chiefs deemed to be unsuitable, notably in Monmouthshire, where Bosanquet proved to be a protected opponent, and in St Helens, but also found themselves circumvented as changing circumstances pointed to the wisdom of regional and national co-operation. The increased use of wireless and forensics in the 1930s are clear examples but it was the need to deal with the problem of large-scale public protest and to prepare for a forthcoming war in the 1930s that provided major stimuli to move beyond localism. Significant change did not come until after the Second World War but the roots of change were to be found in the pre-war period. Despite the questions that surrounded his decision, the words of Justice McCardie in the case of *Fisher v Oldham Corporation* in 1930 are important in capturing the growing official view of the position of the police. McCardie was clear that 'a police constable is...a servant of the State, a ministerial officer of the central power, though subject in some respects, to local supervision and local regulation.'[1]

Much of this debate was conducted in terms of police professionalism. The Desborough Committee identified some major problems that went beyond pay and conditions and argued the need to improve the quality of policing. This was a theme taken up by various politicians,

Home Office officials and leading police figures. Greater emphasis was placed on training but encouragement was given to specialisation. Science was to be enlisted in the fight against crime and specialist detective forces were to be at the forefront. It is important not to overstate the extent of change before 1939. Many forces were too small to have meaningful detective departments and the bulk of crime was solved by traditional means. Nonetheless, in qualitative terms, the basis of a new, more technological, policing was being laid in the 1930s.

The emergence of mass motoring, especially in the 1930s, had a profound effect on the nature of policing. The advent of the motorised criminal, although often exaggerated at the time, brought about a greater degree of co-operation between local police forces and between the Home Office and the police, reinforcing other pressures for change in the balance of power regarding police control. Equally importantly, the rapid growth of road traffic led to increased (and time-consuming) new responsibilities that in turn generated new practices, notably the development of motor patrols, which further encouraged specialisation within the police and led to new practices in police routine. Again, the extent of change must not be overstated. 'Old-fashioned' beat work was still the norm for many constables, especially in the smaller towns as well as in the villages, hamlets and scattered communities that were still a feature of 1930s' Britain. However, fundamental changes were gradually taking place which would culminate in the more publicised developments of the 1960s and 1970s. Finally, the relationship between police and public was profoundly altered by the advent of mass motoring. The drunks and the vagrants disappeared from the courts to be replaced by traffic offenders, many of whom were drawn from the middle classes who were more used to seeing the police as their servants. Once again, a well-known problem of post-Second World War Britain has its roots in the pre-war years. And this is the core of our argument: the inter-war years, and especially the 1930s, constitute a key but neglected period in the development of modern policing.

Notes

1 Introduction

1. See J. C. Weaver (1995), *Crimes, Constables and Courts: Order and Transgression in a Canadian City, 1816–1970* (Montreal: Macgill-Queens University Press) for a discussion of the wider impact of the advent of motorised traffic on police work. The most detailed study of the police response to the newly emerging motor age is E. R. Clapton (2005), *Intersections of Conflict: Policing and Criminalising Melbourne's Traffic, 1890–1930* (Melbourne: University of Melbourne, Department of History).
2. Particularly L. A. Jackson (2006), *Women Police: Gender, Welfare and Surveillance in the Twentieth Century* (Manchester: Manchester University Press) but also see J. Lock (1979), *The British Policewoman* (London: Robert Hale); L. Wyles (1952), *A Woman at Scotland Yard: Reflections on the Struggle and Achievements of Thirty Years in the Metropolitan Police* (London: Faber & Faber); A. Woodeson (1993), 'The first woman police: a force of equality or infringement?', *Women's History Review*, 2, 217–32; P. Levine (1994), ' "Walking the street as no decent woman should". Women police in World War 1', *Journal of Modern History*, 66, 34–78. Occasional references will be made to the women police throughout this book but these will be incidental rather than central to the discussion.
3. C. Emsley (2009), *The Great British Bobby: A History of British Policing from the 18th Century to the Present* (London: Quercus), pp. 224, 228.
4. Emsley, *The Great British Bobby*, pp. 230, 250. The emphasis on the 1960s as a key period of change is to be seen in C. Emsley's earlier survey (1996), *The English Police: A Political and Social History*, 2nd edn (London: Longman), especially Chapter 8. Interestingly the chapter on the inter-war years appears to give greater emphasis on the novelty of the challenges facing the police in the 1920s and 1930s.
5. P. Rawlings (2002), *Policing: A Short History* (Cullompton: Willan), pp. 199–200.
6. T. J. Critchley (1978), *A History of Police in England and Wales* (London: Constable), Chapter 8, 'Reform on an ebb tide 1945–59', and Chapter 10, 'Forward from the Royal Commission'.
7. J. P. Martin and G. Wilson (1969), *The Police: A Study in Manpower: The Evolution of the Service in England and Wales, 1829–1965* (London: Heinemann), p. 36.
8. P. J. Stead (1985), *The Police of Britain* (London: Macmillan), p. 77. It is not unusual for historians of the inter-war years to stress the transitional and changing nature of the period. Look particularly at J. Stevenson and C. Cook (1977), *The Slump* (London: Jonathan Cape), which has run to several editions and two name changes, but there are also many other books that note the rapid changes in the economy and politics of this period.

9. M. Brogden (1991), *On the Mersey Beat Policing Liverpool Between the Wars* (Oxford: Oxford University Press).
10. B. Weinberger (1995), *The Best Police in the World: An Oral History of English Policing* (Aldershot: Scolar Press), p. 63.
11. H. Taylor (1998), 'The politics of the rising crime statistics of England and Wales, 1945–1960', *Crime, History and Societies*, 2, 5–28; H. Taylor (2001), 'Forging the job', *British Journal of Criminology*, 39, 113–35. But see R. M. Morris (2001), 'Lies, damned lies and criminal statistics: reinterpreting the criminal statistics in England and Wales', *Crime, History and Societies*, 5, 111–27.
12. R. Geary (1985), *Policing Industrial Disputes 1893 to 1985* (London and New York: Cambridge University Press), p. 66; J. Morgan (1987), *Conflict and Order: The Police and Labour Disputes in England and Wales, 1900–1939* (Oxford: Oxford University Press); B. Weinberger (1991), *Keeping the Peace? Policing Strikes in Britain 1906–1926* (Oxford: Oxford University Press); B. Weinberger (1987), 'Police perceptions of labour in the inter-war period: the case of the unemployed and miners on strike', in F. Synder and D. Hay (eds), *Labour, Law and Crime: An Historical Perspective* (London: Tavistock Publications), pp. 167–72; K. D. Ewing and C. A. Gearty (2000), *The Struggle for Civil Liberties* (Oxford: Oxford University Press), pp. 155–213.
13. *Report of the Royal Commission on Police Powers and Procedure* (1929), Cmnd. 3297, paras. 299–300.
14. See Chapter 3 on Public Order which discusses the way in which the Home Office advised Bosanquet, the Chief Constable of Monmouthshire, during the General Strike and the coal lock-out in 1926.
15. P. Thorold (2003), *The Motoring Age: The Automobile and Britain, 1896–1939* (London: Profile Books), for example, refers to 'sustained harassment by the police' (p. 15) and AA and RAC 'scouts...employed to sniff out police traps' (p. 197).
16. S. O'Connell (1998), *The Car in British Society: Class, Gender and Motoring, 1896–1939* (Manchester: Manchester University Press); J. Moran (2006), 'Crossing the road in Britain, 1931–76', *Historical Journal*, 49, 477–96. See also, M. M. Ishaque and R. B. Noland (2006), 'Making roads safer for pedestrians or keeping them out of the way?', *Journal of Transport History*, 27, 115–37; B. Luckin and D. Sheen (2009), 'Defining early modern automobility: the road traffic accident crisis in Manchester, 1939–45', *Cultural and Social History*, 6, 211–30. For a more general discussion of governmental attitudes to the car, see W. Plowden (1971), *The Motor Car and Politics, 1896–1970* (London: Bodley).
17. O'Connell, *The Car in British Society*, p. 140. He is also highly critical of the dehumanising of pedestrians by figures such as Alker Tripp of the Metropolitan Police Department (MPD) who referred to 'efficient traffic units', p. 127K.
18. C. Emsley (1993), '"Mother what *did* policemen do when there weren't any motors?" The law, the police and the regulation of motor traffic in England, 1900–1939', *Historical Journal*, 39, 357–81.
19. His Majesty Inspectorate of Constabulary (HMIC), *Annual Report, 1918*, p. 2.
20. HMIC, *Annual Report, 1918*, p. 3
21. The (average) figure of population per constable was one that had been used for many years but its value as a measure of the adequacy of police provision

is debatable, not least because of the considerable local variations to be found in terms of both specific circumstances and police strengths.
22. Dunning wrote that 'the need for economy... has slowed recruiting down to bare necessities'. HMIC, *Annual Report, 1921*, p. 5.
23. HMIC, *Annual Report, 1919*, p. 8.
24. HMIC, *Annual Report, 1923*, p. 4.
25. HMIC, *Annual Report, 1924*, p. 5.
26. HMIC, *Annual Report, 1925*, p. 2. Dunning's partial explanation, that this was due to the fact that 'some people take their impression of a policeman from the policeman of the pantomime and the comic paper' was less than convincing.
27. HMIC, *Annual Report, 1937*, p. 13.
28. Details from HMIC *Annual Reports*. It followed that the population per police constable (PC) figure was significantly higher in Wales. Figures for 1919 show the worst English counties (Rutland and the Isle of Wight) operating at a figure of 1200+:1 and the best (Berkshire and Hertfordshire) operating at less than 700:1. In comparison, only two Welsh counties (Breconshire and Glamorgan) operated at less than 1000:1 and half operated at a figure of 1300:1 or worse.
29. *Report of the Committee on Police Service in England, Wales, and Scotland*, Part II (1920), Cmnd. 574, para. 103, p. 6.
30. Details from HMIC, *Annual Reports*; the quotation is from *Annual Report, 1925*, p. 2.
31. HMIC, *Annual Report, 1928*, p. 4.
32. *Select Committee on Police Forces (Amalgamation) 1931–32*, Cmnd. 106, paras. 43–5 (hereafter *Select Committee on Police Force (Amalgamation)*). Windsor was excepted from the recommendation regarding non-county boroughs.
33. *Select Committee on Police Forces (Amalgamation)*, para. 52. The decision was reached on the grounds that it was not within the terms of reference of the select committee.
34. HMIC, *Annual Report, 1937*, p. 7
35. Ibid.

2 Police Trade Unionism and the Federation

1. R. McKibbin (2010), *Parties and People: England 1914–1951* (Oxford: Oxford University Press), p. 33.
2. A PhD student at the University of Huddersfield, who is a policeman, complains of the brittle nature of the Police Federation when it comes into conflict with Home Office and government. Like many others he supported the police protests throughout London in the summer of 2009.
3. HO 144/3469, Part 2. HO stands for Home Office papers in the National Archives, Kew, London.
4. J. E. Cronin (1982), 'Coping with labour, 1918–1928', in J. E. Cronin and J. Schneer (eds), *Social Conflict and the Political Order in Modern Britain* (London: Routledge), p. 119; J. E. Cronin (1984), *Labour and Society in Britain 1918–1979* (London: Batsford Academic and Educational).

5. R. C. Challinor (1977), *The Origins of British Bolshevism* (London: Croom Helm).
6. P. Evans (1970), *The Police Revolution* (London: George Allen & Unwin); D. Ascoli (1979), *The Queen's Peace: The Origins and Development of the Metropolitan Force 1829–1979* (London: Hamish Hamilton); G. Smith (n.d.), *Bradford City Police* (Bradford: Bradford City Police); W. Clay (ed.) (*c.* 1975), *The Leeds Police* (Leeds: Leeds City Police); D. J. Elliott (1984), *Policing Shropshire* (Location not indicated: K. F. Brewin Books); J. Fairhurst (1966), *Policing Wigan: The Wigan Borough Police Force 1836–1961* (Blackpool: Landy Publishing); B. Edmondson (1985), *Bob's Beat: The Story of a Lancashire Policeman* (Manchester: Neil Richardson).
7. Critchley, *A History of Police in England and Wales*, p. 187.
8. O. Jones, 'The "spirit of Petrograd"? The 1918 and 1919 police strikes', http://www.whatnextjournal.co.uk/Pages/Latest/Police.hml (accessed 14 February 2009). The quote from the radical police is taken from the union paper *The Police and Prison Officers' Magazine*, 2 July 1919.
9. R. Bean (1980), 'Police unrest, unionization and the 1919 strike in Liverpool', *Journal of Contemporary History*, 15, 633–53.
10. Chris A. Williams of the Open University in a book proposal application in 2009.
11. Jack H. Hayes was Labour MP for Edge Hill from 1922, a former policeman and Secretary of the NUPPO.
12. HO 144/3469, Part 2, a memorandum on the Police Strike dated 14 February 1923.
13. HO 45/22806. This contains the details of the cuts. The costs of policing had more than doubled to £20,500,000 between 1918 and 1921. In the discussion between the Police Federation and the Superintendent's Committee, it became clear that in 1922 there would be a cut of £2,387,500 in pay and allowances – rather than more than a 10 per cent cut. In the end it was trimmed to £1,792,000.
14. Joanne Klein (2010), *Invisible Men: The Secret Lives of Police Constables in Liverpool, Manchester, and Birmingham, 1900–1939* (Liverpool: Liverpool University Press), p. 133.
15. Klein, *Invisible Men*, p. 135.
16. MEPO 3/1814, entitled the Metropolitan Police Union, National Archives.
17. The Criminal Investigation Department (CID) report on 21 September 1913 mentions August 1913 but in MEPO 3/1815 the fuller details on John Syme, with picture, indicates 31 January 1910, National Archives.
18. MEPO 3/1814, quoted from a CID report on a meeting held in Trafalgar Square on 1 November 1913, the words being those of Syme.
19. MEPO 3/1814.
20. Cab 23, Cabinet 27 (25), item 20, 'The police: ex-Inspector Syme', 1 April 1921, National Archives.
21. MEPO 3/1814, quoted from the CID report on Syme's speech of 21 September 1913.
22. MEPO 3/1814, quoted from CID report of the meeting at Trafalgar Square, 1 November 1913.
23. MEPO 3/1814, 1 November 1913 meeting at Trafalgar Square.
24. MEPO 3/ 1814, headed letter with the details of the Metropolitan Police Union formed in October 1913.

25. Labour History Archive and Study Centre, Communist Party Archive, IND./MISC/20.29, Syme to Lindsay, 28 December 1920, quoted in Owen Jones, 'The spirit of Petrograd', p. 3.
26. Cab 23, Cabinet 27 (25), item 20; also MEPO 3/257A which contains headed union notepaper with the aims of the union. Both are in the National Archives.
27. MEPO 3/1815.
28. MEPO 3/1815.
29. PCOM Clom 7/705 contains a letter dated 15 February 1917, National Archives.
30. MEPO 3/1815, in a letter dated 15 February 1913.
31. *The Police Review and Parade Gossip*, 2 January 1914, a copy of which can be found in MEPO 3/1815.
32. *Report of the Committee on Police Service in England, Wales and Scotland*, Part I (1920), (London: HMSO), p. 7, para. 24.
33. Desborough Committee, *Report*, Part 1, p. 7, para. 24.
34. MEPO 3/257A in the National Archives contains the statements from the Parliamentary Debates of the House of Lords, vol. 31, no. 73 on the Metropolitan Police Strike, 30 October 1918. The pay details were given by the Marquis of Lansdowne in col. 895.
35. *Westminster Gazette*, 30 August 1918.
36. *Manchester Guardian*, 13 February 1918.
37. MEPO 2/11234, letter in Home Office files addressed to Lord Breadalbane at Taymouth Castle, Aberfeldy. Also look at MEPO 3/257A and the speech of Lord Lansdowne.
38. MEPOL 3/257A contains perhaps a couple of hundred telegrams on the situation throughout the Metropolitan area of London that night. They appear in an indiscriminate order.
39. *Pall Mall Gazette*, 30 August 1918.
40. MEPO 3/257A, debate in the House of Lords after an official report being presented to the House of Lords, vol. 31, no. 73, 30 October 1918.
41. *Workers Dreadnought*, 7 September 1918; also quoted in Jones, 'The "spirit of Petrograd?"'.
42. MEPO 3/257A.
43. MEPO 3/257A, from Parliamentary Debates 35, no. 73, col. 900.
44. House of Lords, Lloyd George Papers, F/30/8, Lloyd George to Bonar Law, 27 January 1919, quoted by Jones, 'The "spirit of Petrograd?"'.
45. MEPO 3 in the evidence to the Mackenzie Committee given by Gen. Macready.
46. MEPO 3.
47. HO 144/3469, Part 1, in a memorandum of 24 December 1918.
48. House of Lords, LG F/36/2/5, letter from Macready to David Lloyd George, 23 January 1919.
49. MEPO 3.
50. MEPO 3, quoting *The Police and Prison Officers Magazine*, 20 February 1919.
51. MEPO 3, Spackman, like some other police officers, had been dismissed for distributing NUPPO literature. He has been brought before the Disciplinary Board of the Metropolitan Police on 1 April 1919.
52. MEPO 3.
53. Hansard, *Parliamentary Debates*, 5th Series, 1918, cx, col. 1001.

54. Hansard, *Parliamentary Debates*, 5th Series, 1919, cxvi, col. 1266.
55. HO 45/15605.
56. Desborough Committee, *Report* (1920, Part 1), p. 9, para. 34.
57. Desborough Committee, *Report* (1920, Part 1), p. 20, Appendix 1.
58. Ibid.
59. Desborough Committee, *Report* (1920), the fine details of all ranks up to that of, but not including, chief constable are on p. 12, para. 50.
60. Desborough Committee, *Report* (1920, Part 1), p. 9, para. 34.
61. Desborough Committee, *Report* (1920, Part 1), p. 10, para. 36, p. 18, para. 88.
62. PCOM, Com 7/705, in a report of 15 February 1917 written by E. Ruggles-Bries.
63. PCOM 7/714.
64. MEPO 2/7649. The second letter was signed by H. W. Widdans, W. H. Halstead, W. Smith, A. C. Hollyer and E. F. Channon.
65. MEPO 3 contains a newspaper article by ex-Inspector Syme, dated 24 July 1920, suggesting that there were 74,000 police officers throughout the country. Our figures in the introduction suggests that the total establishment was less at about 55,000 and that there may have been as few as 35,000 full-time and trained police officers on duty during the Great War. HO 144/3469 contains a small file of evidence given by Macready which indicates the precise voting of the union and other details in other files. HO 144/3469, Part 2, reports on the report of Arthur Henderson indicating that there were about 50,000 police officers and 2000 prison warders in England and Wales. Jones, 'The "spirit of Petrograd"', p. 7, suggests that the vote figures were 44,599 in favour and 4324 against strike action.
66. MEPO 3/1786.
67. MEPOL 3/319 indicates that 1083 members of the Metropolitan Police were dismissed, and that between September 1919 and October 1921, 724 applied for their jobs back, and that another 150 applied before 2 March 1925. HO 144/3469, Part 2, indicates that the Cabinet CP 230 (24) was given figures of 1056 for the Metropolitan Police, the London Police 57, Liverpool 932, Birmingham 118, Birkenhead 106, Bootle 63, Wallasay 1 and 74 prison officers. It also estimated that there were about 50,000 police officer and 2000 prison officers, obviously underestimates.
68. MEPO 3/1786.
69. MEPO 3/1786.
70. HO 144/3469, Part 1, from a report dealing with the 'Threatened General Sympathy Strike in Liverpool' which was going to be called by the trade unions and led by Tom Mann, the famous socialist.
71. MEPO 3/1786; HO 144/3469, Part 2, contains a file on Liverpool, the events, the arrests and the sentencing of some of the rioters.
72. HO 144/3469, Part 1, includes reports on Bootle, Liverpool and other areas of strike activity.
73. MEPO 3/1786.
74. HO 144/3469.
75. HO 144/3469.
76. HO 144/3469.

77. MEPO 3/1786; MEPO 2/10211 deals with reports on meetings of NUPPO, its members and their industrial action from between 1918 to 1925.
78. HO 45/11072/387089 contains evidence that some right-wingers in NUPPO were reluctant to support industrial action.
79. MEPO 2/10211.
80. MEPO 2/10211.
81. MEPO 2/10211.
82. MEPO 2/10211.
83. HO 144/3469, Part 2, a memorandum on the Police Strike dated 14 February 1923.
84. HO 144/3469, Part 2, a memorandum on the Police Strike dated 14 February 1923.
85. MEPO 2/11234, letter in Home Office files addressed to Lord Breadalbane at Taymouth Castle, Aberfeldy. The union executive at this time consisted of J. Marston (President), A Broadway, J. Crisp, G. Halliday, A. Lakey, C. O. Connell, J. Paul, W. Sell, S. Scott, W. Smethwick, G. Wilson, J. Zoller, W. Felgate (Treasurer) and J. H. Hayes (Secretary). Its headquarters were at 191, Bishopgate, London.
86. MEPO 2/11234.
87. MEPO 2/11236, letter 16 June 1920.
88. MEPO 2/11236 and also *The Police Review and Parade Gossip*, 4 June 1920.
89. MEPO 2/11236.
90. MEPO 2/11234.
91. HO 144/3469, Part 2.
92. HO 144/3469, Part 2, papers dated 25 November 1921, 29 December 1921 and 18 January 1922.
93. HO 144/3469, Part 2, several small files deal with these developments. Also *Police Review*, 31 December 1920.
94. HO 144/3469, Part 2.
95. MEPO 2/10211.
96. Cabinet Conclusion CP 230 (24), 4 March 1924, also contained within file HO 144/3469, Part 2. The issue seems to have been raised there and there is attached to it a report to the Cabinet from Henderson dated 31 March 1924.
97. The statement is taken from a Home Office letter to Hayes, dated 12 April 1924, which was mentioned at the Parliamentary Labour Party, 29 May 1924. J. Shepherd and K. Laybourn (2006), *The First Labour Government* (London: Palgrave Macmillan), p. 124, refers to the letter and the events. Also look at HO 144/3469, Part 2.
98. Parliamentary Labour Party, minutes, 29 May 1924. The Mackenzie Committee consisted of Sir W. Mackenzie, Sir Thomas Rodgers, the Rt. Hon. Thomas Richards, and was complemented by A. L. Dixon (a close adviser to the Home Secretary) and one other civil servant.
99. MEPO/3, MEPO 3/227 contain a substantial amount of the evidence given to the Mackenzie Commission on 4, 5, 11, 12 July and 9 and 13 October 1924.
100. MEPO/3 evidence of 12 July 1924.
101. MEPO/3, Mackenzie Committee. The meetings were held on 4 and 5 July 1925 and 11 July 1925.

218 *Notes*

102. MEPO/3, Copy of the Commissioner's evidence to the Committee.
103. MEPO/3, Evidence of the Commissioner of the Metropolitan Police to the Mackenzie Committee, using the evidence of Macready.
104. MEPO/3.
105. MEPO/3. The Spackman letter to the Home Office was dated 7 March 1925 and referred to the suffering of his wife and six children.
106. MEPO/3, evidence given on 9 October 1924.
107. MEPO/3.
108. MEPO/3, evidence of 9 October 1924.
109. MEPO/3, evidence of 12 July 1924.
110. KV2/998.There is also file KV2/999 that indicates that his diaries from 1922 to 1929 had been confiscated and that he was watching MI5 people.
111. *Manchester Evening News*, 19 January 1932.
112. *Daily Dispatch*, 20 January 1932; *Manchester Guardian*, 20 January 1932. The *News Chronicle*, 14 October 1931, indicates that the rates of pay for constables were 70 shillings in September 1931 and 1965s 9d in October 1931, Sergeants' pay was 100 shillings and reduced to 94s 6d. Inspectors had their pay reduced from 125 shillings to 118 shillings and 3d. Constables who had joined in 1931 had their pay reduced to 55 shillings from 70 shillings.
113. The National Archives contain numerous files on the Police Federation including the following: HO 45/12651, Part 1 and Part 2 dealing with 1924 and 1925; HO 45/13821 for 1929; HO 45/13933 for 1930.
114. *The Police Review and Parade Gossip*, 1 June 1928, statement made at a Police Federation meeting at Eastbourne in May 1928.
115. HO 45/13416, Part 1, The Police Federation of England and Wales, *Report of the Sergeants' Central Committee*, Monday, 12 November 1928.
116. *The Police Review and Parade Gossip*, 28 September 1928.
117. HO 45/13933.
118. HO 45/13933.
119. HO 45/13933, Joint Central Meetings for 21–23 January 1930.
120. HO 45/13933.
121. HO 45/13933, meeting 24–26 July 1930.
122. HO 45/13933.
123. HO 45/139333, a meeting on 18, 19 and 20 March 1930.
124. HO 45/139333, a meeting on 18, 19 and 20 March 1930.
125. HO 45/139333.
126. HO 45/139333. Also look at HO 45/19046, copy of the *13th Annual Report of the Police Federation of England and Wales, Containing a Report on the 1931 Central Conference* (London: 1932), p. 16, which expressed the Federation's opposition to women policing, stating that 'it is totally unnecessary to institute a section of women police patrolling the streets in uniform, and to appoint a number of women as Senior Officers.'
127. MEPO 2/7640.
128. City of Liverpool, Liverpool Women Patrols: Report of the Watch Committee, 2 March 1920.
129. MEPO 2/1710; MEPO 2/1910; Jackson, *Women Police*, p. 3.
130. MEPO 2/8103 contains the annual reports of women police of the Metropolitan Police for the 1930s; D. O. G. Peto (1992), *The Memoirs of Miss Dorothy Olivia Georgina Peto* (Brownhill Organising Conference for the European Conference on Equal Opportunities in Policing).

131. MEPO 2/7460.
132. MEPO 2/7460, letter of D. Peto, 26 September 1930 and reply letter of 3 February 1931.
133. MEPO 2/7460, Charles Drummond, letter of 9 January 1941.
134. HO 45/24711.
135. *The Police Review and Parade Gossip*, 20 December 1929.
136. HO 45/24711 contains Popkess's application form.
137. The details of this are given in Chapter 2, which deals with the pay and conditions of policing during the inter-war years.
138. HO 45/12651, Part 1, *The Police Federation of England and Wales: Report of the Joint Central Committee, 1924–25* (1935) (London: HMSO), p. 40.
139. HO 144/6116.
140. *The Police Review and Parade Gossip*, 28 September 1928 reporting on an Open Meeting of the Federation.
141. HO 45/14795, in the deputation to the Home Secretary, Sir Herbert Samuel, 1 September 1932.
142. *Manchester Evening News*, 17 October 1932.
143. HO 45/14795.
144. HO 45/14795, deputation to the Home Secretary, 15 September 1932.
145. HO 45/14795, letter from R. R. Scott, of the Home Office, to the Secretary of the Joint Central Committee of the Federation, 12 October 1932.
146. *The Police Review and Parade Gossip*, 14 October 1932.
147. HO 45/14795, *The Police Review and Parade Gossip*, 14 October 1932.
148. HO 45/14795 contains a file on this deputation.
149. *Daily Herald*, 11 November 1932.
150. The Police Federation of England and Wales Joint Central Committee (1932), *Home Office Reports, November 1919 to October 1932* (London: Home Office). There were 20,000 copies produced at 4d per copy.
151. HO 45/19046, copy of the 1932, *13th Annual Report of the Police Federation of England and Wales, containing a report on the 1931 Central Conference* (London: Police Federation), p. 3.
152. *13th Annual Report of the Police Federation of England and Wales*, p. 3.
153. *13th Annual Report of the Police Federation of England and Wales*, p. 13.
154. HO 45/19046.
155. HO 45/19046, letter of R. R. Scott, of the Home Office, 26 July 1933.
156. HO 45/19046, Home Office Memorandum, 1 August 1933.
157. HO 45/14795, *The Police Review and Parade Gossip*, 16 December 1932.
158. HO 45/12651, Part 1, contains a copy of *The Police and Parade Gossip*, 15 September 1933, which contains the article by Hayes on 'Men and matters of moment'.
159. Robert Reiner (1978), *The Blue-coated Worker: A Sociological Study of Police Unionism* (Cambridge: Cambridge University Press).

3 Policing Public Order in the Inter-war Years

1. There were 56 county forces and 124 borough forces in 1918, as well as the River Police, the Metropolitan Police Force and the City of London Police. These 183 forces had reduced to 178 by 1926, 5 of the borough forces having united into 2 forces. There is a full listing of the police forces

220 Notes

      of England and Wales in HO 144/12050, Part 2, in a document which is related to the circulation of a memorandum seeking precise details of the prosecutions in the General Strike and coal lock-out, dated 17 January 1927.
2. R. Geary (1985), *Policing Industrial Disputes* (London and New York: Cambridge University Press), p. 66.
3. Critchley, *A History of Police in England and Wales*; Morgan, *Conflict and Order*, pp. 117–9, 132–7, 200–19, 276–81; Weinberger, *Keeping the Peace?*, pp. 204–25; Weinberger, 'Police perceptions of labour in the inter-war period: the case of the unemployed and the miners on strike', in F. Snyder and D. Hay (eds) (1987), *Labour, Law and Crime: An Historical Perspective* (London: Tavistock), pp. 167–72.
4. Weinberger, *Keeping the Peace* p. 200; Weinberger, 'Police perceptions', pp. 151, 163.
5. Morgan, *Conflict and Order*, p. 277.
6. K. D. Ewing and C. A. Gearty (2000), *The Struggle for Civil Liberties* (Oxford: Oxford University Press), pp. 155–213, 210.
7. Keith Laybourn (1992), *A History of British Trade Unionism 1770–1990* (Stroud: Sutton), p. 142; James E. Cronin (1979), *Industrial Conflicts in Modern Britain* (London: Croom Helm) stresses the tendency of strikes to concentrate in a few short periods such as 1919–21 and 1926, which mark a moment on the mental framework of workers until working-class political and economic attitudes are remade.
8. Laybourn, *British Trade Unionism*, pp. 125–9.
9. CAB 23, War Cabinet 522, 30 January 1919.
10. CAB 23, War Cabinet 523, 31 January 1919.
11. CAB 23, War Cabinet 529, 7 February 1919.
12. HO 144/4549 is a major file on the government's secret preparations for dealing with strike action.
13. HO 144/4549, a file referring to the Protection (Sub-) Committee meeting of 3 March 1919 and to a subsequently undated meeting.
14. CAB 23, War Cabinet 544, 13 March 1919.
15. HO 144/4549, Part 1, report on the Conference of Chief Constables at the Home Office, 18 February 1919 (hereafter Conference of Chief Constables, 18 February 1919).
16. Conference of Chief Constables, 18 February 1919.
17. Conference of Chief Constables, 18 February 1919.
18. Conference of Chief Constables, 18 February 1919.
19. Conference of Chief Constables, 18 February 1919.
20. HO 144/4549, Part 1, report on the Conference of Chief Constables at the Home Office, 18 February 1919.
21. The Durham Chief Constable indicated at this meeting that he had 3000 specials and that 'several hundred of them have motor cars'.
22. HO 144/4549, a file containing the Chief Constables' Conference, 18 February 1919
23. HO 144/4549, a file containing the Chief Constables' Conference with the Home Office, 7 March 1919. Also referred to in the undated minutes of the Protection Committee that probably took place in the subsequent week.
24. HO 144/4549 Part 1, Conference of Chief Constable at the Home Office, 7 March 1919.

25. HO 144/4549, a file on the meeting of 17 March 1919.
26. HO 144/4549 contains several undated reports on the Protection Committee.
27. HO 144/4549.
28. HO 144/4549.
29. HO 144/4549, file on Post Office.
30. HO 144/4549, Part 2, report on the Protection Committee, 23 July 1919.
31. *Annual Report of the Birmingham City Police, 1919*, pp. 7–8, partly written by the Chief Constable Charles H. Rafter.
32. HO 144/4549, Conference of Chief Constables at the Home Office, 7 March 1919.
33. CAB 23, War Cabinet, 544, 13 March 1919; HO 144/4549.
34. HO 144/4549, Part 2, file on Electricity Undertakings.
35. HO 144/4549, Part 2.
36. HO 144/4549, material in both Part I and Part II of the file.
37. Weinberger, *Keeping the Peace?*, pp. 199–200; Morgan, *Conflict and Order*, pp. 117–9.
38. *Annual Report of the Birmingham City Police, 1926*, p. 6, referred to as Special Constable from 1923 and numbered 4298 during the General Strike when some joined who had vehicles. In this case the Birmingham Special Constabulary Reserve were formed in October 1919.
39. MEPOL 2/42111 is mainly about the work of the Public Order Act of 1936 but contains minutes of the Home Affairs Committee in 1921 and also a Memorandum from the Home Secretary (Edward Shortt) on the Proceedings of the Public Order Bill, dated 23 March 1921, which was in response to the Committee set up on 25 February 1920 to discuss the drafting of a (Public Order) Bill.
40. John McIlroy, Alan Campbell, Keith Laybourn and Quentin Outram (2006), 'The general strike and mining lockout of 1926: a bibliography', *Historical Studies in Industrial Relations*, 21 (spring), pp. 182–206, list upwards of 400 publications on the General Strike. In addition, there are books such as Gordon A. Phillips (1976), *The General Strike: The Politics of Industrial Conflict* (London: Weidenfeld and Nicolson); Patrick Renshaw (1976), *The General Strike Eyre* (London: Methuen); Keith Laybourn (1996), *The General Strike of 1926* (Manchester: Manchester University Press); K. Laybourn (1996), *The General Strike Day by Day* (Sutton: Stroud).
41. Apart from the above there is M. Morris (1976), *The General Strike* (London: The Journeyman Press).
42. Morris, *The General Strike*, p. 55.
43. Morris, *The General Strike*, p. 56.
44. Ibid.
45. Phillips, *The General Strike*, pp. 245, 160.
46. A. Perkins (2006), *A Very British Strike 3 May–12 May 1926* (London: Macmillan), pp. 66, 71–2.
47. HO 144/6116.
48. MEPOL 2/4211, file on the 'Present Law Regarding the Coal Strike'.
49. CAB 27/287, Cabinet proceedings and Memoranda, Cabinet Committee on Public Order & Preservation of Law and Order PO (28)-26 & PLP (1922)

Series, PC(25) 7 Police and Public Meetings, Memorandum by the Home Secretary, 17 December 1925.
50. CAB 27/287 connected with policing and public order.
51. The Civil Constabulary Reserve (CCR) was envisaged as a third line (behind the regular police and special constables) to cope with the General Strike. Described in parliament as a 'semi-military force' (*The Times*, 8 July 1926), the scheme had envisaged a force of 300,000 men across the country. Under Home Office authority, the scheme was run by the War Office and was based upon the organisations of the Territorial Army (TA). However, the TA (nor the Army Reserve) were formally embodied. Rather territorial units (and friends) were asked to volunteer. Pay was 5 shillings per day and 11,000 men joined in London and a further 7000 elsewhere. The CCR was short-lived, being disbanded on 15 May 1926 (following the collapse of the General Strike) but was estimated to have cost some £65,000 (*The Times*, 6 July 1926). Although not discussed in detail here, the history of the CCR is consistent with the more general argument advanced in this book. See also P. Dennis (1981), 'The Territorial Army in Aid of the Civil Power of Britain, 1919–1926', *Journal of Contemporary History*, 16, 705–24.
52. L. Jones (1937, 1978), *Cwmardy* (London: Lawrence & Wishart)
53. *Annual Report of the City of Birmingham Police, 1926*, p. 6.
54. HO 144/6902.
55. Morgan, *Conflict and Order*, p. 117; Weinberger, *Keeping the Peace?*, p. 201; Manchester Watch Committee minutes, 8 June 1926, to be found in the Greater Manchester Police Museum Archive. Also NA, CAB24/181, CP 364 (26), Strength of the police in the coalfields.
56. HO 144/6896, a file on the 'Daily Bulletin: General Strike 3 May 1926', given by the District Officials to the Home Office, North-Eastern Division.
57. HO 144/4549.
58. HO 144/4549.
59. Manchester Police General Orders, 9 October–11 November 1926, GMPMA
60. *Manchester Evening News*, 25 August 1926; Weinberger, *Keeping the Peace?*, p. 185.
61. Greater Manchester Police Museum, a book or report produced by New Scotland Yard entitled *Aspects of the General Strike, 1926*.
62. HO 144/6903.
63. HO 144/12050, Part 2, file on a deputation to the Home Secretary to get the nine-month sentence for Ald. Jenkins to be rescinded.
64. J. Morgan (1988),'Police and labour in the age of Lindsay, 1910–1936', *Llafur*, 5, 1, 20.
65. *Colliery Guardian*, 23 July1926.
66. Weinberger, 'Police perceptions', p. 164. Also look at Stephen Catterall (2004), 'Police', in J. McIlroy, A. Campbell and K. Gildert (eds), *Industrial Politics and the 1926 Mining Lockout and the Struggle for Dignity* (Cardiff: University of Wales Press), pp. 249–68.
67. HO 45/24707, file on the Monmouthshire case.
68. *Police Review and Parade Gossip*, 2 July 1926; *Colliery Guardian*, 23 July 1926.
69. HO 45/24707, letter of 29 May 1926.

70. HO 45/24707, letter of 29 May suggesting that the procession was not illegal and urging prosecution under the Emergency Powers Act and a letter of 23 June 1926 offering Bosanquet the support of the Home Office.
71. *Western Mail*, 26 June 1926.
72. HO 45/24707, letter from W. S. Nash to Bosanquet, 25 June 1926.
73. *Western Mail*, 26 June 1926.
74. *Western Mail*, 1 December 1929, cutting in HO 45/24707.
75. HO 144/6902, file on Bosanquet.
76. Wigan MBC Heritage Services History Workshop, J. Fairhurst, 'Chief Constable Thomas Pey, OBE, a biography', undated typescript, 9 September 1926.
77. *Wigan Examiner*, 20 July, 10 and 19 October 1926.
78. *Wigan Observer*, 4 and 9 September 1926; *Wigan Examiner*, 13 November 1926.
79. *Police Review and Parade Gossip*, 17 December 1926.
80. HO 144/6898.
81. HO 144/6898, report of an inspector of Birmingham CID.
82. HO 144/6898.
83. HO 144/12050, Part 2, file on the 'Conduct of magistrates during the emergency'. This seems to have been drawn up for J. R. Clynes, the Home Secretary, in the second Labour government (1929–31), and produced about 1930 in connection with the appeal of some ex-magistrates to be reinstated.
84. HO 144/12050, Part 1, contains a file on Sam Filer, letter from Bosanquet, 2 June 1926.
85. HO 144/12050, Part 1, file on Rose Davies and William Rees.
86. HO 144/12050, Part 1, file on Rose Davies and William Rees.
87. HO 144/12050, Part 1, file on Heaviside and Trotter.
88. HO 144/12050, Part 1, file on Heaviside and Trotter.
89. HO 144/6896, report of DPS Littleproud, 19 August 1926; N. Warwick to A. Dixon, 4 October 1926.
90. HO 144/6896, report of DPS Lang, 17 October 1926; Lord Cecil to McGurk, 9 November 1926.
91. HO 144/6896 contains numerous examples of this type of action being taken.
92. HO 144/12050, Part 2, contains several files in which the Home Office asks chief constables about candidates to be magistrates.
93. HO 144/12050, Part 1, file on John Beckett and Northampton.
94. HO 144/12050, file on Chief Constables' Returns on Prosecutions arising from the General Strike.
95. HO 144/12050, file on Chief Constables' Returns on Prosecutions arising from the General Strike.
96. HO 144/12050, file on Chief Constables' Returns on Prosecutions arising from the General Strike.
97. HO 144/12050, Part 2, contains a full report of the TUC Delegation to the Home Office on an amnesty.
98. HO 144/12050, Part 1, file on Chief Constables' Returns on Prosecutions arising from the General Strike.

99. HO 144/12050, Part 2, attached to a letter and memorandum to chief constables of England and Wales to bring together up to date all details of prosecutions and so on, 17 January 1927.
100. CAB 24/181, CP 364 (26) Strength of police forces in the coalfields. In the National Archives.
101. HO 144/6116.
102. *Police Review and Parade Gossip*, 19 November 1926.
103. P. Flewers (2009), *The New Civilisation? Understanding Stalin's Soviet Union 1929–1941* (London: Francis Boutle Publishers).
104. *Manchester Guardian*, 13 March 1933.
105. There are numerous accounts of these events but J. Stevenson and C. Cook (1977), *The Slump* (London: Jonathan Cape) has two chapters on fascism and offers as good an account of Olympia as any. Also look at R. Skidelsky (1975), *Oswald Mosley* (London: Macmillan); J. Jacobs (1978), *Out of the Ghetto* (London: Janet Simon); *Daily Worker*, 18 May 1934; Communist Party of Great Britain, Political Bureau minutes, 7 June 1934.
106. MEPOL 2/3098, statement written on the file covers.
107. MEPOL 2/3098.
108. HO 144/6116.
109. CAB 27/610 in the National Archives.
110. HO 45/25388.
111. MEPO 2/8656 contains three-monthly applications to the Home Secretary for the extension of the three-month bans from Philip Game, plus copies of the order, and copies of letters to the main fascists and communist organisations concerned.
112. MEPOL 2/4211.
113. MEPO 2/8656.
114. MEPO 2/8656.
115. MEPOL 2/4211.
116. MEPOL 2/3098.

4 Detective and Scientific Work: A New Vista

1. HO 45/16215, letter to Mr A. L. Dixon, of the Home Office, 25 March 1935.
2. HO 45/16215, letter to A. L. Dixon from C. T. Symons, 22 July 1935.
3. HO 45/16215.
4. C. Emsley (2009), *The Great British Bobby: A History of British Policy from the Eighteenth Century to the Present* (London: Quercus), p. 151.
5. P. Evans (1970), The Police Revolution (London: George Allen and Unwin), p. 108.
6. D. Ascoli (1979), *The Queen's Peace: The Origin and Development of the Metropolitan Force 1829–1876* (London: Hamish Hamilton), p. 181.
7. G. Smith (n.d.), *Bradford City Police* (Bradford: Bradford City Police), pp. 123–4, 126.
8. Clay, *The Leeds Police*; Elliott, *Policing Shropshire*; J. Fairhurst, *Policing Wigan: The Wigan Borough Police Force 1836–1961* (Blackpool: Landy Publishing); B. Edmondson, *Bob's Beat: The Story of a Lancashire Policeman* (Manchester: Neil Richardson).

9. C. Emsley, *The English Police*, pp. 151–2.
10. Eric S. Johnstone (1978), *One Policeman's Story* (London: Berry Row), p. 65, quoted in Emsley, *The English Police*, p. 151.
11. Chief Constables' Association, Annual Report of the 37th General Conference and Special General Conference, held at the Guild Hall, London, 16–17 June 1932, 16 June meeting, p. 20 (hereafter *Chief Constables' Association, Annual Report of 1932* or alternative year). The Chief Constables' Association brought together the county borough, borough forces of England and Wales and the London forces, and was formed in 1896. In 1932 it represented 122 forces of which 120 were represented at the conference in 1932.
12. *Chief Constables' Association, Annual Report of 1937*, p. 23.
13. P. Rawlings (2002), *Policing: A Short History* (Cullompton: Willan), look at chapter 6, and particularly p. 179.
14. *Daily Express*, 23 July 1930.
15. *Chief Constable of Liverpool Annual Police Report* (sometimes referred to as *Watch Committee and Report on the Police* and other titles) *for the year ending 31 December 1925*, p. 5.
16. *Annual Report of the City of Liverpool Police for 1926*, p. 17.
17. *Annual Report of the City of Liverpool Police for 1926*, p. 17.
18. *Annual Report of the City of Liverpool Police for 1926*, p. 18.
19. *Chief Constable of St. Helens' Annual Police Report, 1936*, p. 8.
20. *Chief Constable of Preston Annual Police Report, 1931*, p. 21.
21. *Evening News*, 29 May 1929.
22. *Daily Express*, 23 July 1930.
23. *Police Review and Parade Gossip*, 31 October 1934. Mr J. Lloyd-Williams of the Montgomeryshire Committee was the virulent critic of the Police College idea and the County Council's Association recognised the scientific potential of the Police College.
24. *Police Review and Parade Gossip*, 31 October 1934.
25. *Report of the Royal Commission on Police Powers and Procedures*, 16 March 1929 (1928–29), cmd. 3297, p. 40, para. 102.
26. Ibid.
27. *Manchester Police Constable's Report, 1934, to the Manchester Watch Committee* (hereafter *Annual Report of the City of Manchester Police*).
28. (Manchester) *Evening News*, 18 March 1934.
29. Ascoli, *The Queen's Peace*, pp. 239–40.
30. *Daily Dispatch*, 30 August 1933.
31. *Daily Express*, 4 April 1934.
32. *Report of the Departmental Committee on Detective Work and Procedure* (London: HMSO, 1938), vol. 1, chapters 1–3, opening page (hereafter *Report of the Departmental Committee on Detective Work*).
33. *Daily Herald, Daily Mail* and *Daily Mirror*, all 24 September 1938.
34. *Manchester Guardian*, 24 September 1938; *Police Review and Parade Gossip*, 30 September 1938.
35. *Report of the Departmental Committee on Detective Work*, vol. 1, chapters 1 and 2 (September 1938), p. 12. There are eight chapters in the five reports, the first volume containing two chapters on the existing system of detective work in England and Wales. The full report can be found in HO 45/25052 and also in the Greater Manchester Police Museum, Newton Street, Manchester.

36. Ibid., chapters 1 and 2, p. 18.
37. Ibid., chapters 1 and 2, p. 19, and p. 46, para. 67.
38. Ibid., chapters 1 and 2, p. 43, para. 62.
39. Ibid., chapters 1 and 2, p. 43, para. 62.
40. Ibid., chapters 1 and 2, p. 53, para. 79.
41. Ibid., vol. 1, p. 53, para. 79 and p. 58, para. 89.
42. Ibid., chapters 1 and 2, paras 83 and 85.
43. Ibid., vol. 2, chapter 4, paras 1 and 3.
44. Ibid., vol. 2, chapter 4, para. 127.
45. Ibid., vol. 3, chapter 5, para. 140.
46. Ibid., vol. 4, chapter 6, paras 295 and 309. Seven of the nine regional centres in England and Wales were Brighton, London, Nottingham, Liverpool, Manchester, Wakefield and Newcastle. About five private systems seemed to be operating in London, Wakefield, Glamorganshire, Hertfordshire and Buckinghamshire.
47. Ibid., vol. 4, para. 365.
48. Ibid., vol. 5, chapter 7, para. 410.
49. Ibid.
50. *Chief Constables' Association, Annual Report of 1936*, p. 56.
51. *Chief Constables' Annual Report for Leeds, for the year ending 31 December 1933*, p. 5. This excludes the 37 men employed in the Fire Service.
52. *Annual Report for the City of Leeds Police, 1937*, p. 4.
53. Ibid., 1927, p. 5. There was one superintendent, one chief inspector, four inspectors, one sub-inspector, 13 sergeants and 26 constables.
54. *Ibid.*, 1938, p. 4; *Annual Report for the City of Leeds Police, 1939*, p. 12.
55. *Annual Report of the City of Manchester Police Report 1936*, p. 1.
56. *Daily Express*, 28 March 1934.
57. *Daily Express*, 24 March 1933.
58. *Daily Dispatch*, 24 March 1933.
59. *Annual Report for the City of Manchester Police, 1936*, p. 2.
60. Ibid.; 1937, p. 3.
61. Ibid.; 1938, pp. 2, 4.
62. Ibid., 1938, p. 29.
63. Ibid., pp. 29–30.
64. Ibid., pp. 30–1.
65. *Report of the Departmental Committee on Detective Work*, vol. 1, p. 59, para. 91.
66. Ibid., vol. 1, p. 60, para. 95.
67. Ibid., vol. 1, p. 62, para. 98.
68. Ibid.
69. Emsley, *The English Police*, p. 152, referring to the *Chief Constables' Annual Report of the General Conference and Special Conference, 1939*, pp. 23, 38–47.
70. *Police Review and Parade Gossip*, 1 April 1921.
71. J. J. Buist (1923), 'A Plea for the Improvement in Teaching and in Encouragement in the Study of Legal Medicine', based upon a lecture delivered 8 February 1923, a copy to be found in HO 45/16215.
72. HO 45/16215, letter dated 14 May 1930.
73. *Chief Constables' Association, Annual Report of 1929*, pp. 14–15.
74. Ibid.
75. Ibid., 1930, pp. 28–9.

76. Ibid., p. 29.
77. Ibid., pp. 38–47.
78. Ibid., 1933, pp. 26–7.
79. Ibid., p. 27. Also look at the *Chief Constables' Association Annual Report of 1934*, p. 43, where Mr Harri Heap lectured on 'Some Methods of Science which have been applied to Police Work'.
80. HO 45/16215, letter from Marcan to Trenchard, dated 18 December 1933.
81. HO 45/16215, letter dated 18 December 1933.
82. HO 45/16215, letter dated 26 October 1934.
83. *Evening Chronicle*, 20 September 1933.
84. Ibid.
85. HO 45/16215, file on Scientific Aid in the Detection of Crime, a report of C. T. Symons meeting Mr R. Collett of the Institute of Chemistry in a report on 'The Institute of Chemistry and Posts in Police Laboratories'.
86. HO 45/16215, file and report on Scientific Aid in the Detection of Crime.
87. Ibid., pp. 44–50, paras 64–75.
88. HO 45/16215, letter of 25 July 1935, possibly from the Chief Constable of Birmingham, C.V.A. Moriarty and probably to Tryhorn.
89. HO 45/16215, letter from the Chief Constable of Chesterfield to Mr A. L. Dixon, Home Office, 27 July 1935.
90. HO 45/16215, listing in a letter from the Home Office in August 1935.
91. HO 45/16215, a copy of a report to his chief constable on 25 October 1935.
92. HO 45/16215, report to Mr Baker, Chief Constable of Bristol, 25 October 1935, incorporating the report of Inspector Frederick Carter, and the comments of others.
93. HO 45/16215, Scientific Aid in the Detection of Crime, pp. 30–1, report of Inspector F. Carter, 24 October 1935.
94. HO 45/16215.
95. HO 45/20219, a file which deals with Scientific Aid Returns, 1939; letter of James W. Webster, 10 May 1940.
96. HO 45/20219, from the table on p. 9 of the returns to which James W. Webster is referring. HO 45/20219, letter of Webster, 10 May 1940.

5 'A Mere Traffic Signalling Device'? The Debate on Policing and Traffic Control

1. 'The chariots shall rage in the streets, they shall jostle one another in the broad ways'. *Nahum*, 2:4. The problem in the inter-war years was more one of narrow ways.
2. P. Thorold (2003), *The Motoring Age: The Automobile and Britain 1869–1930* (London: Tavistock Publications), pp. 174 and 210.
3. *Report of the Commissioner of Police of the Metropolis for the Year 1926*, PP 1936/7 (5457), p. 5.
4. The debate continues to the present day. For example, the 1993 White Paper on Police Reform argued that 'the main job of the police is to control criminals' but lamented the fact that 'only about 40% of police officers' time is spent dealing directly with crime'. It detailed the (Tory) government's commitment 'to improve police performance by directing its activities to

"fighting crime" and... encouraging the police to abandon ancillary duties which direct resources away from its core function'. Cited in F. Leishman, B. Loveday and S. P. Savage (eds) (1999), *Core Issues in Policing* (London: Longman), p. 74. The debate rumbles on with no resolution of the issue.
5. *General Regulations, Instructions and Orders of the Metropolitan Police Force* (1851) (London: Clowes & Sons), p. iii.
6. *General Orders*, 7 September 1838 and 1 November 1847.
7. Cited in Anon (1860), 'The Streets of London and How to Make Them Passable', 2nd edn (London: 2000 Library Home Pamphlets HE3/B8), p. 4. The author of this pamphlet was particularly concerned with the inadequacies of the bridges of London.
8. See, for example, evidence of Senior Assistant Commissioner, Metropolitan Police, Sir Alexander Bruce, QQ7405-8064 in which he stressed the great increase in the volume of traffic, the diversity of road users and the outdated nature of police powers; Royal Commission on London Transport, 1906. [Cmnd. 2751], pp. 275–92. See also the reports of the London Traffic Branch of the Board of Trade, especially in the immediate pre-war years.
9. *City of Birmingham Police: Bye Laws, Local Acts etc.* (1903), p. 71. This was issued by the Chief Constable to all members of the city force.
10. R. Peacock (1900), *Police Constables' Duties: Addresses by Robert Peacock, Chief Constable, City of Manchester* (Manchester: Blakelock & Co.), p. 147.
11. Ibid., p. 149.
12. A similar argument is advanced for Melbourne in D. Wilson (2006), *The Beat Policing a Victorian City* (Melbourne: Melbourne Publishing), chapter 8.
13. *The Times*, 23 September 1926.
14. *Judicial Statistics, 1923*, PP 1924–25 [Cmnd. 238], p. 9.
15. *Report of His Majesty's Inspector of Constabulary, 1919*, PP 1920 (91), p. 6.
16. *Report of His Majesty's Inspector of Constabulary, 1922*, PP 1923 (55), p. 7.
17. *Report of His Majesty's Inspector of Constabulary, 1927*, PP 1927 (130), p. 6.
18. T. J. Critchley (1978), *A History of Police in England and Wales* (London: Constable), p. 193.
19. *Committee on the Police Service of England, Wales and Scotland*, PP 1920 (874), p. 9.
20. MT 34/62, Cabinet Economy Committee meeting, 26 February 1926.
21. Ibid.
22. HO 45/24785, minute on traffic wardens.
23. H. Taylor (1998), 'The politics of rising crime statistics in England and Wales, 1945–1960', *Crime, History and Societies*, (2), pp. 9–10.
24. See also R. M. Morris (2001), 'Lies, damned lies and criminal statistics: reinterpreting the criminal statistics of England and Wales', *Crime, Histories and Societies*, (5), pp. 111–27 who talks of the 'implausible degree of concerted conspiracy' in Taylor's argument.
25. *HMIC Report, 1926*, p. 8.
26. *HMIC Report, 1928*, p. 15.
27. *Chief Constables' Association, Annual Report of 1927*.
28. HO 45/24785.
29. Ibid.

30. According to the *Bournemouth Daily Echo* a policeman 'is invested with an authority which an RAC patrolman does not possess' even though he may be as capable in directing traffic. Cited in I. A. Watt (1967), *A History of the Hampshire and Isle of Wight Constabulary, 1839–1966* (Hampshire: Isle of Wight Constabulary), p. 106.
31. HO 45/24785, minute on traffic wardens.
32. *The Times*, 29 August 1928, letter from D. M. Kirby.
33. Ibid.
34. Ibid.
35. Ibid.
36. Ibid.
37. *HMIC Annual Report, 1928*, p. 7.
38. Chief Constable, City of Liverpool Police, *Annual Report of the City of Liverpool Police, 1922*, p. 6. He reiterated his opposition in his 1926 annual report but conceded that 'some sort of auxiliary control... for traffic control' might be a possibility in rural areas, p. 19.
39. HO 45/24785, memorandum, 6 March 1926.
40. HO 45/2478. Atcherley was also concerned with the particular problems associated with sporting fixtures or popular events. Also *HMIC Annual Report, 1929*, p. 11.
41. HO 45/ 24785, minute on traffic wardens. Atcherley made the same point regarding the physical and mental demands of traffic duty; also *HMIC Annual Report, 1927*, p. 11.
42. HO 45/24785, memo to Home Office, 12 March 1926.
43. HO 45/20130, London Traffic, letter to Home Office, 17 April 1930.
44. HO 45/24785, letter to Home Office, 12 March 1926.
45. HO 45/24785, letter to Home Office, 12 March 1926, p. 48.
46. *The Times*, 2 April 1927.
47. Ibid., 13 November 1928.
48. Ibid., 16 November 1928.
49. Quoted in Royal Commission on Transport, *1st Report: The Control of Traffic on Roads*, Parl. Papers 1929/30 (3365), p. 22 (hereafter Royal Commission, Transport, *1st Report: The Control of Traffic on the Roads*).
50. Royal Commission, Transport *1st Report: The Control of Traffic on the Roads*, p. 23.
51. *The Times*, 18 April 1929.
52. Ibid., 16 November 1928.
53. Royal Commission, Transport *1st Report: The Control of Traffic on the Roads*, pp. 22–3.
54. *The Times*, 18 April 1929.
55. Ibid., 15 January 1930.
56. Ibid., 3 May 1932. The question largely disappeared after this with the occasional MP, such as the Tory C. Taylor (Eastbourne), asking for a scheme of traffic wardens to be introduced. *The Times*, 5 March 1936.
57. *Report of the Select Committee of the House of Lords on the Prevention of Road Accidents 1938–9*, Recommendations, Section 4 Police, pp. 15–17. Nonetheless it remained the case that police authorities were concerned at the increasing pressure of traffic work on the police as the result of the

230 Notes

Road Traffic Acts of 1930 and 1934. See, for example, *HMIC Annual Report, 1934*, p. 6.
58. *Annual Report of the City of Liverpool Police, 1929*; *Annual Report of the City of Leeds Police, 1931 and 1934*.
59. *Annual Report of the Metropolitan Police, 1933*, p. 40, *1936*, p. 54 and *1937*, p. 53.
60. *Manchester Evening News*, 18 May 1931. It is not clear how long this experiment at Lingard Road, Northenden, lasted, nor whether it was tried elsewhere.
61. See, for example, *The Times*, 24 April 1936, leader on the 'Massacre of the innocents'.
62. Royal Commission, *Transport 1st Report: The Control of Traffic on the Roads*, p. 39. The report continued to criticise 'motorists who think the road belongs to them' as well as 'cyclists and pedestrians [who] appear to think that all traffic should give way to them', pp. 39–40.
63. *The Times*, 13 January 1937.
64. See particularly S. O'Connell (1998), *The Car in British Society: Class Gender and Motoring, 1896–1939* (Manchester: Manchester University Press).
65. *Saturday Review*, 11 May 1935.
66. *The Times*, 28 June 1921 and 1 December 1930.
67. *The Times*, 15 August 1923. See also 16 August 1926.
68. *Autocar*, 17 September 1926, cited in O'Connell, *Car in British Society*, p. 122.
69. *The Times*, 26 July 1920 and, for example, 31 July 1929.
70. Cited in O'Connell, *Car in British Society*, pp. 54, 57.
71. Ibid., citing *Autocar*, 29 July 1938. There were exceptions. A male correspondent to *The Times* took exception to 'a statement made by a London coroner that all women are dangerous driving cars' on 22 August 1924.
72. *The Times*, 1 December 1930 and 24 November 1936.
73. *The Times*, 5 November 1929.
74. Manchester City Council and written by M. Anderson (1926), *How Manchester is Managed* (Manchester: Manchester City Council), pp. 116–7.
75. *The Times*, 21 August 1923.
76. Ibid., 16 August 1926.
77. Ibid., 29 August 1922 and 17 July 1934.
78. Royal Commission, *Transport 1st Report: The Control of Traffic on the Roads*, pp. 39–40.
79. *Autocar*, 5 February 1937, and *Morris Owner*, October 1932, for the diatribe against idiotic pedestrian, cited in O'Connell, *Car in British Society*, p. 131.
80. *Saturday Review*, 15 June 1935, p. 754.
81. *The Times*, 11 December 1935.
82. Ibid., 6 September 1929.
83. Lt. Col. M. O'Gorman (1943), *The Political Roots of Road Accidents* (London: 21 Embankment Gardens SW, self-published), p. 10.
84. O'Gorman, *The Political Roots of Road Accidents*, p. 10.
85. *The Times*, 5 August 1931 and 24 December 1931.
86. Ibid., 26 March 1927 in a leader entitled 'Traffic responsibilities'.
87. Ibid., 6 November 1929.
88. Ibid., 30 November 1933 in a leader on 'Road accidents'.
89. Ibid., 6 April 1929.

90. Ibid., 20 October 1937.
91. *Hansard, Parliamentary Debates*, 10 April 1934.
92. O'Gorman, *The Political Roots of Road Accidents*, p. 10.
93. A. Tripp (1942), *Town Planning and Road Traffic* (London: E. Arnold).
94. *Annual Report of the City of Leeds Police, 1932*, p. 28.
95. *Annual Report, Metropolitan Police, 1933*, p. 37.
96. Ibid., *1937*, p. 12. A similar point was made by the Chief Constable of Birmingham, Cecil Moriarty, *Annual Report of the City of Birmingham Police, 1936*, p. 6.
97. *Annual Report, Metropolitan Police, 1936*, p. 11.
98. *Annual Report of the City of Birmingham Police, 1937*, p. 7.
99. *Annual Report, Metropolitan Police, 1937*, p. 11.
100. *Annual Report, Metropolitan Police, 1938*, pp. 57–8.
101. See, for example, *Annual Report, Metropolitan Police, 1922*, p. 17; *Annual Report of the City of Birmingham Police, 1926*; *Annual Report of the St. Helens Police, 1937*.
102. The problem was probably most acute in London, where pre-war problems were intensified, but it was not confined to the capital. See, for example, the annual report of the Chief Constables of Liverpool (1926), Leeds (1932), Manchester (1932) and St Helens (1937).
103. *Report of HMIC, 1929, Parl. Papers, 1929/30 (69)*, p. 7.
104. *Annual Report of the Preston Police, 1927*.
105. *Annual Report, Metropolitan Police, 1934*, p. 45.
106. *Annual Report of the City of Liverpool Police, 1928*, p. 15. The problem did not diminish in the following years despite more prosecutions; see *Annual Reports, 1929*, p. 17 and *1930*, p. 15.
107. *Annual Report of the City of Leeds Police, 1932*, p. 24. See also *Annual Report of the St. Helens Police, 1932*, p. 4, and *1936*, p. 3; *Annual Report of the City of Liverpool Police, 1930*, p. 15; *Annual Report of the City of Birmingham Police, 1937*, p. 7; *Annual Report of the City of Bradford Police, 1936*; and *Annual Report of the City of London Police, 1930*, pp. 23, 26, *1936*, pp. 11–12.
108. *Manchester Guardian*, 4 October 1932.
109. *Daily Express*, 8 July 1933. Interestingly, the Manchester area RAC manager, Capt. J. M. Hollis was forced to concede that he was 'driven by experience to look sympathetically upon the police attitude in this matter... the Chief Constable and his traffic officers have done everything possible to mark out appropriate parking places', *Manchester Guardian*, 4 October 1932.
110. See, for example, Capt. Thomas Rawson, Chief Constable of Bradford, *Annual Report of the City of Bradford Police, 1935*, p. 26.
111. The 1896 amendment to the 1878 Locomotives on Highways Act allowed 'light locomotives' on public roads but limited their speed to 14 miles per hour (or less if prescribed by the Local Government Board). The speed limit was raised to 20 mph though local authorities could apply for 10 mph limits in certain towns.
112. Royal Commission, *Transport 1st Report: The Control of Traffic on the Roads*, p. 6. Opinion was equally divided among county and borough chief constables. Somewhat surprisingly, 18 county chief constables were not in favour of the abolition of all speed limits.

232 Notes

113. *Annual Report of the City of Manchester Police, 1925*, p. xxix and *1936*, p. 39.
114. *Annual Report, Metropolitan Police, 1935*, p. 48, and *Annual Report of the City of Bradford Police, 1936*, p. 25. Birmingham is a good example of the often bitter disputes that took place between the Ministry of Transport and local councils and police over deregulation. See Watch Committee minutes, 3 July 1935–18 March 1936.
115. *Annual Report of the St. Helens Police, 1931*. See also *Annual Report of the City of Manchester Police, 1930*, p. x.
116. *Annual Report of the City of Leeds Police, 1932* and see also *1934*.
117. See, for example, *Annual Report of the City of Manchester Police, 1929*, p. vi, and *1936*, p. 30; *Annual Report of the City of Leeds Police, 1929*, p. 23; *Annual Report, Metropolitan Police, 1936*, p. 12.
118. *Annual Report of the Preston Police, 1934*, pp. 11–12.
119. Ibid., *1938*, p. 14.
120. *Annual Report of the Manchester Police, 1938*, p. 43.
121. See, for example, *Annual Report of the St. Helens Police 1935*, p. 4, and *1936*, p. 4.
122. *Annual Report of the St. Helens Police, 1935*, p. 4.
123. Birmingham Watch Committee minutes, 4 February 1934.
124. *Annual Report of the City of Manchester Police, 1938*, p. 44.
125. *Annual Report of the City of Liverpool Police, 1933*, p. 17.
126. *Annual Report, Metropolitan Police, 1936*, p. 15.

6 The Police and the Practicalities of Traffic Management

1. P. Thorold (2003), *Motoring Age: The Automobile and Britain 1898–1939* (London: Profile Books), p. 195.
2. *Report of HMIC, 1921, PP, 1922* (5), pp. 4–5.
3. *HMIC Annual Report, 1938*, p. 14. The problem was not new, having been noted in the early 1920s, but intensified as popular leisure grew during the inter-war years. It was estimated that over seven million people went to Blackpool annually in the mid 1930s and over one million to the more sedate Eastbourne.
4. *HMIC Annual Report, 1927*, p. 11.
5. (Manchester) *Evening News*, 15 July 1931.
6. See *Annual Report of Commissioner of Metropolitan Police, 1921, PP 1922* (1699), p. 17, and *Report of HMIC, 1927, PP 1927* (130), p. 16. Arm signals were codified at a Home Office conference in 1923.
7. Royal Commission on Transport, *1st Report: The Control of Traffic on Roads*, Parl. Papers 1929/30 (3365), p. 24 (hereafter Royal Commission, *Transport, 1st Report: The Control of Traffic on the Roads*).
8. Appendix 1 of the 1935 edition was entitled 'TRAFFIC SIGNALS THAT EVERY ROAD USER SHOULD KNOW. Part 1, SIGNALS TO BE GIVEN BY POLICE CONSTABLES AND OTHERS ENGAGED IN THE REGULATION OF TRAFFIC' comprised two stop signals (which could also be combined) and two proceed signals.
9. *Annual Report, Metropolitan Police, 1935*, p. 55.

10. *Annual Report of the City of Manchester Police, 1928*, Table 5.
11. *Annual Report of the City of Liverpool Police, 1929*.
12. A. L. Dixon, of the Home Office, to the *House of Lords Select Committee on the Prevention of Road Accidents, 1937–8*, Q. 241.
13. *Annual Report of the Preston Police, 1925*, p. 15.
14. *Report of HMIC, 1925, PP 1926* (2), p. 8.
15. Manchester and Preston first installed traffic lights in 1928 and 1929, respectively, but Liverpool and Bradford did not begin experimenting until 1931 and 1932. See also *The Times*, 7 February 1933.
16. *The Times*, 4 March 1924. The lights relied upon gas and were used to flash a continuous red light in each of the four directions at crossroads. A similar experiment was tried in Kent on the London to Folkestone road, *The Times*, 27 October 1927.
17. *Annual Report, Metropolitan Police, 1931*, p. 22. The scheme used a fixed-time cycle which created stop/start problems that were not resolved until the change to vehicular-operated lights in 1934. *The Times*, 10 May 1934.
18. *The Times*, 10 January 1932.
19. Ibid., 22 June 1932.
20. *Annual Reports, Metropolitan Police, 1932*, p. 44, *1935*, p. 55 and 1938, p. 57.
21. *The Times*, 27 March 1933 and 16 November 1937. See also 15 January 1936 and 23 January 1937. The scheme cost £6500 to install.
22. *The Times*, 8 September 1936.
23. *Annual Reports, Metropolitan Police, 1933*, p. 38, and 1937, p. 57.
24. Ibid., p. 38. The increasing problem of negligent cyclists was noted in the *1935 Annual Report*, p. 51.
25. Ibid., *1934*, p. 43.
26. Ibid., *1936*, p. 55.
27. Ibid., *1939*, p. 38.
28. *Annual Report of the City of Manchester Police, 1931*, p. xi.
29. Ibid., *1928*, p. vii.
30. *Annual Report of the City of Manchester Police, 1929*, p. vii.
31. Ibid., *1932*, p. viii.
32. Ibid., *1933*, p. ix.
33. Ibid., *1936*, p. 36.
34. (Manchester) *Evening News*, 15 November 1928.
35. *Annual Report od the City of Manhester Police*, 1929, p. vii.
36. Ibid., p. vii.
37. Ibid., *1933*, pp. xv–xvi.
38. Ibid., *1932*, p. xi.
39. *Annual Report of the Preston Police, 1931*, p. 15.
40. *Annual Report of the City of Leeds Police, 1926*, p. 11.
41. Ibid., *1928*, p. 24.
42. Ibid.
43. Ibid., *1931*, p. 23.
44. *The Times*, 26 September 1933.
45. *Annual Report of the City of Leeds Police, 1934*, p. 26.
46. *The Times*, 7 April 1933 and 17 August 1933.
47. *The Times*, 17 August 1933 and 12 August 1938.
48. *The Times*, 31 January 1934.

49. *Annual Report of St. Helens Police, 1936*, p. 4, the Chief Constable of St Helens in 1936 noted that 'Traffic Signals, Halt Signs and Pedestrian Crossings... are not generally used.'
50. J. Moran (2006), 'Crossing the road in Britain, 1931–1976', *Historical Journal*, 49, pp. 477–96.
51. *The Times*, 7 April 1933.
52. *The Times*, 10 July 1934.
53. *The Times*, 19 September 1934. The beacons were unpopular with many as a blot on the landscape, an easy target for stone-throwing youths and a source of frustration for reformers who wanted to see them illuminated.
54. *The Times*, 29 October 1934.
55. *The Times*, 2 November 1934, 10 November 1934, 6 February 1935 and 11 May 1936.
56. *The Times*, 28 May 1938.
57. *Chief Constables' Association, Annual Report, 1935*, p. 21.
58. *The Times*, 4 and 22 October 1934, 27 August 1935 and 11 April 1938. There was discussion about making jay-walking an offence as in America, but this was never adopted. The new regulations introduced in 1934 did make it an offence to stay longer than necessary on a crossing. *The Times*, 29 October 1934. See also *Annual Report of the City of Leeds Police, 1936*, for 'uncertainty among pedestrians as to their rights'. p. 27.
59. *The Times*, 30 January 1935.
60. Trenchard quoted in *The Times*, 9 January 1935.
61. *Annual Report of the City of Manchester Police, 1934*, p. xxxiv.
62. Ibid., *1936*, p. 30.
63. *Annual Report of the City of Bradford Police, 1935*, p. 28. However, in 1936 Rawson reported some improvement.
64. See, for example, *Annual Report of the City of Leeds, 1934*, p. 26. That this was a general problem is conceded in *HMIC Annual Report, 1936*.
65. *Annual Report of the City of Leeds Police, 1936*, p. 27.
66. Ibid., pp. 27–8.
67. *Annual Report of the Salford Police, 1929*, p. 15.
68. Ibid. One-way systems were a common response to the problems faced in older towns and cities where the roads were clearly inadequate for modern traffic and were introduced in many urban areas. The Salford play street scheme was not introduced into Manchester until 1935.
69. Maxwell was often frustrated by the slow rate of progress that resulted from having to negotiate with various authorities but several chief constables expressed satisfaction with the progress made in conjunction with various local authorities. See, for example, *Annual Report of the Preston Police, 1934*, p. 11, and *Annual Report of the St. Helens Police, 1936*, p. 3.
70. *The Times*, 11 April 1938.
71. *Annual Report of the City of Leeds Police, 1931*, p. 26.
72. *Annual Report of the Middlesbrough Police, 1927*.
73. *Annual Report City of Manchester Police, 1936*, p. 4.
74. C. V. Godfrey (1937), *Road Sense for Children* (Oxford: Oxford University Press).
75. *Annual Report of the Salford Police, 1929*, p. 15.
76. Ibid., p. 37

77. *Annual Report of the City of Leeds Police 1931*, p. 16.
78. *Annual Report of the City of Manchester, 1936*, p. 18.
79. Home Office letter to Salford Chief Constable (Godfrey), 18 February 1937. The same words were used by Sir John Simon, Home Secretary, when he addressed Parliament on the same day.
80. Report of Chief Constable of Lancashire on Home Office Experimental Motor Patrol Scheme, October 1938, p. 3. There is a copy of this in the Greater Manchester Police Museum.
81. Ibid., p. 10.
82. Ibid., p. 12.
83. Ibid., pp. 16, 21.
84. Ibid., p. 26.
85. Ibid., p. 37.
86. Ibid.
87. Ibid., p. 43
88. Chief Constable of Salford Notes for Chief Constables' Meeting at Liverpool, 4 August 1938, regarding Home Office Experimental Motor Patrol Scheme, p. 1. The Home Secretary, unsurprisingly, had used exactly the same language when he addressed the House of Commons on 18 February 1937 on the subject of the police patrols.
89. Chief Constable of Salford, Notes for Chief Constables' Meeting at Liverpool, 4 August 1938, regarding Home Office Experimental Motor Patrol Scheme, p. 2.
90. Metropolitan Police Report on Home Office Experimental Motor Patrol Scheme, October 1938, p. 14.
91. Ibid., p. 7.
92. Ibid., p. 6.

7 Motoring Offences and the Enforcement of the Law

1. *Saturday Review*, 15 December 1928.
2. *The Times*, 9 January 1935.
3. *The Times*, 25 August 1934.
4. Ibid.
5. Both Acts remained on the statute book (and were used) until after the period here under review.
6. Offences Against the Person Act, 1861, Section 35.
7. Cars were required to display number plates and registration was made compulsory. Motorcycles were brought under the provisions of the Act which also made it an offence to fail to stop after, or to report, an accident. Courts were also able to endorse or suspend driving licences.
8. *The Times*, 26 July 1920. See also letter to *The Times*, 11 March 1925 which agreed that 'dangerous driving is a curse, and should be very severely dealt with, but it will not be prevented by a few un-English police "traps".'
9. E. R. Clapton (2000), 'Intersection of conflict: policing and criminalising Melbourne's traffic, 1890–1930', unpublished PhD thesis, University of

Melbourne. As Clapton rightly points out such attitudes were to be found before the advent of motor traffic.
10. Royal Commission on Transport, *1st Report, The Control of Traffic on Roads*, PP 1929/30 (MD 3365), p. 4.
11. Alker Tripp (1935), quoted in J. S. Dean (1947), *Murder Most Foul* (London: Allen & Unwin), p. 21. The Chief Constable of Kendal, in the same year, ascribed the 'town's immunity from road deaths' to its 'winding old-fashioned streets which compel motorists to drive cautiously', see Royal Commission on Transport, *1st report*, p. 4.
12. The 1929 Royal Commission on Transport had rejected the idea of a speed limit in built-up areas largely on the grounds of the 'great difficulty in defining built up areas'.
13. Royal Commission on Transport, *1st Report*, p. 83.
14. *Hansard*, House of Lords, 21 April 1937, vol. 104, cols 980–1032.
15. *The Times*, 13 January 1937, felt that 'the speed limit is another of those precautions whose familiarity seems to be breeding contempt'.
16. *Annual Report, Metropolitan Police, 1937*, PP 1937/38 (5761), p. 53.
17. *The Times*, 17 August 1937.
18. *Annual Report of the Preston Police, 1938*, p. 10.
19. *The Times*, 15 August and 21 August 1923.
20. Royal Commission on Transport (1929), *1st Report*, p. 6.
21. Chief Constables' Association, *Annual Report of 1932*, p. 27, the General Conference Section.
22. Ibid., p. 27; See also editorial 'Motorists and manslaughter', *The Times*, 23 April 1937.
23. *Andrew v DPP*, 1937. House of Lords, 8 and 9 March and 22 April 1937.
24. *Saturday Review*, 6 July 1935, p. 857.
25. Solicitor, 'Motoring offences', *Saturday Review*, 16 November 1929, p. 572.
26. *The Times*, 2 December 1935.
27. *The Times*, 27 February 1935.
28. Stringer was appealing on the ground that an acquittal for manslaughter was incompatible with a conviction for dangerous driving.
29. In fact the unfortunate William Burton was carried for several yards on the bonnet of Andrews's van before being thrown forward onto the road and run over again. To compound matters, Andrews did not stop after the accident.
30. *Andrews v DPP*, judgment of Lord Atkins.
31. See, for example, William Hunt in *The Times*, 18 February 1937, p. 19.
32. *The Times*, 24 October 1932.
33. Patrick Donnelly was found not guilty of manslaughter at Gloucester Assizes in 1934 but sentenced to four months' imprisonment for dangerous driving and disqualified for five years. The fact that he had 41 previous motoring convictions and was a known criminal may have played some part in the decision. Lord du Clifford was acquitted of dangerous driving when tried at the Old Bailey following his acquittal for manslaughter. Similarly, Charles Pratt who had killed two schoolgirls and injured two more when his car had mounted the pavement was acquitted of manslaughter but found guilty of dangerous driving, for which he was fined £5 and ordered to meet the costs of prosecution, not exceeding the sum of £35.
34. *The Times*, 29 January 1937, p. 11.

35. *The Times*, 1 July 1931, p. 10.
36. *The Times*, 29 October 1937, p. 4.
37. See, for example, *House of Lords Select Committee on the Prevention of Accidents*, Q. 255.
38. *The Times*, 27 June 1939.
39. *The Times*, 11 January 1935, p. 11.
40. The failure rate in Liverpool was even higher at *c.* 44 per cent. Ibid.
41. Royal Commission on Police Procedures, *Report* (1929).
42. Ibid.
43. *Hansard*, House of Lords, 16 December 1929.
44. Ibid.
45. Ibid., 18 February 1930.
46. Ibid., 17 December 1929.
47. King's Bench Division, 13 January 1938, *The Times*, 14 January 1938.
48. Ibid.
49. See, for example, *Annual Report of the City of Leeds Police*, 1925 and 1931.
50. *Annual Report of the City of Liverpool Police*, 1935, p. 19. Three years later he was still writing that there was a need for 'the imposition of more severe penalties', in *Annual Report, 1938*, p. 16.
51. HMIC, *Annual Report 1928*, pp. 8–9.
52. Ibid., quoting the Chair of the Hove Watch Committee, speaking at the 1928 meeting of the Chief Constables' Association (Cities and Boroughs).
53. See, for example, the *Daily Express*, 15 February 1934 which reported one case of drunken driving being thrown out at Liverpool Assizes by the judge who had condemned police measures as 'inroads on our British freedoms'. In a second case in London the use of the bow tie test (i.e., tying one without the use of a mirror) as a test of drunkenness was roundly ridiculed.
54. *The Times*, 13 October 1933.
55. *Annual Report of the City of Manchester Police, 1932*, p. x.
56. Ibid. See also the situation in Liverpool noted above.
57. *Annual Report of the City of Liverpool Police, 1932*, p. 14.
58. Ibid., p. 24.
59. Ibid., p. 19.
60. *Annual Report of the City of Leeds Police, 1935*, p. 57.
61. House of Lords Select Committee on the Prevention of Accidents (1937–38), *Report*, QQ 5124, 5133, 5195.
62. *The Times*, 27 February 1933 and 3 March 1933, though in the latter they criticised the police as well as magistrates for their inability or unwillingness to enforce the law. A similar complaint was made 23 September 1936.
63. *The Times*, 10 December 1935.
64. P. Donovan and P. Lawrence (2008), 'Road traffic offending and an inner London Magistrates' Court (1913–1963)', *Crime, History and Societies*, 12, 119–40. The following details are taken from this article.
65. It is not insignificant that many defendants were well off and well informed and willing to defend themselves in court.
66. This provides a useful but crude measure. A more sensitive indicator would relate prosecutions to vehicle ownership, but even this would not take into account other important factors such as differences in the physical environment.

67. *The Times*, 22 and 23 September 1936 and 8 May 1937.
68. *The Times*, 24 November 1936. Letter writers to *The Times* joined in to identify magistrates who allegedly took a harsh line against motorists. Those in Swindon aroused particular anger.
69. *Hansard*, House of Lords, 21 April 137, House of Commons, 1 December 1937. The House of Lords Select Committee on the Prevention of Accidents (1937–38) were told by Dixon that regarding the law and motorists the problem was more 'in the execution of the law than in the law itself'. *Report*, Q 270. See also Q 5124 but see evidence of Captain Holder, Chief Constable of Lancashire, who recognised that justices were becoming less inconsistent. Q 7860.
70. *The Times*, 17 August 1937.
71. See, for example, Gamon's description of the Western and Eastern views of the police in Edwardian London. H R. P. Gamon (1907), *The London Police Court, Today and Tomorrow* (London: Dent).
72. *The Times*, 29 March 1934.
73. Various correspondents to *The Times* spoke of 'a sense of injustice' towards the police as a result of their enforcement of the speed limit in particular. See, for example, letters 29 March 1935 and 15 October 1935.
74. Royal Commission on Policing, *Final Report* (May 1962), PP 1961/2 cmd. 1728, pp. 114–7. The commissioners were criticised at the time for their conservative (if not misleading) interpretation of the findings of this survey. See Ben Whitaker (1960), *The Police* (London: Eyre and Spottisswode).

8 Cars, Crime and Coppers: Combating the 'Smash and Grab' Raider

1. *Hansard*, House of Commons Parliamentary Debates, 24 March 1933.
2. Ibid., 22 January 1930. See also questions in the House of Commons, 29 January 1931 and 11 December 1931 on prevalence of smash and grab raids.
3. *Hansard*, House of Commons Parliamentary Debate, 15 April 1932.
4. For example, *The Times* reported jewellery raids in London on 19 December 1928; 4 January, 2 February, 30 May and 23 December 1929; 17, 28 February, 19, 21, 26 April 1930; 1, 11 July, 28 October, 1 November, 2, 18 December 1930; 19 February, 24 March, 30 April, 12, 21 August, 30 September, 6 November, 8 December 1931; 11 February, 1 March, 1 August, 5 September 1932; 25 May, 23 June, 4 October, 19 October 1933; 14, 15, 22 February 1934; 18 May, 14, 31 August, 5, 22 September 1935; 24 September 1936; 22 March, 13, 14, 23, 30 December 1937; 25 July, 1 November 1938; and 24 August 1939. Outside London raids were reported in North Walsham (4 June 1929), Orpington (5 September 1933), Glasgow (20 September 1933, 6 January 1934), Thame (4 October 1933), Lowestoft (9 August 1934), Dover (4 September 1934), Liverpool (13 September 1934), Aldershot (31 December 1935), Bournemouth (1, 30 January 1936), Manchester (10 January 1936), Newhaven (1, 16 June 1936), Edinburgh (21 July, 22 August 1936), Dudley (2 December 1938) and Yeovil (16 August 1938). Among the less obvious items stolen were waterproofs (Streatham,

28 December 1935) and piano accordions (Kentish Town, 5 September 1935, and Harrow, 25 January 1937).
5. Detective-Sergeant Weir at Central Criminal Court. *The Times*, 27 September 1929.
6. For example, *The Times*, 18 December 1930, 23 June 1933 and especially 19 October 1933 for large hauls; 17 February 1930 for fast cars, but see *The Times* 15 August 1932 for the case of 19-year-old hairdresser, Joseph Gambardella, who stole a slower moving hearse and used it in an attack on a jeweller's shop in Great Dover Street, London; 1 May 1935 for a car chase across London and a fight with the thieves.
7. For example, the speedy action of a flying squad patrol car ensured the rescue of Christmas parcels, *The Times*, 23 December 1929.
8. *The Times*, 3 October 1932.
9. For advocacy of the right to shoot to kill, see letters, 11 and 17 May 1932. For paint-filled glass balls, see 29 April 1932. Less than a month later the following advert appeared: 'Smash and grab – inventor of the new "eggshell" colour bomb would like to get in touch with a firm of manufacturers able and willing to manufacture and market the same'. No manufacturer appears to have been forthcoming.
10. Mr Paul Griffiths, *The Times*, 6 November 1931. See also the enthusiasm of one MP (Mr Hales) to 'put up both hands for the reintroduction of the cat-o'-nine-tails for the punishment of men convicted of offences of that description' (i.e., smash and grab raids), *Hansard*, House of Commons Parliamentary Debates, 30 June 1932.
11. Letter to *The Times*, 4 August 1932.
12. Letter to *The Times*, 6 August 1932.
13. Letter to *The Times*, 19 October 1932.
14. *Hansard*, House of Commons, 15 April 1932. Grenfell also asked for a political census of prisoners, reassuring his audience with his belief that 'the majority of "old lags" [would call] themselves good, sound Conservatives'.
15. *Annual Report, Metropolitan Police, 1932*, p. 19.
16. *The Times*, 27 September 1929. See also 23 December 1929, 17 February 1930, 30 April 1931, 1 May 1935 and 18 January 1938.
17. *The Times*, 19 April 1930. It was also claimed that less experienced thieves had taken their place but were easier to arrest. Less reassuring was the statement that some criminals had turned their attention to provincial targets.
18. *The Times*, 6 June 1934.
19. Ibid., 2 April 1935.
20. Ibid.
21. Ibid.
22. *The Times*, 'The wireless hue and cry', editorial, 11 October 1935. See also 'Cars and crime', 29 March 1938 and 'Crime in 1938', 2 January 1939.
23. *The Times*, 13 April 1937.
24. Ibid.
25. C. Williams (2008), 'Trains, planes then automobiles: the advent of the police control room in the UK, 1907–1975, sent to authors by C. Williams (hereafter Williams, Trains, planes and automobiles).

26. Williams, 'Trains, planes and automobiles'.
27. HMIC, *Annual Report, 1931*, p. 5.
28. Ibid., *1934*, p. 11.
29. Ibid., *1936*, pp. 14–5.
30. *Annual Report, Metropolitan Police, 1924*, which referred to the flying squad's 'excellent results', p. 15.
31. *Annual Report of the City of Manchester Police, 1937*, p. 22; *Annual Reports of the Leeds Police, 1938*, p. 22.
32. Records of the Lancashire County Police, located in the Lancashire County Record Office, Preston, reference 5335. These photographs were often used in the Chief Constables' Association's various annual reports for advertising purposes.
33. *Annual Report of the Preston Police, 1938*, p. 16.
34. This was particularly a problem in certain rural areas where police houses were some distance from the nearest phone, private or public.
35. *Annual Report, Metropolitan Police, 1929*, p. 7. The problem continued. Reports of the Commissioner of the Metropolis, 1933, p. 29, *1934*, p. 29 and *1935*, p. 40.
36. Ibid., p. 17, *1932*, p. 35.
37. Ibid., *1934*, p. 32.
38. Ibid., *1936*, p. 44 and *1937*.
39. *Annual Report of the City of Leeds Police 1931*, p. 20, and *1932*, p. 20, *1933*, p. 20, *1934*, p. 24.
40. Ibid., 1935, p. 20.
41. *Annual Report of the Salford Police, 1928*, pp. 13–14; also *1930*, p. 13.
42. *Annual Report of the Preston Police, 1934*, p. 13.
43. Ibid., *1937*, p. 10.
44. *Annual Report of the City of Manchester Police, 1928*, p. 11.
45. *Manchester Guardian*, 27 April 1928.
46. Ibid., 5 May 1928.
47. Ibid., 1 November 1928.
48. Ibid., 11 November 1928; Manchester City Police (1929), 'Police Box System: Reorganization of C Division' (Manchester: Chief Constables' Office) a 58-page pamphlet. Also look at Manchester City Police, 'Police Box System: Internal Book C Division' (Manchester: Manchester City Police).
49. *Annual Report of the City of Manchester Police, 1929*, p. vi.
50. Ibid., p. vii.
51. *Daily Herald*, 4 November 1932.
52. Ibid., 11 November 1932.
53. (Manchester) *Evening Chronicle*, 9 September 1933.
54. Manchester City Police (1938), 'Telephone Pillar System: B Division' (Manchester: Manchester City Police), pp. 3–4.
55. HMIC, *Annual Report, 1936*, p. 15.
56. HMIC, *Annual Report, 1933*, p. 30.
57. *Annual Report, Metropolitan Police, 1934*, pp. 16–7. 'It was also claimed that the new system improved morale across the force as all could feel part of a new way and with new efficiency in crime prevention and detection.'

58. There is a scrapbook of cuttings on him, many of them without dates, that was presented to the Greater Manchester Police Museum, Newton Street, Manchester, shortly after his death. It has no reference listing.
59. *Annual Report of the City of Manchester Police, 1935*, p. xxv.
60. Ibid., p. xxxiv.
61. Chief Constables' Association, *Annual Report*, 13 June 1935 and 10 June 1936.
62. *Annual Reports, Metropolitan Police, 1918, 1919*, p. 12.
63. Ibid., *1926*, p. 16.
64. *Crime Statistics, 1928*, p. xii.
65. *Crime Statistics, 1928*, p. xii; *Annual Report of the City of Leeds Police, 1931*, made a similar point regarding the growth of suburbs in this city. Other chief constables in Bradford, Liverpool, Manchester, Salford and Preston did not share this concern – at least, not to the extent of raising it publicly in their annual reports.
66. *Annual Report, Metropolitan Police, 1930*, p. 17.
67. Ibid., *1932*, p. 39.
68. *Annual Report of the City of Bradford Police, 1932*, p. 10; *Annual Reports of the City of Manchester Police 1934*, p. i and *1935*, pp. v–vi.
69. *Annual Report of the City of Leeds Police, 1936*, p. 7.
70. *Annual Report of the City of Bradford Police, 1932*, p. 10 and *Annual Report of the Preston Police 1930*, p. 20.
71. *Annual Report of the Liverpool Police, 1932*, p. 18. The concern with juvenile delinquency, unsurprisingly, was to be found in many towns and cities.
72. *Annual Report of the City of Liverpool Police, 1929*, p. 15.
73. HMIC, *Annual Report, 1925*, p. 9.
74. HMIC, *Annual Report, 1926*, p. 12.
75. HMIC, *Annual Report, 1933*, p. 10.
76. HMIC, *Annual Report, 1936*, p. 14.
77. Ibid.
78. HMIC, *Annual Report, 1937*, p. 16.
79. HMIC, *Annual Report, 1938*, p. 10.
80. *Annual Report, Metropolitan Police, 1918/19*, p. 6.
81. Ibid., *1921*, p. 12. By 1924 'light motor cars' had replaced motorcycles, no doubt to the relief of all concerned.
82. K. Rivers (1972), *History of the Traffic Department of the Metropolitan Police* (London: Metropolitan Police), p. 15. This considerable increase in the size of the overall motor transport section put considerable pressure on those responsible for maintaining the fleet of cars and motorcycles on the road. Motor patrol officers were expected to be able to carry out minor repairs and to use the Barnes garage facility only for more serious mechanical problems.
83. Rivers, *History of the Traffic Department of the Metropolitan Police*, p. 18. Trenchard was a firm believer in the need for more cars for traffic work and this was one of the conclusions of the internal Tomlin Committee, which he set up in January 1932.
84. Rivers, *History of the Traffic Department of the Metropolitan Police*, p. 21.
85. Ibid., p. 34.
86. Ibid.

87. See, for example, *Annual Reports of the City of Leeds Police, 1932*, p. 17 and *1933*, p. 17.
88. *Annual Report of the City of Leeds Police, 1935*, p. 16.
89. Ibid., *1931*, p. xiv.
90. Ibid., *1937*, p. 22.
91. Ibid., p. 24; M. Anderson (1926), *How Manchester is Managed* (Manchester: Manchester City Council), p. 200.
92. *Annual Report of the Preston Police, 1932*, p. 15.
93. *Annual Reports of St. Helens' Police, 1932*, p. 2.
94. T. S. Madigan (1993), *The Men Who Wore Straw Helmets: Policing Luton* (Dunstable: Book Castle), p. 47. Essex Police Museum, http://www.essex.police.uk/mseum/history_25.htm (accessed 19 November 2010).
95. Bob Dobson (1989), *Policing Lancashire* (Blackpool, Landy: Bob Dobson), p. 52; L. C. Jacobs (1992), *Constables of Suffolk* (Suffolk: Suffolk Constabulary), p. 55.
96. *Annual Report of Luton Police, 1928*, quoted in A. R. Richer (1991), *Policing Bedfordshire* (Bedford: Bedfordshire Magazine), p. 115.
97. R. Inglton (2002), *Policing Kent* (Chichester: Phillimore), pp. 97–8.
98. L. C. Jacobs (1992), *Constables of Suffolk* (Ipswich: Suffolk Constabulary), pp. 55, 77.
99. M. Scollan (1993), *Sworn to Serve: Police in Essex* (Chichester: Phillimore), p. 16; J. Woodgate (1985), *The Essex Police* (Suffolk: Terence Dalton), pp. 144–5.
100. *Annual Report of the City of Leeds Police, 1938*, p. 22.
101. C. Emsley (2009), *The Great British Bobby A History of British Policing from the 18th Century to the Present* (London: Quercus), pp. 224, 228.
102. Ibid., pp. 224, 228, 230.
103. *Hansard*, House of Commons, 14 April 1937.
104. *Annual Report, Metropolitan Police, 1938*, p. 52.

9 Conclusion

1. Demos (2000), *A Force for Change: Policing 2020*, April 2006, p. 20.

Bibliography

Primary sources

Manuscript sources
Lloyd George Papers (House of Lords).
National Archives, Kew.
CAB 23 War Cabinet, CAB 24/181, CAB 27/287, CAB 27/610.
Home Office 45/11072/387089, Home Office 45/12651, Part 1,Home Office 45/13933, Home Office 45/14795, Home Office 45/16125, Home Office 45/19406, Home Office 45/20130, Home Office 45/20219, Home Office 45/22806, Home Office 45/24707, Home Office 45/24711, Home Office 45/24785, Home Office 45/25388, Home Office 45/3469, Home Office 45/6215, Home Office 144/12050 Part 1 and Part 2, Home Office 144/3469, Part 1 and Part 2, Home Office 144/4549 Part 1, Part 2, Home Office 144/6116, Home Office 144/6896, Home Office 144/6898, Home Office 144/6902.
Home Office 144/6903, KV 2/998.
KV 2/999, MEPO 1/1126.
MEPO 2/10211, MEPO 2/11234.
MEPO 2/1910, MEPOL 2/4211.
MEPOL 2/3098, MEPOL 2/3908.
MEPO 2/4211, MEP0 2/7640.
MEPO 2/7649, MEPO 2/8103.
MEPO 2/8656, MEPO 3.
MEPO 3/1710, MEPO 3/1786.
MEPO 3/1814, MEPO 3/1815.
MEPO 3/257A, MEPO 3/319.
MT 34/62, Cabinet Economy Committee.
PCOM 7/714, PCOM CLOM 7/705.

Parliamentary papers and government papers
Committee on the Police Service in England and Wales and Scotland, PP 1920(874).
Crime Statistics, 1928.
Hansard, *Parliamentary Debates.*
His Majesty's Inspectorate of Constabulary, *Annual Reports* from 1918, 1919, 1921, 1923, 1924, 1925, 1926, 1927, 1928, 1929, 1932, 1933, 1936, 1937, 1938.
Judicial Statistics, 1923 PP 1924–25.
Report of the Committee on Police Service in England, Wales, and Scotland, Part 1 (920), Part II (1920), known as the Desborough Report.
Report of the Departmental Committee on Detective Work and Procedure (1938), vols 1–5 (London: HMSO).
Report of His Majesty's Inspector of Constabulary, 1919, PP 1920 (91); 1922, PP 1923 (55); 1927, PP 1927 (130).

Report of the Royal Commission on Police Powers and Procedures (1929), (Cmnd. 3297).
Select Committee on Police Forces (Amalgamation) 1931–2 (Cmnd. 106).
Report of the Select Committee of the House of Lords on the Prevention of Road Accidents, 1937 to 1938, copy in the Library of the House of Lords.
Royal Commission on Transport, *1st Report: The Control of Traffic on the Roads*, PP 1929–1930 (Cmnd. 3365).
Royal Commission on Police, *Final Report* (May 1962), (Cmnd. 1728).

Books, pamphlets and reports

Annual Reports of the Birmingham City Police, 1918–1939 (Birmingham Central Library).
Annual Reports of the Bradford City Police, 1918–1939 (West Yorkshire Archives).
Annual Reports of the City of Leeds Police, 1918–1939 (West Yorkshire Archives).
Annual Reports of the City of London Police (various reports via Parliamentary Papers).
Annual Reports of the Lancashire Constabulary, 1918–1939 (Lancashire Records Office, Preston).
Annual Reports of the City of Liverpool Police, 1918–1939 (Liverpool Record Office).
Annual Reports of the City of Manchester Police, 1918–1939 (Greater Manchester Police Museum).
Annual Reports of the Metropolitan Police (various from National Archives and Parliamentary Papers).
Annual Report of the Middlesbrough Police, 1918–1939, and various (Cleveland County Archive).
Annual Reports of the Preston Police, 1918–1939 (Lancashire Record Office, Preston).
Annual Reports of the Salford Police, 1918–1939 (Greater Manchester Police Museum).
Annual Report of the St. Helens' Police, 1918–1939 (Lancashire Record Office, Preston).
Annual Reports of the West Riding Police, 1918–1939 (West Yorkshire Archives).
Anon (1860), *The Streets of London and How to Make Them Passable*, 2nd edn (London: 2000 Library Home Pamphlets HE3/B8).
Birmingham Watch Committee, Minutes.
Buist, J. J. (1923), *A Plea for the Improvement in Teaching and in Encouragement in the Study of Legal Medicine* (n.d.).
Chief Constables' Association, *Annual Reports and Conference Reports, 1918–1939*.
City of Birmingham Police: Bye Laws, Local Acts etc (1903).
Gamon, R. P. (1907), *The London Police Court, Today and Tomorrow* (London: Dent).
General Orders, 1838 and 1839.
General Regulations, Instructions and Orders of the Metropolitan Police Force (1951) (London: Clowes & Sons).
Godfrey, C. V. (1937), *Road Sense for Children* (Oxford: Oxford University Press).
O'Gorman, Lt. Col. (1943), *The Political Roots of Road Accidents* (London: 21 Embankment Gardens, SW, self-published).
Peacock, R. (1900), *Police Constables' Duties: Addresses by Robert Peacock, Chief Constable, City of Manchester* (Manchester: Blakelock & Co).

Police Federation of England and Wales, *Reports of then Joint Central Committee Report of the Commissioner of Police of the Metropolis for the Year 1926, PP 1936/7* (5457).
Report of the Chief Constable of Lancashire on Home Office Experimental Motor Patrol Scheme, October 1938, copy in the Greater Manchester Police Museum, Newton Street, Manchester.
Tripp, A. (1942), *Town Planning and Road Traffic* (London: E. Arnold).

Newspapers

Autocar
Colliery Guardian
Daily Dispatch
Daily Express
Daily Herald
Daily Mail
Daily Mirror
Daily Worker
(Manchester) *Evening News*
Manchester Evening News
Manchester Guardian
Pall Mall Gazette
Saturday Review
The Police and Prison Officers' Magazine
The Police Review and Parade Gossip
The Times
Western Mail
Westminster Gazette
Wigan Examiner
Wigan Observer
Workers' Dreadnought

Secondary sources

Books

Ascoli, D. (1979), *The Queen's Peace: The Origins and Development of the Metropolitan Police Force 1829–1979* (London: Hamish Hamilton).
Brogdon, M. (1991), *On the Mersey Beat: Policing Liverpool between the Wars* (Oxford: Oxford University Press).
Challinor, R. C. (1977), *The Origins of British Bolshevism* (London: Croom Helm).
Clapton, E. R. (2005), *Intersections of Conflict: Policing and Criminalising Melbourne's Traffic, 1890–1930* (Melbourne: University of Melbourne, Department of History).
Clay, W. (ed.) (c. 1975), *The Leeds Police* (Leeds: Leeds City Police).
Critchley, T. J. (1978), *A History of Police in England and Wales* (London: Constable).
Cronin, James E. (1979), *Industrial Conflict in Modern Britain* (London: Croom Helm).

———(1984), *Labour and Society in Britain 1918–1979* (London: Batsford Academic and Education).
Dean, J. S. (1947), *Murder Most Foul* (London: Allen & Unwin).
Dobson, B. (1989), *Policing Lancashire* (Blackpool: Landy Publishing).
Edmondson, B. (1985), *Bob's Beat: The Story of a Lancashire Policeman* (Manchester: Neil Richardson).
Elliott, D. E. (1984), *Policing Shropshire* (no publisher details).
Emsley, C. (1996), *The English Police: A Political and Social History*, 2nd edn (London: Longman).
———(2009), *The Great British Bobby: A history of British Policing from the 18th Century to the Present* (London: Quercus).
Evans, P. (1970), *The Police Revolution* (London: George Allen & Unwin).
Ewing, K. D. and Gearty, C. A. (2000), *The Struggle for Civil Liberties* (Oxford: Oxford University Press).
Fairhurst, J. (1966), *Policing Wigan: The Wigan Borough Police Force 1836–1961* (Blackpool: Landy Publishing).
Flewers, P. (2009), *The New Civilisation? Understanding Stalin's Soviet Union 1929–1941* (London: Francis Boutle Publishers).
Geary, R. (1985), *Policing Industrial Disputes 1893 to 1985* (London and New York: Cambridge University Press).
Hay, D. (ed.) (1987), *Labour, Law and Crime: An Historical Perspective* (London: Tavistock Publications).
Ingleton, R. (2002), *Policing Kent* (Chichester: Phillimore).
Jackson, L. A. (2006), *Women Police: Gender, Welfare and Surveillance in the Twentieth Century* (Manchester: Manchester University Press).
Jacobs, J. (1978), *Out of the Ghetto* (London: Janet Simon).
Jacobs, L. C. (1992), *Constables in Suffolk* (Ipswich: Ipswich Constabulary).
Johnstone, Eric S. (1978), *One Policeman's Story* (London, Berry Row).
Klein, Joanne (2010), *Invisible Men: The Secret Lives of Police Constables in Liverpool, Manchester and Birmingham, 1900–1939* (Liverpool: Liverpool University Press).
Laybourn, K. (1992), *A History of British Trade Unionism 1770–1990* (Stroud: Sutton).
———(1993), *The General Strike of 1926* (Manchester: Manchester University Press).
———(1996), *The General Strike Day by Day* (Stroud: Sutton).
Leishman, F., Loveday B., and Savage, S. P. (eds) (1999), *Core Issues in Policing* (London: Longman).
Lock, J. (1979), *British Policewomen* (London: Robert Hale).
Madigan, T. S. (1993), *The Men Who Wore Straw Helmets: Policing Luton* (Dunstable: Book Castle).
Martin, J. F. and Wilson, G. (1969), *The Police: A Study of Manpower: The Evolution of the Service in England and Wales, 1829–1965* (London: Heinemann).
McKibbin, R. (2010), *Parties and People in England 1914–1951* (Oxford: Oxford University Press).
Morgan, J. (1987), *Conflict and Order: The Police and Labour Disputes in England and Wales, 1900–1939* (Oxford: Oxford University Press).
Morris, M. (1976), *The General Strike* (London: The Journeyman Press).
O'Connell, S. (1998), *The Car in British Society: Class, Gender and Motoring, 1896–1939* (Manchester: Manchester University Press).

Perkins, A. (2006), *A Very British Strike 3 May–12 May 1926* (London: Macmillan).
Peto, D. O. G. (1992), *The Memoirs of Miss Dorothy Olivia Georgina Peto* (London: Brownhill Organising Conference for the European Conference of Equal Opportunities in Policing).
Phillips, Gordan A. (1976), *The General Strike: The Politics of Industrial Conflict* (London: Weidenfeld and Nicolson).
Plowden, W. (1971), *The Motor Car and Politics, 1896–1970* (London: Bodley).
Rawlings, P. (2002), *Policing: A Short History* (Cullompton: Willan).
Reiner, R. (1978), *The Blue-coated Worker: A Sociological Study of Police Unionism* (Cambridge: Cambridge University Press).
Renshaw, P. (1976), *The General Strike* (London: Methuen).
Richer, A. R. (1991), *Policing Bedfordshire* (Bedford: Bedfordshire Magazine).
Rivers, K. (1972), *History of the Traffic Department of the Metropolitan Police* (London: Metropolitan Police).
Scollan, M. (1993), *Sworn to Serve: Police in Essex* (Chichester: Phillimore).
Shepherd, J. and Laybourn, K. (2006), *The First Labour Government* (Basingstoke: Palgrave Macmillan).
Skidelsky, O. (1975), *Oswald Mosley* (London: Macmillan).
Smith, G. (n.d.), *Bradford City Police* (Bradford: Bradford City Police).
Stead, P. J. (1985), *The Police in Britain* (London: Macmillan).
Stevenson, J. and Cook, C. (1977), *The Slump* (London: Jonathan Cape).
Thorold, P. (2003), *The Motoring Age: The Automobile and Britain, 1896–1939* (London: Tavisock Publications).
Weaver, J. C. (1995), *Crimes, Constables and Courts: Order and Transgression in a Canadian City, 1816–1970* (Montreal: MacGill-Queens University Press).
Weinberger, B. (1995), *The Best Police in the World: An Oral History of English Policing* (Aldershot: Scolar Press).
Wilson, D. (2006), *The Beat Policing a Victorian City* (Melbourne: Melbourne Publishing).
Woodgate, J. (1985), *The Essex Police* (Suffolk: Terence Dalton).
Wyles, L. (1952), *A Woman at Scotland Yard: Reflections on the Struggle and Achievements of Thirty Years in the Metropolitan Police* (London: Faber & Faber).

Book chapters

Catterall, S. (2004), 'Police', in J. McIlroy, A. Campbell, and K. Gildert (eds), *Industrial Politics and the 1926 Mining Lockout and the Struggle for Dignity* (Cardiff: University of Wales Press), pp. 249–68.
Cronin, J. E.(1982), 'Coping with Labour, 1918–1928', in J. E. Cronin and J. Schneer (eds), *Social Conflict and Political Order in Modern Britain* (London: Routledge), pp. 110–30.
Weinberger, B. (1987) 'Police perceptions of labour in the inter-war period: the case of the unemployed and the miners; strike', in F. Snyder and D. Hay (eds), *Labour, Law and Crime: An Historical Perspective* (London: Tavistock Publications).

Articles

Bean, R. (1980), 'Police unrest, unionization and the 1919 strike in Liverpool', *Journal of Contemporary History*, 15, 633–53.

Dennis, P. (1981), 'The Territorial Army in aid of the civil power in Britain, 1919–1926', *Journal of Contemporary History*, 16, 705–24.
Donovan, P. and Lawrence, P. (2008), 'Road traffic offending and an inner London Magistrates' Court (1913–1963), *Crime, History and Societies*, 12, 119–40.
Emsley, C. (1993), '"Mother what *did* policemen do when there weren't any motors?" The law, the police and regulation of motor traffic in England, 1900–1939', *Historical Journal*, 39, 357–81.
Ishaque, M. M. and Noland, R. B. (2006), 'Making roads safer for pedestrians or keeping them out of the way?', *Journal of Transport History*, 27, 115–37.
Levine, P. (1994), ' "Walking the street as no decent woman should", women in World War 1', *Journal of Modern History*, 66, 34–78.
Luckin, B. and Sheen, D. (2009), 'Defining early modern automobility: the road traffic accident crisis in Manchester, 1939–1945', *Cultural and Social History*, 6, 211–30.
McIlroy, J., Campbell, A., Laybourn, K., and Outram, Q. (2006), 'The general strike and mining lockout of 1926: a bibliography', *Historical Studies in Industrial Relations*, 21 (Spring), 182–206.
Moran, J. (1988), 'Police and labour in the age of Lindsay, 1910–1936', *Llafur*, 5, 1.
——(2006), 'Crossing the road in Britain, 1931–1976', *Historical Journal*, 49, 477–96.
Morris, R. M. (2001), 'Lies, damned lies and criminal statistics: reinterpreting the criminal statistics in England and Wales', *Crime, History and Societies*, 5, 111–27.
Taylor, H. (1998), 'The politics of rising crime statistics in England and Wales, 1945–1960', *Crime, History and Societies*, 2, 5–28.
Taylor, H., (2001), 'Forging the job', *British Journal of Criminology*, 39, 113–35.
Woodeson, A. (1993), 'The first women police: a force of equality or infringement?', *Women's History Review*, 2, 217–32.

Unpublished dissertations, theses and other works

Clapton, E. R. (2000), 'Intersection of conflict: policing and criminalising Melbourne's traffic, 1890–1930', unpublished PhD thesis, University of Melbourne.
Williams, C. (2008), 'Trains, planes then automobiles: the advent of the police control room in the UK, 1907–1975', sent to the authors by C. Williams.

Websites

Jones, O., ' "The spirit of Petrograd"? The 1918 and 1919 Police Strikes', http. www.whatnext journal.co,uk/Pages/Latest/Police.hml (accessed 14 February 2009).

Index

Note: The letter 'n' followed by the locators refers to notes cited in the text.

Aberdere City Police Athletic and Recreation Unit, 38
Adams, James, 166
Allen, Lt. Col. W. D., 87
All-Russian Co-operative Society, 15
Amalgamated Society of Engineers, 28
America, 4
Anderson, M., 123, 230n, 242n
  How Manchester is Managed, 123, 230n, 242n
Anderson, Sir John, 39–40
Andrews v DPP (1937), 165, 236n
Ascoli, D., 214n, 224–5n
Association of Municipal Corporations, 117
Atcherley, Major General (sometimes Lt. Col), W. L., 24, 42, 54, 60, 87, 116, 137–8, 190, 201
Atkin, Lord, 162, 165–6, 168
Atkinson, E. H. Tindall, 162
Attlee, Clem(ent), 32
Auchterlonie, Ian Douglas, 195
Auchterlonie, John, 32
Autocar, 122, 158, 230n
Automobile Association (AA), 113–14, 117–18, 130, 137, 155, 159, 178–9, 191
  scouts, 212n

Baldwin, Stanley, 11, 58–9, 62–3
Battle of Cable Street (1936), 76–7
Bean, R., 14, 214n
Beckett, John, 70
Belisha Beacons, 144
Bennett MP, Captain E. N., 95
Birmingham Strike Bulletin, 70
Blacker, Chief Inspector, 92
Bolshevik/ism, 23, 35, 48, 63–4, 77–9
Bosanquet, Victor, 63–5, 67, 69, 209, 212n, 223n

Brabazon, Lt. Col. Moore, 125
Breadalbane, Lord, 21
British Association for the Advancement of Science, 107
British fascism, 76–9
British Union of Fascists, 76–9
British Worker, 69
Brodrip, Prison Warden, 30
Brogdon, M., 2, 212n
Brook, Lt. Col. F., 190, 201
Brown, Edgar Percy, 26–7
Browne, T. B. (Chief Constable of Bootle), 34
Buchanan, C. D., 136
  Mixed Blessings: The Motor in Britain, 136
Buist, J. J., 95, 226n
Byng, General Julian, 116

Cabinet, 52–3, 61
  Supply and Transport Committee, 61
Caine, Hall, 186
Caldwell, Chief Constable F., 115–16
Campbell, A., 221n
Campbell, Sir Malcolm, 146, 202–3
Carter, Inspector Frederick, 100
Cecil, Lord, 169
Challinor, Raymond, 13–14, 214n
  The Origins of British Bolshevism, 13–14
Chief Constables' Association (CCA), 38, 43, 47, 54, 83, 91, 114, 132, 148, 162, 221n, 225–7n, 234n, 236n, 241n
chief constable/s and reports, 3, 6, 8–9, 15, 17, 24, 48, 55, 87, 99, 113, 115, 117, 225–49 *passim*
  Bedfordshire, 113, 242n
  Birmingham, 128, 231n

249

chief constable/s and reports –
  continued
  Bradford, 53, 83, 130, 231n,
    233n, 241n
  Bristol, 98
  Carmarthenshire, 63
  Chesterfield, 98, 227n
  Dewsbury, 56
  Durham, 220n
  East Riding, 98
  Glamorgan, 63, 69
  Glasgow, 63
  Lancashire, 147, 240n
  Leeds, 53, 131, 138, 142, 145, 172,
    226n, 230–4n, 237n, 240–2n
  Leicester, 144, 192
  Lincoln, 59
  Liverpool, 115, 129, 132, 225n,
    229n, 231–2n, 237n, 241n
  Luton, 242n
  Manchester, 98, 110, 140, 145, 171,
    226n, 231–4n, 238n, 240n
  Middlesbrough, 194, 234n
  Monmouthshire, 62–4
  Newcastle on Tyne, 53, 87, 192
  Northampton, 70
  Oldham, 6, 83
  Preston, 131, 138, 142, 160, 192,
    231–4n, 236n, 240n, 242n
  St. Helens, 66, 225n, 231–2n, 234n,
    242n
  Salford, 4, 126, 131, 234n, 241n
  Sheffield, 144, 192
  Sunderland, 59
  Surrey, 126
  Warwickshire, 126
  West Riding, 56
  Wigan, 65–6
  York, 57
Churchill, W., 52, 112, 116
City of London Police, 231n
  annual reports, 231n
Civil Constabulary Reserve, 61, 222n
Clapton, E. R., 235n
Clark, Sidney, 164
Clay. W., 212n, 224n
Clynes, J. R., 39, 95
coal dispute, 1921, 52
coal lock-out, 1926, 58, 63

Cole, J. B., 144
Cole, Oswald, 192
Collett, R. L., 98
Colliery Guardian, 222n
Common Police Service Fund, 94
Communist Party of Great Britain, 15,
  72, 76, 224n
communist/s, 30, 72, 76
Cook, C., 224n
Cook, Sir Stenson, 179
Cottenham, Lord, 203
County Council's Association, 117
Courtesy Cops Scheme, 178
Crawley. F.W., 87, 97, 192
Crime Act (1885), 17
Criminal Investigation Department
  (CID), 82, 84–5, 87, 89, 91–3,
  97–8, 100, 191, 205
Criminal Justice Act, 170
Criminal Registrar, 151
Critchley, T.A., 2, 14, 50, 211n, 214n,
  220n, 228n
Cronin, James, 13–14, 213n
Cummings, Sefton, 121, 124
Cunnington, Arthur, 187
cyclists, 132–3, 233n

Daily Dispatch, 87, 225n
Daily Express, 85, 87, 92, 97, 225–6n
Daily Herald, 88, 194, 219n, 240n
Daily Worker, 224n
Dale, Walter Edwin, 35–6
dangerous, careless and drunken
  driving, 160–81
Davidson, Dr. James, 97
Davis, R., 223
de Clifford, Lord, 164
Defence of the Realm Act (DORA), 52, 56
Demos, 242n
  *A Force for Change: Policing 2020
    (April 2006)*, 242n
Departmental Committee on
  Detective Work for England and
  Wales (1933–1938), 83, 87–91,
  96–7
  report, 87–91
Desborough Committee (1918–1919),
  5, 7, 13, 25–6, 36, 47, 83, 89, 108,
  110, 112, 209, 215–16n

detective (and scientific work), 81–104
  numbers, 83–4, 93–4
Dickens, Sir Henry, 187
Diness, ex-Police Sergeant
  Daniel, 30
Director of Public Prosecutions,
  162
Dixon, A. L., 8, 39, 54, 81, 87, 91,
  95–6, 104, 116, 118, 227n,
  233n
Dobson, B., 242n
Donnelly, P., 236n
Donovan, P., 237n
Drummond, C., 219n
drunken drivers, 170–2
Dunning, Leonard, 6, 24, 39, 54,
  110–12, 190, 213n

Earl of Plymouth, 139
Edmondson, B., 214n, 224n
Ellington, Chief Constable A. R., 66,
  130
Elliott, D. J., 214n, 224n
Else, W.M., 97–8
Emergency Powers Act (1920), 49–51,
  57–8, 70, 72
Emsley, Clive, 2, 4, 82, 205, 211n,
  224–6n, 242n
  The English Police, 82
  The Great British Bobby, 2, 82, 205,
    242n
Evans, P., 214n, 224n
Evening Chronicle, 194
Evening News, 85, 225n
Ewing, Keith, 51, 212n, 220n

Fairhurst, J., 214n, 224n
fascism, 76–9
Fields, Gracie, 146
Filer, Sam, 68–9
First World War (or Great War), 1, 11,
  19, 36, 47, 105, 120, 138, 155,
  183–4, 191, 196, 207
Fisher v Oldham, 209
Flewers, P., 224n
flying squad, 71, 75, 190–1
Fontes, Luis, 164

Game, Sir Philip, 78–9, 107, 127, 133,
  181, 224n
Gamon, H. P., 238n
  *The London Police Court Today and
  Tomorrow (London, 1907)*, 238n
Garrow, J. M., 97
Gearty, Conor, 51, 212n, 220n
Geary, Richard, 50, 212n, 220n
Geddes Axe (1921), 4, 35, 42, 60,
  113
General Strike (1926), 2–3, 11–12, 49,
  51, 57–63, 70–6, 222–4n
  prosecutions, 73–4, 222–4n
George, David Lloyd, 21–5, 31, 47,
  49–51, 215n
Germany, 4
Gilmour, Sir John, 44–5
Goddard, Thomas, 173
Godfrey, Major (Chief Constable of
  Salford) C. V., 4, 126, 131, 145–6,
  148, 193, 234n
Goodsell, J., 44
governments
  inter-war, 15
  national, 4, 14
  wartime coalition, 14
Great War, *see* First World War
Great Western Railway, 190
Greenwood, Sir Hamer, 54
Grenfell, David, 188
Grimsby Borough Police Athletic
  Club, 38

Hambrook, Inspector Walter, 190
Hansard, 215n, 237–9n, 242n
Hardley, PC, 43
Harrison, W.R., 95–6
Hay, D., 212n
Hayes, Colonel, H. M. A., 187
Hayes, Jack H., 15, 20, 22, 28–34, 36,
  46–7, 214n, 217n
Heaviside, H. F., 68–70, 223n
Henderson, Arthur, 32–3
Henry, Sir Edward, 17, 22–3, 82
Highway Code, 137, 145, 147, 158,
  178 (1931), 145
Highways Act (1935), 156

His Majesty's Inspectors of Constabulary, and reports, 5–8, 212–14n, 228n
Hollis, Captain J. M., 231n
Holmes, J., 44
Home Affairs Committee, 58
Home Office, 1, 3, 8, 11, 27, 30, 35, 38–40, 42, 45, 48, 50–1, 55–6, 58, 60, 64–5, 67, 69, 72, 82–3, 85–6, 91, 94, 97–8, 100–1, 104, 112, 114–15, 117–18, 178–9, 203, 206, 210, 213–29n, 232n, 235n
Home Office Experimental Motor Patrol Scheme, 147–50
  Metropolitan Police Report on the Experimental Patrol Scheme (1938), 235n
  Notes of Salford Chief Constables on the Home Office Experimental Motor Patrol Scheme (1938), 235n
  Report of the Chief Constable of Lancashire on Home Experimental Motor Patrol scheme (1938), 235n
Home Secretary, 22, 25, 32–5, 39, 44, 58, 61–4, 70, 77–9, 88, 95, 117–18, 124
Hordern, Captain, Sir Archibald, 147–9
Hore-Belisha, Mr, 143, 146
Horne, R. M., 87
Horwood, Brigadier-General, 116
House of Commons, 186, 188
House of Lords, 159, 164
House of Lords Select Committee on the Prevention of Accidents (1937–1938), 167, 171–2, 233n, 237n
Howard, ex-PC Frederick W., 29–30, 32
Humphries, Justice, 166–7

Incitement to Mutiny Act (1797), 60
Independent Labour Party, 28
Inglton, R., 242n
Institute of Transport, 135
Ishaque, M. M., 212n

Jackson, L. A., 211n
Jacobs, J., 224n
Jacobs, L. C., 242n
Johnson, Charles Henry, 32
Johnstone, Eric S., 225n
Jones, Aaron, 68, 70
Jones, L., 222n
Jones, Owen, 14, 214n
  'Spirit of Petrograd', 14, 214n
Joynson-Hicks, Sir William, 44, 60, 117
Judicial Statistics, 110

Kempster, John, 17
Kirkby (sometimes known as Kirby), 2
Klein, Joanne, 17, 214n
  Invisible Men: The Secret Lives of Police Constables in Liverpool, Manchester, and Birmingham, 1900–1939, 17, 214n
Klishko, Nicholas, 30

Labour
  Conference (1919), 32
  Government (1924), 32
  magistrates, 66–72
  Party, 32, 46–8, 72
Lakey, ex-Police Sergeant Arthur, 30, 217n
Laurie, Lt. Col. P. R., 55
Law, Major, 113
Lawrence, P., 237n
Lawther, W., 59
Laybourn, K., 220–1n
Leeds 'Safety First Council', 146
Leishman, F., 228n
Lenin, V. I., 14
Levine, P., 211n
Liberal Party, 11
Lindsay, Lionel, 63, 69
Liverpool Daily Post, 27
Liverpool and District Police Orphanage, 38
Lloyd-Williams, J., 225n
Locker-Lampson, Commander, 206
Lock, J., 211n
Locomotive Act (1861), 156
  amended, 1865, 156

Loveday, B, 228n
Luckin, B, 212n

Macfall, J. E. W., 96
Mackenzie Committee (1924–1925), 15, 32–5, 217n
Mackenzie, Sir William, 32, 217n
Macready, General Sir C. F. Neville, 23–5, 29, 34, 53
Madigan, T. S., 242n
magistrates, 117, 156, 167, 169–70, 173, 179
Manchester Evening News, 141, 219n, 222n, 230n, 232n
Manchester Guardian, 88, 215n, 224–5n, 231n, 240n
Manchester Police Force, 21–3
Manchester Police Regional Wireless Station, 195
Manchester 'Safety First' Committee, 146
Manslaughter, 162–6
Marcan, A., 96
Marsden, James, 30
Marston, James, 24, 29
Martin, J. P., 2, 211n
marxism, 29–30
Matthews, Robert, 131, 145, 192
Maxwell, John (Chief Constable of Manchester), 43–4, 86–7, 89, 129–32, 140–1, 145, 171, 193, 195
Mayall, A. K., 83
McCardie, Justice, 209
McCrone v Riding, 169–70
McGurk, John, 70
McIlroy, J., 221n
McKenna, Sir Reginald, 19
McKibbin, Ross, 11, 213n
Metropolitan police, 7, 16–22, 27–30, 40–1, 60, 77–9, 82–3, 87, 89–90, 107, 116, 127–32, 160, 189–90, 195, 197, 199, 206, 214–21n, 232–3n, 239–42n
    college at Hendon, 86, 90, 94, 97–8, 203
    flying squad, 190–1
    metropolis/itan annual reports, 227n, 229–33n, 239–42n

mobile patrol experiment (1921), 190
Police Strike (1918), 13–16, 21–4
Police Union (MPU), 17–19
Representative Board/s, 24–5, 31
Special Branch, 29–30
women, 40–1
Ministry of Transport, 140, 143–4, 158, 197, 232n
Mond, Sir Alfred, 30
Moran, J., 3, 234n
Morgan, Jane, 50–1, 59, 212n, 220n, 222n
Moriarty, C.V., 227n
Morris, Margaret, 59, 221n
Morrison, Herbert, 145–6
Morris, R. M., 212n, 228n
Mosley, Sir Oswald, 76
Motor Car Act (1903), 109, 157–8, 160
Motor Car Club, 157
motoring offences and the law, 151–85, 198–200
motorists, 1, 105–211 *passim*
    numbers, 105
    patrolling, 200–5
motor-vehicles, 105– 134, 198, 200

National Police Fund, 38
National 'Safety-First' Association, 146
National Union of Police and Prison Officers (NUPPO), 13–36, 46
    ballot, 27
    The Police and Prison Officers' Magazine, 24
National Union of Railwaymen, 22
    Ilford branch, 22
Nichols, Inspector E., 43
Noland, R. B., 212n
non-County Boroughs Association, 7
Northern Light, 70
Northern Police Orphanage, 37

Ockey, Inspector, 188
O'Connell, S., 3–4, 126, 132, 212n, 230n
Offences Against the Person Act (1861), 156, 162
O'Gorman, Lt. Col. M., 230n
Old Swan Station (transmitting), 196

Olympia, 76
Outram, Quentin, 221n

Pall Mall Gazette, 215n
Palmer, Sir Alfred, 70
Pankhurst, Sylvia, 22
Parliamentary Labour Party (PLP), 33, 217n
Parry, HMI, 112–13
Peacock, Robert, 110, 228n
Pease, Sir Alfred, 187
pedestrians, 119–33
Pedestrians' Association, 123
Penfold, J. R., 18
Perkins, Anne, 59, 221n
Peto, Dorothy Olivia Georgina, 40, 218–19n
Pey, Thomas, 65
Philcox, Sergeant, 38
Phillips, G.A., 221n
Phillips, Picton, 63
Police
  Act or Bill (1919), 2–3, 26–8, 30–1, 36–8, 47, 49, 208
  amalgamations/mergers, 7–9
  borough and county forces, 4–7; numbers or size, 4–5, 8
  boxes, 191–4
  College Scheme, 39–40
  Council, 36, 42, 47, 83
  Disabilities Removal Act (1887), 208
  Federation of England and Wales, 3, 12–15, 24, 26, 30–1, 36–48, 208–9, 218–19n
  flying squads, 62
  Gazette, 88
  officers, 13
  order, 49–80
  pay and pensions, 12, 19–22, 25–6; cuts (1922, 1931/2), 12, 35–7, 42–3
  pensioners, 61
  Pensions Bill (1890), 17
  and Police Strike (1919), 13, 27–9
  professionalisation, 1, 11–12
  public, 1, 184–5
  recruitment, 6
  Reserve, 61

Review and Parade Gossip, later simply Police Review, 17–18, 44–5, 75, 88, 90, 95, 215n, 218–19n, 222–3n, 225–6n
  scientific and detective work, 12
  specials, 62
  strikers (1919), 27–31, 33, 47
  strikes (1918 and 1919), 11, 13–36, 52, 208
  strikes, 51–2; days lost, 51–2; see also Police, strikes (1918 and 1919)
  Superannuation Act (1906), 17, 32
  Superannuation Act (1926), 321
  trade unionism, 16–36
  war record, 31
  women, 1, 4, 40–1
Police Review and Parade Gossip (later *Police Review*), 17–18, 44–5, 75, 95
Pomeroy, Thomas, 173
Popkess, Captain Athelston N., 42, 92, 99, 189, 196
prison wardens, 13
Public Order, 3, 49–80 *passim*
  Act (1936), 77
  Policies, 3
Punch, 107, 120, 126

'Q' cars, or 'mystery cars', 188–9, 195, 207

Rafter, Charles Houghton (Chief Constable of Birmingham), 34
Randall, Leslie, 97–8
Rawlings, Philip, 2, 211n, 225n
  Policing: A Short History, 2, 211n, 225n
  'road holocaust', 9
Rawson, T., 83, 231n
Rees, W., 223n
Reiner, R., 48, 218n
Renshaw, Patrick, 221n
Rentoul, Sir Gervais, 169
Report of the Committee on Police Service in England and Wales, and Scotland, Part 2, 1920) Cmnd 574, 214–15n, 228n
  see also Desborough Committee (1918–1919)

Index 255

Report of the Departmental Committee on Detective Work and Procedures (1933–1938), 87–8, 225–6n
Report of the Royal Commission on Police Powers and Procedures (1929), 3, 40, 85–7, 212n, 225n
Reynolds and Brown, 81
Richardson, Lt. Col. A. W. C., 124
Riches, Henry, 194, 199
Rigby, ex-PC, 32
Rivers, K., 241n
  History of the Traffic Department of the Metropolitan Police (London, 1972), 241n
road hog, 127
road safety, 119–26
Road Traffic Act (1930), 130, 143, 158, 161, 166, 170–1, 184, 199, 201, 203–4
Road Traffic Act (1934), 130, 143, 147, 151, 159, 165, 169, 173, 184, 203
road wardens, 112
Ross, Roderick, 203
Royal Air Force, 55–7
Royal Automobile Club (RAC), 113–14, 130, 155, 159, 178, 231n
Royal Commission on London Transport (1906), 109, 118
Royal Commission on Motor Cars (1906), 157
Royal Commission on Policing (1960–1962), 2, 184–5, 238n
Royal Commission on Transport (1929), 120, 124, 137, 158, 160, 168, 229n, 232n, 236n
Russell, Lord, 168
Russian revolutions, 23
Russian Trade Delegation, 30
R v Bateman (1925), 165
R v Stringer (1931), 165–6, 236n

Salford City Police and Fire Brigade Athletic Society, 38
Salter, Dr. Alfred, 67
Samuel, Sir Herbert, 44, 118, 186–8
Sant, Captain Mowbray, 113
Saturday Review, 121, 154–5, 230n, 235–6n
Saunders, Miss Dorothy, 35
Savage, S.P., 228n
Schneer, J., 213
Scientific Acts to Criminal Investigation (HO, 1926), 95
scientific (and detective) work, 81–104
  statistics, 102
Scollan, M., 242n
Scotland Yard, 15, 84–5, 88, 92, 95, 188
Scot, Thomas John Currie, 30
Scott, R. R., 44, 46, 219n
Special Branch, 15
Seager, William, 167
Second World War, 2, 47, 78–9, 101, 104, 210
Select Committee of the House of Commons on Police Forces (Amalgamation) (1932), 8–9, 213n
Self-propelled Traffic Association, 157
Sell, ex-Police Sergeant (sometime Superintendent) W., 30, 217n
Sheen, D., 212n
Shepperson, Harry, 29
Siam Police Journal, 96
Sillitoe, Percy, 192
Simpson, H. B., 112
Skidelsky, R., 224n
smash and grab, 186–90
Smith, Gordon, 82, 214n, 224n
  Bradford City Police, 82
Snyder, F., 212n
Soviet House, 30
Soviet Union, 11, 13
Spackman, PC, 25, 34
special constables, 77
Special Constables Act (1923), 57
Special Constabulary Reserve, 56, 71
speeding, 157–60
  offences, 157–60
speed limits, 130
Spilsbury, Sir Bernard, 95
Stage Carriage Act (1832), 156
Stalybridge Borough Police Recreation Club, 38
Stead, Philip, 2, 221n
Stevens, Major Frank, 204
Stevenson, J., 224n
Strangeways, Staff Sergeant, 37–9
'Sunderland' boxes, 192–4

Syme, John, 17–19
  Fighting Officialdom, 18
  League, 17–18
Symons, C. T., 81, 98, 227n

Taylor, ex-PC Rupert, 30
Taylor, Howard, 2, 112, 118–19, 212n, 228n
telegraphic communications, 194–6
The Outfitter, 129
The Psychologist, 91, 122
The Times, 110–11, 117, 121–2, 130, 155, 160, 167, 181, 184, 186–7, 189
Thiel, Tommy, 21–2, 29
Thompson, Kenneth, 167
Thomson, Sir Basil, 58
Thorold, P., 3, 212n, 227n, 232n
  The Motoring Age, 3, 212n, 227n, 232n
Town Police Clauses Act (1847), 156
Trades Union Congress, 32, 48
  Conference (1919), 32
  Red Friday, 60
  Triple Alliance, 54
traffic management, 135–50
traffic policing, 2, 41, 105–34, 135–207 *passim*
Trenchard, Lord, 46, 86–7, 90, 96–7, 127, 139, 155, 202, 234n
  Advisory Committee on Scientific Investigation, 90
Tripp, Alker, 126, 149–50, 231n, 236n
Trotter, F. L., 68–70, 223n
Troup, Sir Edward, 54

Tryhorn, Professor E. H., 81, 98–101, 127n
Turnbull, Sir Hugh, 87

Valentine, Superintendent, 86
Vennel, Police Sergeant, 31
Vitty, Major, 95

Watson, John, 193
Watt, I. A., 229n
Weaver, J. C., 211n
Webster, James, 101
Weinberger, Barbara, 50–1, 58–9, 212n, 220n, 222n
Wells, H. G., 107
Western Mail, 64–5, 223n
Westminster Gazette, 215n
West Riding Police Report, 90, 92
West Wickham Wireless Transmitting Station, 195
Wheeler, ex-PC, 30
Wigan Examiner, 223n
Wigan Observer, 223n
Williams, C.A., 214n, 239n
Wilson, Archibald, 170
Wilson, G., 2, 211n
wireless, 194–6
Woodeson, A., 211n
Woodgate, J., 242n
Workers' Dreadnought, 22
Wormwood Scrubs Prison, 26
Wyles, L., 211n

Yeomans, Dr, 81

Z Cars, 2, 207